Office for Disarmament Affairs
New York, 2018

The United Nations
DISARMAMENT YEARBOOK

Volume 42 (Part I): 2017

Disarmament Resolutions and Decisions
of the Seventy-second Session
of the United Nations General Assembly

Guide to the user

To facilitate early analysis of the resolutions and decisions on disarmament adopted at the seventy-first session of the General Assembly, the United Nations Office for Disarmament Affairs offers Part I of the Yearbook as a handy, concise reference tool, containing the full texts of all the resolutions and decisions, the date of adoption by the Assembly and the First Committee, the agenda item number, the symbol number of the Report of the Rapporteur, the main sponsors and the voting patterns in the Assembly. For a snapshot of this information in a convenient chart, see "Quick view of votes by cluster". For a list of agenda items and their corresponding reports, see the Annex.

Bold type in the list of sponsors indicates the State(s) that submitted the draft resolution or decision.

Voting statistics in this publication are presented as three sets of numbers separated by two dashes, where the first figure represents the total of votes in favour, followed by votes against and abstentions.

> Electronically available in PDF or database
> format at
> **www.un.org/disarmament**

UNITED NATIONS PUBLICATION
Sales No. E.18.IX.5

ISBN 978-92-1-142328-0
eISBN 978-92-1-363298-7
Print ISSN 0252-5607
Online ISSN 2412-1193

Contents

Decisions

Annex

Preface

The *United Nations Disarmament Yearbook* is now in its forty-second year of publication. Part I presents the official texts of the 54 resolutions and 4 decisions related to disarmament, arms control and international security that were debated in the First Committee and forwarded to the General Assembly for adoption at its seventy-second session.

Part I is issued as a separate publication to provide early access to the resolutions and decisions, each presented with key information: relevant agenda items, main sponsors and co-sponsors, vote counts, including voting patterns in the First Committee and the General Assembly, adoption and meeting number dates and draft resolution numbers.

A *Quick view by cluster* gives the reader an easy handle (using the First Committee's "cluster" arrangement of agenda items) on resolution numbers, titles and votes in the First Committee and in the Assembly.

We hope that Part I furnishes the reader with a handy, consolidated reference book on multilateral disarmament, in print and electronic form.

Part II of the Yearbook will contain main multilateral issues under consideration, including their trends, summaries of First Committee and General Assembly actions taken on resolutions and a convenient issue-oriented timeline. Part II is forthcoming in October 2018.

Quick view of votes by cluster (54 resolutions and 4 decisions)*

No.	Title	GA action, 4 Dec. (vote)	First Cttee action (vote, date)
Cluster 1: Nuclear weapons			
72/22	African Nuclear-Weapon-Free Zone Treaty	w/o vote	w/o vote 27 Oct.
72/24	Establishment of a nuclear-weapon-free zone in the region of the Middle East	w/o vote	w/o vote 27 Oct.
72/25	Conclusion of effective international arrangements to assure non-nuclear-weapon States against the use or threat of use of nuclear weapons	125-0-62	118-0-59 27 Oct.
72/29	Follow-up to nuclear disarmament obligations agreed to at the 1995, 2000 and 2010 Review Conferences of the Parties to the Treaty on the Non-Proliferation of Nuclear Weapons	118-44-17 125-5-47, p.p. 6	112-44-15 115-5-47, p.p. 6 27 Oct.
72/30	Humanitarian consequences of nuclear weapons	141-15-27	134-15-25 27 Oct.
72/31	Taking forward multilateral nuclear disarmament negotiations	125-39-14	118-39-11 27 Oct.
72/37	Ethical imperatives for a nuclear-weapon-free world	130-36-15 125-37-13, p.p. 11	122-36-14 118-37-11, p.p. 11 27 Oct.
72/38	Nuclear disarmament	119-41-20 123-38-11, p.p. 32 172-1-5, o.p. 16	110-41-18 114-37-11, p.p. 32 159-1-6, o.p. 16 1 Nov.
72/39	Towards a nuclear-weapon-free world: accelerating the implementation of nuclear disarmament commitments	137-31-16 127-37-11, p.p. 10 169-4-6, o.p. 14 128-37-11, o.p. 22	127-32-14 118-37-10, p.p. 10 157-4-6, o.p. 14 121-37-10, o.p. 22 27 Oct.
72/41	Reducing nuclear danger	124-49-11	116-49-10 27 Oct.
72/45	Nuclear-weapon-free southern hemisphere and adjacent areas	149-5-29 128-35-12, p.p. 6	142-4-29 121-35-11, p.p. 6 27 Oct.

---

* Abbreviations: o.p. = operative paragraph; p.p. = preambular paragraph.

No.	Title	GA action, 4 Dec. (vote)	First Cttee action (vote, date)
72/50	United action with renewed determination towards the total elimination of nuclear weapons	156-4-24 158-1-17, p.p. 19 166-1-8, p.p. 20 142-7-27, o.p. 2 169-4-5, o.p. 5 157-2-16, o.p. 8 164-3-11, o.p. 20 154-4-19, o.p. 21 164-1-11, o.p. 28	144-4-27 147-1-19, p.p. 19 155-2-10, p.p. 20 128-7-27, o.p. 2 161-4-3, o.p. 5 149-2-16, o.p. 8 155-4-11, o.p. 20 143-4-22, o.p. 21 155-2-9, o.p. 28 27 Oct.
72/51	International Day against Nuclear Tests	w/o vote	w/o vote 27 Oct.
72/52	Prohibition of the dumping of radioactive wastes	w/o vote	w/o vote 27 Oct.
72/58	Follow-up to the advisory opinion of the International Court of Justice on the legality of the threat or use of nuclear weapons	131-31-18 125-35-13, p.p. 16 123-35-15, o.p. 2	124-31-17 117-35-13, p.p. 16 117-35-14, o.p. 2 1 Nov.
72/59	Convention on the Prohibition of the Use of Nuclear Weapons	123-50-10	115-50-11 27 Oct.
72/67	The risk of nuclear proliferation in the Middle East	157-5-20 173-3-2, p.p. 5 172-3-1, p.p. 6	150-4-19 164-3-2, p.p. 5 164-3-2, p.p. 6 27 Oct.
72/70	Comprehensive Nuclear-Test-Ban Treaty	180-1-4 169-0-11, p.p. 4 174-0-6, p.p. 7	174-1-4 164-0-11, p.p. 4 167-0-7, p.p. 7 27 Oct.
72/251	Follow-up to the 2013 high-level meeting of the General Assembly on nuclear disarmament	114-30-14 97-29-18, p.p. 12 23 Dec.	129-30-12 123-26-17, p.p. 12 1 Nov.
72/513	Treaty banning the production of fissile material for nuclear weapons or other nuclear explosive devices (decision)	182-1-4	174-1-4 27 Oct.
72/514	Nuclear disarmament verification (decision)	w/o vote	w/o vote 27 Oct.
72/515	Treaty on the South-East Asia Nuclear-Weapon-Free Zone (Bangkok Treaty) (decision)	w/o vote	w/o vote 1 Nov.

No.	Title	GA action, 4 Dec. (vote)	First Cttee action (vote, date)
Cluster 2: Other weapons of mass destruction			
72/42	Measures to prevent terrorists from acquiring weapons of mass destruction	w/o vote	w/o vote 30 Oct.
72/43	Implementation of the Convention on the Prohibition of the Development, Production, Stockpiling and Use of Chemical Weapons and on Their Destruction	159-7-14 142-9-23, p.p. 4 133-12-25, o.p. 2 138-10-26, o.p. 15	150-6-12 134-7-19, p.p. 4 122-11-24, o.p. 2 123-9-27, o.p. 15 2 Nov.
72/71	Convention on the Prohibition of the Development, Production and Stockpiling of Bacteriological (Biological) and Toxin Weapons and on Their Destruction	w/o vote	w/o vote 30 Oct.
Cluster 3: Outer space (disarmament aspects)			
72/26	Prevention of an arms race in outer space	182-0-3	175-0-2 30 Oct.
72/27	No first placement of weapons in outer space	131-4-48	122-4-48 30 Oct.
72/56	Transparency and confidence-building measures in outer space activities	w/o vote	w/o vote 30 Oct.
72/250	Further practical measures for the prevention of an arms race in outer space	108-5-47 23 Dec.	121-5-45 30 Oct.
Cluster 4: Conventional weapons			
72/36	Countering the threat posed by improvised explosive devices	w/o vote	w/o vote 31 Oct.
72/40	Assistance to States for curbing the illicit traffic in small arms and light weapons and collecting them	w/o vote	w/o vote 31 Oct.
72/44	The Arms Trade Treaty	155-0-29	144-0-29 31 Oct.
72/53	Implementation of the Convention on the Prohibition of the Use, Stockpiling, Production and Transfer of Anti-Personnel Mines and on Their Destruction	167-0-17	158-0-16 31 Oct.
72/54	Implementation of the Convention on Cluster Munitions	142-2-36	134-2-36 31 Oct.

No.	Title	GA action, 4 Dec. (vote)	First Cttee action (vote, date)
72/55	Problems arising from the accumulation of conventional ammunition stockpiles in surplus	w/o vote	w/o vote 31 Oct.
72/57	The illicit trade in small arms and light weapons in all its aspects	w/o vote	w/o vote 31 Oct.
72/68	Convention on Prohibitions or Restrictions on the Use of Certain Conventional Weapons Which May Be Deemed to Be Excessively Injurious or to Have Indiscriminate Effects	w/o vote	w/o vote 31 Oct.

Cluster 5: Other disarmament measures and international security

No.	Title	GA action, 4 Dec. (vote)	First Cttee action (vote, date)
72/20	Objective information on military matters, including transparency of military expenditures	w/o vote	w/o vote 31 Oct.
72/28	Role of science and technology in the context of international security and disarmament	w/o vote	w/o vote 31 Oct.
72/32	Compliance with non-proliferation, arms limitation and disarmament agreements and commitments	173-1-11	165-1-11 31 Oct.
72/46	Relationship between disarmament and development	w/o vote	w/o vote 31 Oct.
72/47	Observance of environmental norms in the drafting and implementation of agreements on disarmament and arms control	w/o vote	w/o vote 31 Oct.
72/48	Promotion of multilateralism in the area of disarmament and non-proliferation	130-4-51	120-4-49 31 Oct.
72/512	Developments in the field of information and telecommunications in the context of international security (decision)	185-0-1	173-0-1 31 Oct.

Cluster 6: Regional disarmament and security

No.	Title	GA action, 4 Dec. (vote)	First Cttee action (vote, date)
72/21	Implementation of the Declaration of the Indian Ocean as a Zone of Peace	132-3-46	126-3-45 1 Nov.
72/33	Confidence-building measures in the regional and subregional context	w/o vote	w/o vote 1 Nov.

No.	Title	GA action, 4 Dec. (vote)	First Cttee action (vote, date)
72/34	Regional disarmament	w/o vote	w/o vote 1 Nov.
72/35	Conventional arms control at the regional and subregional levels	184-1-2 140-1-39, o.p. 2	174-1-2 131-1-38, o.p. 2 1 Nov.
72/69	Strengthening of security and cooperation in the Mediterranean region	w/o vote	w/o vote 1 Nov.

Cluster 7: Disarmament machinery

No.	Title	GA action, 4 Dec. (vote)	First Cttee action (vote, date)
72/23	Prohibition of the development and manufacture of new types of weapons of mass destruction and new systems of such weapons: report of the Conference on Disarmament	180-3-0	173-3-0 1 Nov.
72/49	Convening of the fourth special session of the General Assembly devoted to disarmament	181-0-3	170-0-3 1 Nov.
72/60	United Nations Regional Centre for Peace and Disarmament in Africa	w/o vote	w/o vote 1 Nov.
72/61	United Nations Regional Centre for Peace, Disarmament and Development in Latin America and the Caribbean	w/o vote	w/o vote 1 Nov.
72/62	United Nations Regional Centre for Peace and Disarmament in Asia and the Pacific	w/o vote	w/o vote 1 Nov.
72/63	Regional confidence-building measures: activities of the United Nations Standing Advisory Committee on Security Questions in Central Africa	w/o vote	w/o vote 1 Nov.
72/64	United Nations regional centres for peace and disarmament	w/o vote	w/o vote 1 Nov.
72/65	Report of the Conference on Disarmament	w/o vote	w/o vote 1 Nov.
72/66	Report of the Disarmament Commission	w/o vote	w/o vote 1 Nov.

Agenda item 90 (b)

72/20 Objective information on military matters, including transparency of military expenditures

Text

The General Assembly,

Recalling its resolutions 53/72 of 4 December 1998, 54/43 of 1 December 1999, 56/14 of 29 November 2001, 58/28 of 8 December 2003, 60/44 of 8 December 2005, 62/13 of 5 December 2007, 64/22 of 2 December 2009, 66/20 of 2 December 2011, 68/23 of 5 December 2013 and 70/21 of 7 December 2015 on objective information on military matters, including transparency of military expenditures,

Recalling also its resolution 35/142 B of 12 December 1980, which introduced the United Nations system for the standardized reporting of military expenditures, its resolutions 48/62 of 16 December 1993, 49/66 of 15 December 1994, 51/38 of 10 December 1996 and 52/32 of 9 December 1997, in which the General Assembly called upon all Member States to participate in the system, and its resolution 47/54 B of 9 December 1992, in which the Assembly endorsed the guidelines and recommendations for objective information on military matters and invited Member States to provide the Secretary-General with relevant information regarding their implementation,

Noting that, since then, national reports on military expenditures and on the guidelines and recommendations for objective information on military matters have been submitted by a number of Member States belonging to different geographical regions,

Convinced that the improvement of international relations forms a sound basis for promoting further openness and transparency in all military matters,

Convinced also that transparency in military matters is an essential element for building a climate of trust and confidence between States worldwide and that a better flow of objective information on military matters can help to relieve international tension and is therefore an important contribution to conflict prevention,

Noting the role of the standardized reporting system, as instituted through its resolution 35/142 B, as an important instrument to enhance transparency in military matters,

Conscious that the value of the standardized reporting system would be enhanced by a broader participation of Member States,

Noting that a periodic review of the United Nations Report on Military Expenditures could facilitate its further development and maintain its continued relevance and operation, and recalling that, in its resolution 66/20, the General Assembly recommended the establishment of a process for periodic reviews,

Recalling, in that regard, the report of the Secretary-General on ways and means to implement the guidelines and recommendations for objective information on military matters, including, in particular, on how to strengthen and broaden participation in the standardized reporting system,[1]

Recalling also the report of the Group of Governmental Experts on the Operation and Further Development of the United Nations Standardized Instrument for Reporting Military Expenditures on further ways and means to implement the guidelines and recommendations for objective information on military matters, including, in particular, on how to strengthen and broaden participation in the standardized reporting system,[2]

Welcoming the work of the Secretariat on migrating data submitted on military expenditures to its new, interactive web platform, which includes an online reporting feature, thus increasing user-friendliness and facilitating the submission of reports,[3] in accordance with resolution 66/20,

Noting the efforts of several regional organizations to promote transparency of military expenditures, including standardized annual exchanges of relevant information among their member States,

Emphasizing the continuing importance of the Report on Military Expenditures under the current political and economic circumstances,

Recalling that, in its resolution 66/20, the General Assembly recommended that, for the purpose of reporting by Member States of their national military expenditures in the framework of the Report on Military Expenditures, "military expenditures" be commonly understood to refer to all financial resources that a State spends on the uses and functions of its military forces and information on military expenditures represents an actual outlay in current prices and domestic currency,

Mindful of the provisions of the Charter of the United Nations, including its Article 26,

---

[1] A/54/298.
[2] A/66/89 and A/66/89/Corr.1, A/66/89/Corr.2 and A/66/89/Corr.3.
[3] Available from www.un-arm.org/Milex/home.aspx.

1.   *Endorses* the report of the Group of Governmental Experts to Review the Operation and Further Development of the United Nations Report on Military Expenditures;[4]

2.   *Calls upon* Member States, with a view to achieving the broadest possible participation, to provide the Secretary-General, by 30 April annually, with a report on their military expenditures for the latest fiscal year for which data are available, using, preferably and to the extent possible, one of the online reporting forms, including, if appropriate, a nil report or the "single figure" report on military expenditures or any other format developed in the context of similar reporting on military expenditures to other international or regional organizations;

3.   *Recommends* the guidelines and recommendations for objective information on military matters to all Member States for implementation, fully taking into account specific political, military and other conditions prevailing in a region, on the basis of initiatives and with the agreement of the States of the region concerned;

4.   *Invites* Member States in a position to do so to supplement their reports, on a voluntary basis, with explanatory remarks regarding submitted data to explain or clarify the figures provided in the reporting forms, such as the total military expenditures as a share of gross domestic product, major changes from previous reports and any additional information reflecting their defence policy, military strategies and doctrines;

5.   *Invites* Member States to provide, preferably with their annual report, information on their national points of contact;

6.   *Encourages* relevant international bodies and regional organizations to promote transparency of military expenditures and to enhance complementarities among reporting systems, taking into account the particular characteristics of each region, and to consider the possibility of an exchange of information with the United Nations;

7.   *Takes note* of the annual reports of the Secretary-General;[5]

8.   *Requests* the Secretary-General, within available resources:

(a)   To continue the practice of sending an annual note verbale to Member States requesting the submission of their report on military expenditures;

---

[4] A/72/293.

[5] A/58/202 and A/58/202/Add.1, A/58/202/Add.2 and A/58/202/Add.3, A/59/192 and A/59/192/Add.1, A/60/159 and A/60/159/Add.1, A/60/159/Add.2 and A/60/159/Add.3, A/61/133 and A/61/133/Add.1, A/61/133/Add.2 and A/61/133/Add.3, A/62/158 and A/62/158/Add.1, A/62/158/Add.2 and A/62/158/Add.3, A/63/97 and A/63/97/Add.1 and A/63/97/Add.2, A/64/113 and A/64/113/Add.1 and A/64/113/Add.2, A/65/118 and A/65/118/Corr.1 and A/65/118/Add.1 and A/65/118/Add.2, A/66/117 and A/66/117/Add.1, A/67/128 and A/67/128/Add.1, A/68/131 and A/68/131/Add.1, A/69/135 and A/69/135/Add.1, A/70/139 and A/70/139/Add.1 and A/71/115 and A/71/115/Add.1.

(b)   To circulate annually a note verbale to Member States detailing which reports on military expenditures were submitted and are available online;

(c)   To circulate to Member States the questionnaire contained in annex I to the report of the Group of Governmental Experts[4] and to collect the responses from Member States and provide a summary thereof in advance of the seventy-fourth session of the General Assembly;

(d)   To continue consultations with relevant international bodies, with a view to ascertaining requirements for adjusting the present instrument in order to encourage wider participation, and to make recommendations, based on the outcome of those consultations and taking into account the views of Member States, on necessary changes to the content and structure of the standardized reporting system;

(e)   To encourage relevant international bodies and organizations to promote transparency of military expenditures and to consult with those bodies and organizations with emphasis on examining possibilities for enhancing complementarities among international and regional reporting systems and for exchanging related information between those bodies and the United Nations;

(f)   To continue to foster further cooperation with relevant regional organizations, with a view to raising awareness of the United Nations Report on Military Expenditures and its role as a confidence-building measure;

(g)   To encourage the United Nations regional centres for peace and disarmament in Africa, in Asia and the Pacific and in Latin America and the Caribbean to assist Member States in their regions in enhancing their knowledge of the standardized reporting system;

(h)   To promote international and regional or subregional symposiums and training seminars and to support the development of an online training course by the Office for Disarmament Affairs of the Secretariat, with the financial and technical support of interested States, with a view to explaining the purpose of the standardized reporting system, facilitating the electronic filing of reports and providing relevant technical instructions;

(i)   To report on experiences gained during such symposiums and training seminars;

(j)   To provide, upon request, technical assistance to Member States lacking the capacity to report data and to encourage Member States to voluntarily provide bilateral assistance to other Member States;

9.   *Encourages* Member States:

(a)   To inform the Secretary-General about possible problems with the standardized reporting system and their reasons for not submitting the requested data;

(b)   To continue to provide the Secretary-General with their views and suggestions on ways and means to improve the future functioning of and broadened participation in the standardized reporting system, including necessary changes to its content and structure, as well as recommendations to facilitate its further development;

(c)   To complete the questionnaire contained in annex I to the report of the Group of Governmental Experts and to return it to the Secretary-General within the deadline to be set by him;

10.   *Recommends* that the matter of the establishment of a process of periodic reviews of the Report on Military Expenditures and the timing of the next review be considered at the seventy-fourth session of the General Assembly, taking into account the results of the questionnaire referred to in paragraphs 8 (c) and 9 (c) above;

11.   *Decides* to include in the provisional agenda of its seventy-fourth session, under the item entitled "Reduction of military budgets", the sub-item entitled "Objective information on military matters, including transparency of military expenditures".

Action by the General Assembly

Date: 4 December 2017   Meeting: 62nd plenary meeting
Vote: Adopted without a vote   Report: A/72/400

Sponsors

Albania, Angola, Australia, Austria, Belgium, Bulgaria, Canada, Croatia, Czech Republic, Estonia, Finland, Germany, Greece, Hungary, Ireland, Italy, Japan, Latvia, Lithuania, Luxembourg, Malta, Montenegro, the Netherlands, Norway, Poland, Portugal, Republic of Moldova, **Romania**, Slovakia, Slovenia, Spain, Sweden, Switzerland, Thailand, United Kingdom

Co-sponsors

Andorra, Argentina, Armenia, Bosnia and Herzegovina, Chile, Cyprus, Denmark, France, Haiti, Liechtenstein, Monaco, Republic of Korea, San Marino, Sierra Leone, the former Yugoslav Republic of Macedonia, Turkey, United States

Action by the First Committee

Date: 31 October 2017   Meeting: 26th meeting
Vote: Adopted without a vote   Draft resolution: A/C.1/72/L.24

Agenda item 91

72/21 Implementation of the Declaration of the Indian Ocean as a Zone of Peace

Text

> *The General Assembly,*
>
> *Recalling* the Declaration of the Indian Ocean as a Zone of Peace, contained in its resolution 2832 (XXVI) of 16 December 1971, and recalling also its resolutions 54/47 of 1 December 1999, 56/16 of 29 November 2001, 58/29 of 8 December 2003, 60/48 of 8 December 2005, 62/14 of 5 December 2007, 64/23 of 2 December 2009, 66/22 of 2 December 2011, 68/24 of 5 December 2013 and 70/22 of 7 December 2015 and other relevant resolutions,
>
> *Recalling also* the report of the Meeting of the Littoral and Hinterland States of the Indian Ocean, held in New York from 2 to 13 July 1979,[1]
>
> *Recalling further* paragraph 102 of the Final Document of the Thirteenth Conference of Heads of State or Government of Non-Aligned Countries, held in Kuala Lumpur on 24 and 25 February 2003,[2] in which it was noted, inter alia, that the Chair of the Ad Hoc Committee on the Indian Ocean would continue his informal consultations on the future work of the Committee,
>
> *Emphasizing* the need to foster consensual approaches that are conducive to the pursuit of such endeavours,
>
> *Noting* the initiatives taken by countries of the region to promote cooperation, in particular economic cooperation, in the Indian Ocean area and the possible contribution of such initiatives to overall objectives of a zone of peace,
>
> *Convinced* that the participation of all permanent members of the Security Council and the major maritime users of the Indian Ocean in the work of the Ad Hoc Committee is important and would assist the progress of a mutually beneficial dialogue to develop conditions of peace, security and stability in the Indian Ocean region,
>
> *Considering* that greater efforts and more time are required to develop a focused discussion on practical measures to ensure conditions of peace, security and stability in the Indian Ocean region,

---

[1] *Official Records of the General Assembly, Thirty-fourth Session, Supplement No. 45* and corrigendum (A/34/45 and A/34/45/Corr.1).

[2] A/57/759-S/2003/332, annex I.

Having considered the report of the Ad Hoc Committee,[3]

1.   *Takes note* of the report of the Ad Hoc Committee on the Indian Ocean;[3]

2.   *Reiterates its conviction* that the participation of all permanent members of the Security Council and the major maritime users of the Indian Ocean in the work of the Ad Hoc Committee is important and would greatly facilitate the development of a mutually beneficial dialogue to advance peace, security and stability in the Indian Ocean region;

3.   *Requests* the Chair of the Ad Hoc Committee to continue his informal consultations with the members of the Committee and to report through the Committee to the General Assembly at its seventy-fourth session;

4.   *Requests* the Secretary-General to continue to render, within existing resources, all necessary assistance to the Ad Hoc Committee, including the provision of summary records;

5.   *Decides* to include in the provisional agenda of its seventy-fourth session the item entitled "Implementation of the Declaration of the Indian Ocean as a Zone of Peace".

Action by the General Assembly

Date: 4 December 2017   Meeting: 62nd plenary meeting
Vote: 132-3-46   Report: A/72/401

Sponsors

> **Indonesia** (on behalf of the States Members of the United Nations that are members of the Movement of Non-Aligned Countries)

Recorded vote

In favour:

> Afghanistan, Algeria, Angola, Antigua and Barbuda, Argentina, Armenia, Australia, Azerbaijan, Bahamas, Bahrain, Bangladesh, Barbados, Belarus, Belize, Benin, Bhutan, Bolivia (Plurinational State of), Botswana, Brazil, Brunei Darussalam, Burkina Faso, Burundi, Cabo Verde, Cambodia, Cameroon, Chile, China, Colombia, Comoros, Congo, Costa Rica, Côte d'Ivoire, Cuba, Democratic People's Republic of Korea, Democratic Republic of the Congo, Djibouti, Dominican Republic, Ecuador, Egypt, El Salvador, Eritrea, Ethiopia, Fiji, Gabon, Gambia, Ghana, Guatemala, Guinea, Guyana, Honduras, India, Indonesia, Iran (Islamic Republic of), Iraq, Jamaica, Japan, Jordan, Kazakhstan, Kenya, Kiribati, Kuwait, Kyrgyzstan, Lao People's Democratic Republic, Lebanon, Lesotho, Liberia, Libya, Madagascar, Malawi, Malaysia,

---

[3] *Official Records of the General Assembly, Seventy-second Session, Supplement No. 29* (A/72/29).

Maldives, Mali, Mauritania, Mauritius, Mexico, Mongolia, Morocco, Mozambique, Myanmar, Namibia, Nauru, Nepal, Netherlands, New Zealand, Nicaragua, Nigeria, Oman, Pakistan, Panama, Papua New Guinea, Paraguay, Peru, Philippines, Qatar, Republic of Korea, Russian Federation, Rwanda, Saint Kitts and Nevis, Saint Lucia, Saint Vincent and the Grenadines, Samoa, Saudi Arabia, Senegal, Sierra Leone, Singapore, Solomon Islands, Somalia, South Africa, Sri Lanka, Sudan, Suriname, Swaziland, Syrian Arab Republic, Tajikistan, Thailand, Timor-Leste, Togo, Tonga, Trinidad and Tobago, Tunisia, Turkmenistan, Uganda, United Arab Emirates, United Republic of Tanzania, Uruguay, Uzbekistan, Vanuatu, Venezuela (Bolivarian Republic of), Viet Nam, Yemen, Zambia, Zimbabwe

Against:

France, United Kingdom, United States

Abstaining:

Albania, Andorra, Austria, Belgium, Bosnia and Herzegovina, Bulgaria, Canada, Central African Republic, Croatia, Cyprus, Czech Republic, Denmark, Estonia, Finland, Georgia, Germany, Greece, Hungary, Iceland, Ireland, Israel, Italy, Latvia, Liechtenstein, Lithuania, Luxembourg, Malta, Micronesia (Federated States of), Monaco, Montenegro, Norway, Palau, Poland, Portugal, Republic of Moldova, Romania, San Marino, Serbia, Slovakia, Slovenia, Spain, Sweden, Switzerland, the former Yugoslav Republic of Macedonia, Turkey, Ukraine

Action by the First Committee

Date: 1 November 2017   Meeting: 27th meeting
Vote: 126-3-45   Draft resolution: A/C.1/72/L.29

Agenda item 92

72/22   African Nuclear-Weapon-Free Zone Treaty

Text

The General Assembly,

Recalling its resolutions 51/53 of 10 December 1996 and 56/17 of 29 November 2001 and all its other relevant resolutions, as well as those of the Organization of African Unity and of the African Union,

Recalling also the signing of the African Nuclear-Weapon-Free Zone Treaty (Treaty of Pelindaba) in Cairo on 11 April 1996,[1]

Recalling further the Cairo Declaration adopted on that occasion,[2] in which it was emphasized that nuclear-weapon-free zones, especially in regions of tension, such as the Middle East, enhance global and regional peace and security,

Recalling the statement made by the President of the Security Council on behalf of the members of the Council on 12 April 1996,[3] in which the Council affirmed that the signature of the Treaty constituted an important contribution by the African countries to the maintenance of international peace and security,

Considering that the establishment of nuclear-weapon-free zones, especially in the Middle East, would enhance the security of Africa and the viability of the African nuclear-weapon-free zone,

1.   *Recalls with satisfaction* the entry into force of the African Nuclear-Weapon-Free Zone Treaty (Treaty of Pelindaba)[1] on 15 July 2009;

2.   *Calls upon* African States that have not yet done so to sign and ratify the Treaty as soon as possible;

3.   *Recalls* the convening of the first Conference of States Parties to the African Nuclear-Weapon-Free Zone Treaty (Treaty of Pelindaba), on 4 November 2010, the second Conference of States Parties, on 12 and 13 November 2012, and the third Conference of States Parties, on 29 and 30 May 2014, all held in Addis Ababa;

4.   *Expresses its appreciation* to the nuclear-weapon States that have signed the Protocols to the Treaty[1] that concern them, and calls upon those that have not yet ratified the Protocols that concern them to do so as soon as possible;

---

[1] A/50/426, annex.
[2] A/51/113-S/1996/276, annex.
[3] S/PRST/1996/17; see *Resolutions and Decisions of the Security Council*, 1996 (S/INF/52).

5. *Calls upon* the States contemplated in Protocol III to the Treaty that have not yet done so to take all measures necessary to ensure the speedy application of the Treaty to territories for which they are, de jure or de facto, internationally responsible and which lie within the limits of the geographical zone established in the Treaty;

6. *Calls upon* the African States parties to the Treaty on the Non-Proliferation of Nuclear Weapons[4] that have not yet done so to conclude comprehensive safeguards agreements with the International Atomic Energy Agency pursuant to the Treaty, thereby satisfying the requirements of article 9 (b) and annex II to the Treaty of Pelindaba, and encourages them to conclude additional protocols to their safeguards agreements on the basis of the model protocol approved by the Board of Governors of the Agency on 15 May 1997;

7. *Expresses its gratitude* to the Secretary-General of the United Nations, the Chairperson of the African Union Commission and the Director General of the International Atomic Energy Agency for the diligence with which they have rendered effective assistance to the signatories to the Treaty;

8. *Decides* to include in the provisional agenda of its seventy-third session the item entitled "African Nuclear-Weapon-Free Zone Treaty".

Action by the General Assembly

Date: 4 December 2017   Meeting: 62nd plenary meeting
Vote: Adopted without a vote   Report: A/72/402

Sponsors

Australia, Austria, Kazakhstan, Mexico, **Nigeria** (on behalf of the States Members of the United Nations that are members of the Group of African States), Portugal

Co-sponsors

Georgia, Haiti, Turkey

Action by the First Committee

Date: 27 October 2017   Meeting: 24th meeting
Vote: Adopted without a vote   Draft resolution: A/C.1/72/L.37

---

[4] United Nations, *Treaty Series*, vol. 729, No. 10485.

Agenda item 93

72/23 Prohibition of the development and manufacture of new types of weapons of mass destruction and new systems of such weapons: report of the Conference on Disarmament

Text

The General Assembly,

Recalling its previous resolutions on the prohibition of the development and manufacture of new types of weapons of mass destruction and new systems of such weapons,

Recalling also its resolutions 51/37 of 10 December 1996, 54/44 of 1 December 1999, 57/50 of 22 November 2002, 60/46 of 8 December 2005, 63/36 of 2 December 2008, 66/21 of 2 December 2011 and 69/27 of 2 December 2014 relating to the prohibition of the development and manufacture of new types of weapons of mass destruction and new systems of such weapons,

Recalling further paragraph 77 of the Final Document of the Tenth Special Session of the General Assembly,[1]

Determined to prevent the emergence of new types of weapons of mass destruction that have characteristics comparable in destructive effect to those of weapons of mass destruction identified in the definition of weapons of mass destruction adopted by the United Nations in 1948,[2]

Noting with appreciation the discussions which have been held in the Conference on Disarmament under the item entitled "New types of weapons of mass destruction and new systems of such weapons; radiological weapons",[3]

Noting the desirability of keeping the matter under review, as appropriate,

1. *Reaffirms* that effective measures should be taken to prevent the emergence of new types of weapons of mass destruction;

---

[1] Resolution S-10/2.

[2] The definition was adopted by the Commission for Conventional Armaments (see S/C.3/32/Rev.1 and S/C.3/32/Rev.1/Corr.1).

[3] *Official Records of the General Assembly, Sixty-fourth Session, Supplement No. 27* (A/64/27), chap. III, sect. E; ibid., Sixty-fifth Session, Supplement No. 27 (A/65/27), chap. III, sect. E; ibid., *Sixty-sixth Session, Supplement No. 27* (A/66/27), chap. III, sect. E; ibid., *Sixty-seventh Session, Supplement No. 27* (A/67/27), chap. III, sect. E; ibid., *Sixty-eighth Session, Supplement No. 27* (A/68/27), chap. III, sect. E; ibid., *Sixty-ninth Session, Supplement No. 27* (A/69/27), chap. III, sect. E; ibid., *Seventieth Session, Supplement No. 27* (A/70/27), chap. III, sect. E; ibid., *Seventy-first Session, Supplement No. 27* (A/71/27), chap. III, sect. E; and ibid., *Seventy-second Session, Supplement No. 27* (A/72/27), chap. III, sect. E.

2.   *Requests* the Conference on Disarmament, without prejudice to further overview of its agenda, to keep the matter under review, as appropriate, with a view to making, when necessary, recommendations on undertaking specific negotiations on identified types of such weapons;

3.   *Calls upon* all States, immediately following any recommendations of the Conference on Disarmament, to give favourable consideration to those recommendations;

4.   *Requests* the Secretary-General to transmit to the Conference on Disarmament all documents relating to the consideration of this item by the General Assembly at its seventy-second session;

5.   *Requests* the Conference on Disarmament to report the results of any consideration of the matter in its annual reports to the General Assembly;

6.   *Decides* to include in the provisional agenda of its seventy-fifth session the item entitled "Prohibition of the development and manufacture of new types of weapons of mass destruction and new systems of such weapons: report of the Conference on Disarmament".

Action by the General Assembly

Date: 4 December 2017   Meeting: 62nd plenary meeting
Vote: 180-3-0   Report: A/72/403

Sponsors

Angola, Armenia, Azerbaijan, **Belarus**, Cuba, Ecuador, Indonesia, Kazakhstan, Madagascar, Nicaragua, Philippines, Russian Federation, Syrian Arab Republic, Tajikistan, Thailand, Turkmenistan, Venezuela (Bolivarian Republic of)

Co-sponsors

Bangladesh, Benin, Bolivia (Plurinational State of), Chad, Congo, Côte d'Ivoire, Egypt, Eritrea, Ethiopia, Ghana, Honduras, Kenya, Kyrgyzstan, Lesotho, Maldives, Nigeria, Pakistan, Senegal, Uzbekistan

Recorded vote

In favour:

Afghanistan, Albania, Algeria, Andorra, Angola, Antigua and Barbuda, Argentina, Armenia, Australia, Austria, Azerbaijan, Bahamas, Bahrain, Bangladesh, Barbados, Belarus, Belgium, Belize, Benin, Bhutan, Bolivia (Plurinational State of), Bosnia and Herzegovina, Botswana, Brazil, Brunei Darussalam, Bulgaria, Burkina Faso, Burundi, Cabo Verde, Cambodia, Cameroon, Canada, Central African Republic, Chad, Chile, China, Colombia, Comoros, Congo, Costa Rica, Côte d'Ivoire, Croatia, Cuba, Cyprus, Czech Republic, Democratic People's Republic of Korea, Democratic Republic of the Congo, Denmark, Djibouti, Dominican Republic, Ecuador, Egypt, El Salvador, Equatorial Guinea, Eritrea, Estonia, Ethiopia, Fiji, Finland, France, Gabon, Gambia, Georgia, Germany, Ghana, Greece, Guatemala, Guinea, Guyana, Honduras, Hungary, Iceland, India, Indonesia, Iran (Islamic Republic of), Iraq, Ireland, Italy, Jamaica, Japan, Jordan, Kazakhstan, Kenya, Kiribati, Kuwait, Kyrgyzstan, Lao People's Democratic Republic, Latvia, Lebanon, Lesotho, Liberia, Libya, Liechtenstein, Lithuania, Luxembourg, Madagascar, Malawi, Malaysia, Maldives, Mali, Malta, Marshall Islands, Mauritania, Mauritius, Mexico, Monaco, Mongolia, Montenegro, Morocco, Mozambique, Myanmar, Namibia, Nepal, Netherlands, New Zealand, Nicaragua, Nigeria, Norway, Oman, Pakistan, Palau, Panama, Papua New Guinea, Paraguay, Peru, Philippines, Poland, Portugal, Qatar, Republic of Korea, Republic of Moldova, Romania, Russian Federation, Rwanda, Saint Kitts and Nevis, Saint Lucia, Saint Vincent and the Grenadines, Samoa, San Marino, Saudi Arabia, Senegal, Serbia, Sierra Leone, Singapore, Slovakia, Slovenia, Solomon Islands, Somalia, South Africa, Spain, Sri Lanka, Sudan, Suriname, Swaziland, Sweden, Switzerland, Syrian Arab Republic, Tajikistan, Thailand, the former Yugoslav Republic of Macedonia, Timor-Leste, Togo, Tonga, Trinidad and Tobago, Tunisia, Turkey, Turkmenistan, Tuvalu, Uganda, United Arab Emirates, United Kingdom, United Republic of Tanzania, Uruguay, Uzbekistan, Vanuatu, Venezuela (Bolivarian Republic of), Viet Nam, Yemen, Zambia, Zimbabwe

Against:
Israel, Ukraine, United States

Abstaining:
None

Action by the First Committee

Date:	1 November 2017	Meeting:	27th meeting
Vote:	173-3-0	Draft resolution:	A/C.1/72/L.9

Agenda item 95

72/24   Establishment of a nuclear-weapon-free zone in the region of the Middle East

Text

The General Assembly,

Recalling its resolutions 3263 (XXIX) of 9 December 1974, 3474 (XXX) of 11 December 1975, 31/71 of 10 December 1976, 32/82 of 12 December 1977, 33/64 of 14 December 1978, 34/77 of 11 December 1979, 35/147 of 12 December 1980, 36/87 A and B of 9 December 1981, 37/75 of 9 December 1982, 38/64 of 15 December 1983, 39/54 of 12 December 1984, 40/82 of 12 December 1985, 41/48 of 3 December 1986, 42/28 of 30 November 1987, 43/65 of 7 December 1988, 44/108 of 15 December 1989, 45/52 of 4 December 1990, 46/30 of 6 December 1991, 47/48 of 9 December 1992, 48/71 of 16 December 1993, 49/71 of 15 December 1994, 50/66 of 12 December 1995, 51/41 of 10 December 1996, 52/34 of 9 December 1997, 53/74 of 4 December 1998, 54/51 of 1 December 1999, 55/30 of 20 November 2000, 56/21 of 29 November 2001, 57/55 of 22 November 2002, 58/34 of 8 December 2003, 59/63 of 3 December 2004, 60/52 of 8 December 2005, 61/56 of 6 December 2006, 62/18 of 5 December 2007, 63/38 of 2 December 2008, 64/26 of 2 December 2009, 65/42 of 8 December 2010, 66/25 of 2 December 2011, 67/28 of 3 December 2012, 68/27 of 5 December 2013, 69/29 of 2 December 2014, 70/24 of 7 December 2015 and 71/29 of 5 December 2016 on the establishment of a nuclear-weapon-free zone in the region of the Middle East,

Recalling also the recommendations for the establishment of a nuclear-weapon-free zone in the region of the Middle East consistent with paragraphs 60 to 63, and in particular paragraph 63 (d), of the Final Document of the Tenth Special Session of the General Assembly,[1]

Emphasizing the basic provisions of the above-mentioned resolutions, in which all parties directly concerned are called upon to consider taking the practical and urgent steps required for the implementation of the proposal to establish a nuclear-weapon-free zone in the region of the Middle East and, pending and during the establishment of such a zone, to declare solemnly that they will refrain, on a reciprocal basis, from producing, acquiring or in any other way possessing nuclear weapons and nuclear explosive devices and from permitting the stationing of nuclear weapons on their territory by any third party, to agree to place their nuclear facilities under International Atomic Energy Agency safeguards and to declare their support for the establishment

---

[1] Resolution S-10/2.

of the zone and to deposit such declarations with the Security Council for consideration, as appropriate,

Reaffirming the inalienable right of all States to acquire and develop nuclear energy for peaceful purposes,

Emphasizing the need for appropriate measures on the question of the prohibition of military attacks on nuclear facilities,

Bearing in mind the consensus reached by the General Assembly since its thirty-fifth session that the establishment of a nuclear-weapon-free zone in the region of the Middle East would greatly enhance international peace and security,

Desirous of building on that consensus so that substantial progress can be made towards establishing a nuclear-weapon-free zone in the region of the Middle East,

Welcoming all initiatives leading to general and complete disarmament, including in the region of the Middle East, and in particular on the establishment therein of a zone free of weapons of mass destruction, including nuclear weapons,

Noting the peace negotiations in the Middle East, which should be of a comprehensive nature and represent an appropriate framework for the peaceful settlement of contentious issues in the region,

Recognizing the importance of credible regional security, including the establishment of a mutually verifiable nuclear-weapon-free zone,

Emphasizing the essential role of the United Nations in the establishment of a mutually verifiable nuclear-weapon-free zone,

Having examined the report of the Secretary-General on the implementation of resolution 71/29,[2]

1.   *Urges* all parties directly concerned seriously to consider taking the practical and urgent steps required for the implementation of the proposal to establish a nuclear-weapon-free zone in the region of the Middle East in accordance with the relevant resolutions of the General Assembly, and, as a means of promoting this objective, invites the countries concerned to adhere to the Treaty on the Non-Proliferation of Nuclear Weapons;[3]

2.   *Calls upon* all countries of the region that have not yet done so, pending the establishment of the zone, to agree to place all their nuclear activities under International Atomic Energy Agency safeguards;

3.   *Takes note* of resolution GC(61)/RES/14, adopted on 21 September 2017 by the General Conference of the International Atomic Energy Agency at

---

[2] A/72/340 (Part I).
[3] United Nations, *Treaty Series*, vol. 729, No. 10485.

its sixty-first regular session, concerning the application of Agency safeguards in the Middle East;

4.   *Notes* the importance of the ongoing bilateral Middle East peace negotiations and the activities of the multilateral Working Group on Arms Control and Regional Security in promoting mutual confidence and security in the Middle East, including the establishment of a nuclear-weapon-free zone;

5.   *Invites* all countries of the region, pending the establishment of a nuclear-weapon-free zone in the region of the Middle East, to declare their support for establishing such a zone, consistent with paragraph 63 (d) of the Final Document of the Tenth Special Session of the General Assembly,[1] and to deposit those declarations with the Security Council;

6.   *Also invites* those countries, pending the establishment of the zone, not to develop, produce, test or otherwise acquire nuclear weapons or permit the stationing on their territories, or territories under their control, of nuclear weapons or nuclear explosive devices;

7.   *Invites* the nuclear-weapon States and all other States to render their assistance in the establishment of the zone and at the same time to refrain from any action that runs counter to both the letter and the spirit of the present resolution;

8.   *Takes note* of the report of the Secretary-General on the implementation of resolution 71/29;[2]

9.   *Invites* all parties to consider the appropriate means that may contribute towards the goal of general and complete disarmament and the establishment of a zone free of weapons of mass destruction in the region of the Middle East;

10.   *Requests* the Secretary-General to continue to pursue consultations with the States of the region and other concerned States, in accordance with paragraph 7 of resolution 46/30 and taking into account the evolving situation in the region, and to seek from those States their views on the measures outlined in chapters III and IV of the study annexed to the report of the Secretary-General of 10 October 1990[4] or other relevant measures, in order to move towards the establishment of a nuclear-weapon-free zone in the region of the Middle East;

11.   *Also requests* the Secretary-General to submit to the General Assembly at its seventy-third session a report on the implementation of the present resolution;

12.   *Decides* to include in the provisional agenda of its seventy-third session the item entitled "Establishment of a nuclear-weapon-free zone in the region of the Middle East".

---

[4] A/45/435.

Action by the General Assembly

    Date: 4 December 2017   Meeting: 62nd plenary meeting

    Vote: Adopted without a vote   Report: A/72/405

Sponsors

   Egypt

Action by the First Committee

    Date: 27 October 2017   Meeting: 24th meeting

    Vote: Adopted without a vote   Draft resolution: A/C.1/72/L.1

Agenda item 96

72/25 Conclusion of effective international arrangements to assure non-nuclear-weapon States against the use or threat of use of nuclear weapons

Text

The General Assembly,

Bearing in mind the need to allay the legitimate concern of the States of the world with regard to ensuring lasting security for their peoples,

Convinced that nuclear weapons pose the greatest threat to mankind and to the survival of civilization,

Noting that the renewed interest in nuclear disarmament should be translated into concrete actions for the achievement of general and complete disarmament under effective international control,

Convinced that nuclear disarmament and the complete elimination of nuclear weapons are essential to remove the danger of nuclear war,

Determined to abide strictly by the relevant provisions of the Charter of the United Nations on the non-use of force or threat of force,

Recognizing that the independence, territorial integrity and sovereignty of non-nuclear-weapon States need to be safeguarded against the use or threat of use of force, including the use or threat of use of nuclear weapons,

Considering that, until nuclear disarmament is achieved on a universal basis, it is imperative for the international community to develop effective measures and arrangements to ensure the security of non-nuclear-weapon States against the use or threat of use of nuclear weapons from any quarter,

Recognizing that effective measures and arrangements to assure non-nuclear-weapon States against the use or threat of use of nuclear weapons can contribute positively to the prevention of the spread of nuclear weapons,

Bearing in mind paragraph 59 of the Final Document of the Tenth Special Session of the General Assembly, the first special session devoted to disarmament,[1] in which it urged the nuclear-weapon States to pursue efforts to conclude, as appropriate, effective arrangements to assure non-nuclear-weapon States against the use or threat of use of nuclear weapons, and desirous of promoting the implementation of the relevant provisions of the Final Document,

---

[1] Resolution S-10/2.

Recalling the relevant parts of the special report of the Committee on Disarmament[2] submitted to the General Assembly at its twelfth special session, the second special session devoted to disarmament,[3] and of the special report of the Conference on Disarmament submitted to the Assembly at its fifteenth special session, the third special session devoted to disarmament,[4] as well as the report of the Conference on its 1992 session,[5]

Recalling also paragraph 12 of the Declaration of the 1980s as the Second Disarmament Decade, contained in the annex to its resolution 35/46 of 3 December 1980, in which it is stated, inter alia, that all efforts should be exerted by the Committee on Disarmament urgently to negotiate with a view to reaching agreement on effective international arrangements to assure non-nuclear-weapon States against the use or threat of use of nuclear weapons,

Noting the in-depth negotiations undertaken in the Conference on Disarmament and its Ad Hoc Committee on Effective International Arrangements to Assure Non-Nuclear-Weapon States against the Use or Threat of Use of Nuclear Weapons,[6] with a view to reaching agreement on this question,

Taking note of the proposals submitted under the item in the Conference on Disarmament, including the drafts of an international convention,

Taking note also of the relevant decision of the Thirteenth Conference of Heads of State or Government of Non-Aligned Countries, held in Kuala Lumpur on 24 and 25 February 2003,[7] which was reiterated at the Seventeenth Conference of Heads of State or Government of Non-Aligned Countries, held on Margarita Island, Bolivarian Republic of Venezuela, from 13 to 18 September 2016, as well as the relevant recommendations of the Organization of Islamic Cooperation,

Taking note further of the unilateral declarations made by all the nuclear-weapon States on their policies of non-use or non-threat of use of nuclear weapons against the non-nuclear-weapon States,

Noting the support expressed in the Conference on Disarmament and in the General Assembly for the elaboration of an international convention to assure non-nuclear-weapon States against the use or threat of use of nuclear weapons, as well as the difficulties pointed out in evolving a common approach acceptable to all,

---

[2] The Committee on Disarmament was redesignated the Conference on Disarmament as from 7 February 1984.
[3] *Official Records of the General Assembly, Twelfth Special Session, Supplement No. 2* (A/S-12/2), sect. III.C.
[4] Ibid., *Fifteenth Special Session, Supplement No. 2* (A/S-15/2), sect. III.F.
[5] Ibid., *Forty-seventh Session, Supplement No. 27* (A/47/27), sect. III.F.
[6] Ibid., *Forty-eighth Session, Supplement No. 27* (A/48/27), sect. III.E.
[7] See A/57/759-S/2003/332, annex I.

Taking note of Security Council resolution 984 (1995) of 11 April 1995 and the views expressed on it,

Recalling its relevant resolutions adopted in previous years, in particular resolutions 45/54 of 4 December 1990, 46/32 of 6 December 1991, 47/50 of 9 December 1992, 48/73 of 16 December 1993, 49/73 of 15 December 1994, 50/68 of 12 December 1995, 51/43 of 10 December 1996, 52/36 of 9 December 1997, 53/75 of 4 December 1998, 54/52 of 1 December 1999, 55/31 of 20 November 2000, 56/22 of 29 November 2001, 57/56 of 22 November 2002, 58/35 of 8 December 2003, 59/64 of 3 December 2004, 60/53 of 8 December 2005, 61/57 of 6 December 2006, 62/19 of 5 December 2007, 63/39 of 2 December 2008, 64/27 of 2 December 2009, 65/43 of 8 December 2010, 66/26 of 2 December 2011, 67/29 of 3 December 2012, 68/28 of 5 December 2013, 69/30 of 2 December 2014, 70/25 of 7 December 2015 and 71/30 of 5 December 2016,

1.   *Reaffirms* the urgent need to reach an early agreement on effective international arrangements to assure non-nuclear-weapon States against the use or threat of use of nuclear weapons;

2.   *Notes with satisfaction* that in the Conference on Disarmament there is no objection, in principle, to the idea of an international convention to assure non-nuclear-weapon States against the use or threat of use of nuclear weapons, although the difficulties with regard to evolving a common approach acceptable to all have also been pointed out;

3.   *Appeals* to all States, especially the nuclear-weapon States, to work actively towards an early agreement on a common approach and, in particular, on a common formula that could be included in an international instrument of a legally binding character;

4.   *Recommends* that further intensive efforts be devoted to the search for such a common approach or common formula and that the various alternative approaches, including, in particular, those considered in the Conference on Disarmament, be further explored in order to overcome the difficulties;

5.   *Also recommends* that the Conference on Disarmament actively continue intensive negotiations with a view to reaching early agreement and concluding effective international agreements to assure the non-nuclear-weapon States against the use or threat of use of nuclear weapons, taking into account the widespread support for the conclusion of an international convention and giving consideration to any other proposals designed to secure the same objective;

6.   *Decides* to include in the provisional agenda of its seventy-third session the item entitled "Conclusion of effective international arrangements to assure non-nuclear-weapon States against the use or threat of use of nuclear weapons".

Action by the General Assembly

    Date: 4 December 2017   Meeting: 62nd plenary meeting
    Vote: 125-0-62   Report: A/72/406

Sponsors

Algeria, Chad, Cuba, Egypt, Eritrea, Ghana, Iraq, Libya, Nicaragua, **Pakistan**, Peru, Saudi Arabia, Swaziland, Syrian Arab Republic, Venezuela (Bolivarian Republic of)

Co-sponsors

Angola, Bangladesh, Bolivia (Plurinational State of), Colombia, Honduras, Iran (Islamic Republic of), Kazakhstan, Kuwait, Paraguay, Sierra Leone, Sri Lanka, Uganda, Uzbekistan

Recorded vote

In favour:

Afghanistan, Algeria, Angola, Antigua and Barbuda, Azerbaijan, Bahamas, Bahrain, Bangladesh, Barbados, Belarus, Belize, Benin, Bhutan, Bolivia (Plurinational State of), Botswana, Brunei Darussalam, Burkina Faso, Burundi, Cabo Verde, Cambodia, Cameroon, Central African Republic, Chad, Chile, China, Colombia, Comoros, Congo, Costa Rica, Côte d'Ivoire, Cuba, Democratic Republic of the Congo, Djibouti, Dominican Republic, Ecuador, Egypt, El Salvador, Equatorial Guinea, Eritrea, Ethiopia, Fiji, Gabon, Gambia, Ghana, Guatemala, Guinea, Guinea-Bissau, Guyana, Haiti, Honduras, India, Indonesia, Iran (Islamic Republic of), Iraq, Jamaica, Japan, Jordan, Kazakhstan, Kenya, Kiribati, Kuwait, Kyrgyzstan, Lao People's Democratic Republic, Lebanon, Lesotho, Liberia, Libya, Madagascar, Malawi, Malaysia, Maldives, Mauritania, Mauritius, Mexico, Mongolia, Morocco, Mozambique, Myanmar, Namibia, Nauru, Nepal, Nicaragua, Oman, Pakistan, Panama, Papua New Guinea, Paraguay, Peru, Philippines, Qatar, Rwanda, Saint Kitts and Nevis, Saint Lucia, Saint Vincent and the Grenadines, Samoa, Saudi Arabia, Senegal, Sierra Leone, Singapore, Solomon Islands, Somalia, Sri Lanka, Sudan, Suriname, Swaziland, Syrian Arab Republic, Tajikistan, Thailand, Timor-Leste, Togo, Tonga, Trinidad and Tobago, Tunisia, Turkmenistan, Uganda, United Arab Emirates, United Republic of Tanzania, Uruguay, Uzbekistan, Vanuatu, Venezuela (Bolivarian Republic of), Viet Nam, Yemen, Zambia, Zimbabwe

Against:

None

Abstaining:

Albania, Andorra, Argentina, Armenia, Australia, Austria, Belgium, Bosnia and Herzegovina, Brazil, Bulgaria, Canada, Croatia, Cyprus, Czech Republic, Democratic People's Republic of Korea, Denmark, Estonia, Finland, France, Georgia, Germany, Greece, Hungary, Iceland, Ireland, Israel, Italy, Latvia, Liechtenstein, Lithuania, Luxembourg, Mali, Malta, Marshall Islands, Micronesia (Federated States of), Monaco, Montenegro, Netherlands, New Zealand, Nigeria, Norway, Palau, Poland, Portugal, Republic of Korea, Republic of Moldova, Romania, Russian Federation, San Marino, Serbia, Slovakia, Slovenia, South Africa, Spain, Sweden, Switzerland, the former Yugoslav Republic of Macedonia, Turkey, Tuvalu, Ukraine, United Kingdom, United States

Action by the First Committee

Date:	27 October 2017	Meeting:	24th meeting
Vote:	118-0-59	Draft resolution:	A/C.1/72/L.10/Rev.1

Agenda item 97 (a)

72/26 Prevention of an arms race in outer space

Text

The General Assembly,

Recognizing the common interest of all mankind in the exploration and use of outer space for peaceful purposes,

Reaffirming the will of all States that the exploration and use of outer space, including the Moon and other celestial bodies, shall be for peaceful purposes and shall be carried out for the benefit and in the interest of all countries, irrespective of their degree of economic or scientific development,

Reaffirming also the provisions of articles III and IV of the Treaty on Principles Governing the Activities of States in the Exploration and Use of Outer Space, including the Moon and Other Celestial Bodies,[1]

Recalling the obligation of all States to observe the provisions of the Charter of the United Nations regarding the use or threat of use of force in their international relations, including in their space activities,

Reaffirming paragraph 80 of the Final Document of the Tenth Special Session of the General Assembly,[2] in which it is stated that, in order to prevent an arms race in outer space, further measures should be taken and appropriate international negotiations held in accordance with the spirit of the Treaty,

Recalling its previous resolutions on this issue, the most recent of which is resolution 71/31 of 5 December 2016, and taking note of the proposals submitted to the General Assembly at its tenth special session and at its regular sessions and of the recommendations made to the competent organs of the United Nations and to the Conference on Disarmament,

Recognizing that the prevention of an arms race in outer space would avert a grave danger for international peace and security,

Emphasizing the paramount importance of strict compliance with existing arms limitation and disarmament agreements relevant to outer space, including bilateral agreements, and with the existing legal regime concerning the use of outer space,

Considering that wide participation in the legal regime applicable to outer space could contribute to enhancing its effectiveness,

Noting that the Ad Hoc Committee on the Prevention of an Arms Race in Outer Space, taking into account its previous efforts since its establishment in 1985 and seeking to enhance its functioning in qualitative terms, continued

---

[1] United Nations, *Treaty Series*, vol. 610, No. 8843.

[2] Resolution S-10/2.

the examination and identification of various issues, existing agreements and existing proposals, as well as future initiatives relevant to the prevention of an arms race in outer space, and that this contributed to a better understanding of a number of problems and to a clearer perception of the various positions,

Noting also that there were no objections in principle in the Conference on Disarmament to the re-establishment of the Ad Hoc Committee, subject to re-examination of the mandate contained in the decision of the Conference on Disarmament of 13 February 1992,[3]

Emphasizing the mutually complementary nature of bilateral and multilateral efforts for the prevention of an arms race in outer space, and hoping that concrete results will emerge from those efforts as soon as possible,

Convinced that further measures should be examined in the search for effective and verifiable bilateral and multilateral agreements in order to prevent an arms race in outer space, including the weaponization of outer space,

Stressing that the growing use of outer space increases the need for greater transparency and better information on the part of the international community,

Recalling, in this context, its previous resolutions, in particular resolutions 45/55 B of 4 December 1990, 47/51 of 9 December 1992 and 48/74 A of 16 December 1993, in which, inter alia, it reaffirmed the importance of confidence-building measures as a means conducive to ensuring the attainment of the objective of the prevention of an arms race in outer space,

Conscious of the benefits of confidence- and security-building measures in the military field,

Recognizing that negotiations for the conclusion of an international agreement or agreements to prevent an arms race in outer space remain a priority task of the Conference on Disarmament and that the concrete proposals on confidence-building measures could form an integral part of such agreements,

Noting with satisfaction the constructive, structured and focused debate on the prevention of an arms race in outer space at the Conference on Disarmament in 2009, 2010, 2011, 2012, 2013, 2014, 2015, 2016 and 2017,

Noting the introduction by China and the Russian Federation at the Conference on Disarmament of the draft treaty on the prevention of the

---

[3] See *Official Records of the General Assembly, Forty-seventh Session, Supplement No. 27* (A/47/27), para. 76.

placement of weapons in outer space and of the threat or use of force against outer space objects in 2008 and the submission of its updated version in 2014,[4]

Taking note of the decision of the Conference on Disarmament to establish for its 2009 session a working group to discuss, substantially, without limitation, all issues related to the prevention of an arms race in outer space,

1.   *Reaffirms* the importance and urgency of preventing an arms race in outer space and the readiness of all States to contribute to that common objective, in conformity with the provisions of the Treaty on Principles Governing the Activities of States in the Exploration and Use of Outer Space, including the Moon and Other Celestial Bodies;[1]

2.   *Reaffirms its recognition*, as stated in the report of the Ad Hoc Committee on the Prevention of an Arms Race in Outer Space, that the legal regime applicable to outer space by itself does not guarantee the prevention of an arms race in outer space, that the regime plays a significant role in the prevention of an arms race in that environment, that there is a need to consolidate and reinforce that regime and enhance its effectiveness and that it is important to comply strictly with existing agreements, both bilateral and multilateral;

3.   *Emphasizes* the necessity of further measures with appropriate and effective provisions for verification to prevent an arms race in outer space;

4.   *Calls upon* all States, in particular those with major space capabilities, to contribute actively to the objective of the peaceful use of outer space and of the prevention of an arms race in outer space and to refrain from actions contrary to that objective and to the relevant existing treaties in the interest of maintaining international peace and security and promoting international cooperation;

5.   *Reiterates* that the Conference on Disarmament, as the sole multilateral disarmament negotiating forum, has the primary role in the negotiation of a multilateral agreement or agreements, as appropriate, on the prevention of an arms race in outer space in all its aspects;

6.   *Invites* the Conference on Disarmament to establish a working group under its agenda item entitled "Prevention of an arms race in outer space" as early as possible during its 2018 session;

7.   *Recognizes*, in this respect, the growing convergence of views on the elaboration of measures designed to strengthen transparency, confidence and security in the peaceful uses of outer space;

8.   *Urges* States conducting activities in outer space, as well as States interested in conducting such activities, to keep the Conference

---

[4] See CD/1839 and CD/1985.

on Disarmament informed of the progress of bilateral and multilateral negotiations on the matter, if any, so as to facilitate its work;

9.   *Decides* to include in the provisional agenda of its seventy-third session the item entitled "Prevention of an arms race in outer space".

Action by the General Assembly

Date: 4 December 2017   Meeting: 62nd plenary meeting
Vote: 182-0-3   Report: A/72/407

Sponsors

Algeria, Angola, Belarus, China, Cuba, **Egypt**, Indonesia, Iraq, Kenya, Mongolia, Myanmar, Nigeria, **Sri Lanka**, Syrian Arab Republic, Thailand

Co-sponsors

Armenia, Bangladesh, Brazil, Burkina Faso, Ecuador, Ghana, Honduras, India, Kazakhstan, Kyrgyzstan, Malaysia, Nepal, Pakistan, Panama, Russian Federation, Samoa, Sierra Leone, Suriname, Uruguay, Uzbekistan, Zimbabwe

Recorded vote

In favour:

Afghanistan, Albania, Algeria, Andorra, Angola, Antigua and Barbuda, Argentina, Armenia, Australia, Austria, Azerbaijan, Bahamas, Bahrain, Bangladesh, Barbados, Belarus, Belgium, Belize, Benin, Bhutan, Bolivia (Plurinational State of), Bosnia and Herzegovina, Botswana, Brazil, Brunei Darussalam, Bulgaria, Burkina Faso, Burundi, Cabo Verde, Cambodia, Cameroon, Canada, Central African Republic, Chad, Chile, China, Colombia, Comoros, Congo, Costa Rica, Côte d'Ivoire, Croatia, Cuba, Cyprus, Czech Republic, Democratic People's Republic of Korea, Democratic Republic of the Congo, Denmark, Djibouti, Dominican Republic, Ecuador, Egypt, El Salvador, Equatorial Guinea, Eritrea, Estonia, Ethiopia, Fiji, Finland, France, Gabon, Gambia, Georgia, Germany, Ghana, Greece, Guatemala, Guinea, Guinea-Bissau, Guyana, Honduras, Hungary, Iceland, India, Indonesia, Iran (Islamic Republic of), Iraq, Ireland, Italy, Jamaica, Japan, Jordan, Kazakhstan, Kenya, Kiribati, Kuwait, Kyrgyzstan, Lao People's Democratic Republic, Latvia, Lebanon, Lesotho, Liberia, Libya, Liechtenstein, Lithuania, Luxembourg, Madagascar, Malawi, Malaysia, Maldives, Mali, Malta, Marshall Islands, Mauritania, Mauritius, Mexico, Micronesia (Federated States of), Monaco, Mongolia, Montenegro, Morocco, Mozambique, Myanmar, Namibia, Nauru, Nepal, Netherlands, New Zealand, Nicaragua, Nigeria, Norway, Oman, Pakistan, Panama, Papua New Guinea, Paraguay, Peru, Philippines, Poland, Portugal, Qatar, Republic of Korea, Republic of Moldova, Romania, Russian Federation, Rwanda, Saint Kitts and Nevis, Saint Lucia, Saint Vincent and the Grenadines, Samoa, San Marino, Saudi Arabia, Senegal, Serbia, Sierra Leone, Singapore, Slovakia, Slovenia, Solomon Islands, Somalia, South Africa, Spain, Sri Lanka, Sudan, Suriname, Swaziland, Sweden, Switzerland, Syrian Arab Republic, Tajikistan, Thailand, the former Yugoslav Republic of Macedonia, Timor-Leste, Togo, Tonga, Trinidad and Tobago, Tunisia, Turkey, Turkmenistan, Uganda, Ukraine, United Arab Emirates, United Kingdom, United Republic of Tanzania, Uruguay, Uzbekistan, Vanuatu, Venezuela (Bolivarian Republic of), Viet Nam, Yemen, Zambia, Zimbabwe

Against:
None

Abstaining:
Israel, Palau, United States

Action by the First Committee

Date: 30 October 2017   Meeting: 25th meeting
Vote: 175-0-2   Draft resolution: A/C.1/72/L.3

Agenda item 97 (b)

72/27   No first placement of weapons in outer space

Text

The General Assembly,

Recognizing the common interest of all humankind in the exploration and use of outer space for peaceful purposes,

Seriously concerned about the possibility of an arms race in outer space and of outer space turning into an arena for military confrontation, and bearing in mind the importance of articles III and IV of the Treaty on Principles Governing the Activities of States in the Exploration and Use of Outer Space, including the Moon and Other Celestial Bodies,[1]

Conscious that the prevention of an arms race in outer space would avert a grave danger to international peace and security,

Reaffirming that practical measures should be examined and taken in the search for agreements to prevent an arms race in outer space in a common effort towards a community of shared future for humankind,

Emphasizing the paramount importance of strict compliance with the existing legal regime providing for the peaceful use of outer space,

Reaffirming its recognition that the legal regime applicable to outer space by itself does not guarantee prevention of an arms race in outer space and that there is a need to consolidate and reinforce that regime,

Welcoming, in this regard, the draft treaty on the prevention of the placement of weapons in outer space and of the threat or use of force against outer space objects, introduced by China and the Russian Federation at the Conference on Disarmament in 2008,[2] and the submission of its updated version in 2014,[3]

Considering that transparency and confidence-building measures in outer space activities are an integral part of the draft treaty referred to above,

Recalling its resolutions 69/32 of 2 December 2014, 70/27 of 7 December 2015 and 71/32 of 5 December 2016, and its resolutions 45/55 B of 4 December 1990 and 48/74 B of 16 December 1993, which, inter alia, confirm the importance of transparency and confidence-building measures as a means conducive to ensuring the attainment of the objective of the prevention of an arms race in outer space,

---

[1] United Nations, *Treaty Series*, vol. 610, No. 8843.
[2] See CD/1839.
[3] See CD/1985.

Noting the importance of the political statements made by a number of States[4] that they would not be the first to place weapons in outer space,

1.   *Reaffirms* the importance and urgency of the objective to prevent an arms race in outer space and the willingness of States to contribute to reaching this common goal;

2.   *Reiterates* that the Conference on Disarmament, as the single multilateral negotiating forum on this subject,[5] has the primary role in the negotiation of a multilateral agreement, or agreements, as appropriate, on the prevention of an arms race in outer space in all its aspects;

3.   *Urges* an early commencement of substantive work based on the updated draft treaty on the prevention of the placement of weapons in outer space and of the threat or use of force against outer space objects,[3] introduced by China and the Russian Federation at the Conference on Disarmament in 2008,[2] under the agenda item entitled "Prevention of an arms race in outer space";

4.   *Stresses* that, while such an agreement is not yet concluded, other measures may contribute to ensuring that weapons are not placed in outer space;

5.   *Encourages* all States, especially space-faring nations, to consider the possibility of upholding, as appropriate, a political commitment not to be the first to place weapons in outer space;

6.   *Decides* to include in the provisional agenda of its seventy-third session the item entitled "No first placement of weapons in outer space".

Action by the General Assembly

Date: 4 December 2017   Meeting: 62nd plenary meeting
Vote: 131-4-48   Report: A/72/407

Sponsors

Algeria, Angola, Argentina, Armenia, Belarus, Brazil, China, Cuba, Democratic People's Republic of Korea, Egypt, El Salvador, Guinea, Kazakhstan, Kenya, Lao People's Democratic Republic, Mali, Myanmar, Nicaragua, **Russian Federation**, Sudan, Suriname, Syrian Arab Republic, Tajikistan, Turkmenistan, Venezuela (Bolivarian Republic of), Zimbabwe

Co-sponsors

Bangladesh, Benin, Bolivia (Plurinational State of), Cambodia, Eritrea, Honduras, Indonesia, Kyrgyzstan, Morocco, Namibia, Nigeria, Pakistan, Senegal, Sri Lanka, Thailand, Uganda, Uzbekistan, Viet Nam

---

[4] Argentina, Armenia, Belarus, Bolivia (Plurinational State of), Brazil, Cuba, Ecuador, Indonesia, Kazakhstan, Kyrgyzstan, Nicaragua, Russian Federation, Sri Lanka, Tajikistan, Uruguay, Venezuela (Bolivarian Republic of) and Viet Nam.

[5] See resolution S-10/2.

Recorded vote

In favour:

Afghanistan, Algeria, Angola, Antigua and Barbuda, Argentina, Armenia, Azerbaijan, Bahamas, Bahrain, Bangladesh, Barbados, Belarus, Belize, Benin, Bhutan, Bolivia (Plurinational State of), Botswana, Brazil, Brunei Darussalam, Burkina Faso, Burundi, Cabo Verde, Cambodia, Cameroon, Central African Republic, Chad, Chile, China, Colombia, Comoros, Congo, Costa Rica, Côte d'Ivoire, Cuba, Democratic People's Republic of Korea, Democratic Republic of the Congo, Djibouti, Dominican Republic, Ecuador, Egypt, El Salvador, Equatorial Guinea, Eritrea, Ethiopia, Fiji, Gabon, Gambia, Ghana, Guatemala, Guinea, Guinea-Bissau, Guyana, Honduras, India, Indonesia, Iran (Islamic Republic of), Iraq, Jamaica, Jordan, Kazakhstan, Kenya, Kiribati, Kuwait, Kyrgyzstan, Lao People's Democratic Republic, Lebanon, Lesotho, Liberia, Libya, Madagascar, Malawi, Malaysia, Maldives, Mali, Mauritania, Mauritius, Mexico, Mongolia, Morocco, Mozambique, Myanmar, Namibia, Nauru, Nepal, Nicaragua, Nigeria, Oman, Pakistan, Panama, Papua New Guinea, Paraguay, Peru, Philippines, Qatar, Russian Federation, Rwanda, Saint Kitts and Nevis, Saint Lucia, Saint Vincent and the Grenadines, Samoa, Saudi Arabia, Senegal, Serbia, Sierra Leone, Singapore, Solomon Islands, Somalia, South Africa, Sri Lanka, Sudan, Suriname, Swaziland, Syrian Arab Republic, Tajikistan, Thailand, Timor-Leste, Togo, Trinidad and Tobago, Tunisia, Turkmenistan, Uganda, United Arab Emirates, United Republic of Tanzania, Uruguay, Uzbekistan, Vanuatu, Venezuela (Bolivarian Republic of), Viet Nam, Yemen, Zambia, Zimbabwe

Against:

Georgia, Israel, Ukraine, United States

Abstaining:

Albania, Andorra, Australia, Austria, Belgium, Bosnia and Herzegovina, Bulgaria, Canada, Croatia, Cyprus, Czech Republic, Denmark, Estonia, Finland, France, Germany, Greece, Hungary, Iceland, Ireland, Italy, Japan, Latvia, Liechtenstein, Lithuania, Luxembourg, Malta, Monaco, Montenegro, Netherlands, New Zealand, Norway, Palau, Poland, Portugal, Republic of Korea, Republic of Moldova, Romania, San Marino, Slovakia, Slovenia, Spain, Sweden, Switzerland, the former Yugoslav Republic of Macedonia, Turkey, Tuvalu, United Kingdom

Action by the First Committee

Date: 30 October 2017   Meeting: 25th meeting

Vote: 122-4-48   Draft resolution: A/C.1/72/L.53

Agenda item 98

72/28 Role of science and technology in the context of international security and disarmament

Text

The General Assembly,

Recognizing that scientific and technological developments can have both civilian and military applications and that progress in science and technology for civilian applications needs to be maintained and encouraged,

Underlining the keen interest of the international community to keep abreast of the latest developments in science and technology of relevance to international security and disarmament and to channel scientific and technological developments for beneficial purposes,

Mindful of the need to regulate the transfer of technologies for peaceful uses, in accordance with relevant international obligations, to address the risk of proliferation by States or non-State actors,

Acknowledging the need to continue the exchange of technologies for peaceful uses, including in accordance with relevant international obligations,

Cognizant of the discussions on developments in science and technology at the International Atomic Energy Agency and the Organisation for the Prohibition of Chemical Weapons and under the standing agenda item on science and technology of the intersessional programme established by the Seventh Review Conference of the States Parties to the Convention on the Prohibition of the Development, Production and Stockpiling of Bacteriological (Biological) and Toxin Weapons and on Their Destruction,

Mindful of the discussions in other forums, such as the Committee on the Peaceful Uses of Outer Space, on the long-term sustainability of outer space activities and on the prevention of an arms race in outer space in the United Nations disarmament machinery,

Noting the discussions on various dimensions of emerging technologies under the framework of the Convention on Prohibitions or Restrictions on the Use of Certain Conventional Weapons Which May Be Deemed to Be Excessively Injurious or to Have Indiscriminate Effects,[1]

Noting also the discussions within the United Nations and the specialized agencies on developments in the field of information and communications technologies, including in the context of international security,

Acknowledging that the accelerating pace of technological change necessitates a system-wide assessment of the potential impact of developments

---

[1] United Nations, *Treaty Series*, vol. 1342, No. 22495.

in science and technology on international security and disarmament, with due regard to avoiding duplication and complementing efforts already under way in United Nations entities and in the framework of the relevant international conventions,

1.   *Invites* Member States to continue efforts to apply developments in science and technology for disarmament-related purposes, including the verification of disarmament, arms control and non-proliferation instruments, and to make disarmament-related technologies available to interested States;

2.   *Requests* the Secretary-General to submit to the General Assembly at its seventy-third session a report on current developments in science and technology and their potential impact on international security and disarmament efforts, with an annex containing submissions from Member States giving their views on the matter;

3.   *Decides* to include in the provisional agenda of its seventy-third session the item entitled "Role of science and technology in the context of international security and disarmament".

Action by the General Assembly

Date: 4 December 2017   Meeting: 62nd plenary meeting
Vote: Adopted without a vote   Report: A/72/408

Sponsors

Angola, Bangladesh, Bhutan, Brazil, **India**, Mauritius, Sierra Leone

Co-sponsors

Austria, Canada, Croatia, Finland, Germany, Italy, Montenegro, Netherlands, Paraguay, Spain, Sweden, Switzerland

Action by the First Committee

Date: 31 October 2017   Meeting: 26th meeting
Vote: Adopted without a vote   Draft resolution: A/C.1/72/L.52/Rev.1

Agenda item 99 (w)

72/29 Follow-up to nuclear disarmament obligations agreed to at the 1995, 2000 and 2010 Review Conferences of the Parties to the Treaty on the Non-Proliferation of Nuclear Weapons

Text

The General Assembly,

Recalling its various resolutions in the field of nuclear disarmament, including resolutions 60/72 of 8 December 2005, 62/24 of 5 December 2007, 64/31 of 2 December 2009, 66/28 of 2 December 2011, 68/35 of 5 December 2013, 69/43 and 69/48 of 2 December 2014 and 70/38 of 7 December 2015,

Bearing in mind its resolution 2373 (XXII) of 12 June 1968, the annex to which contains the Treaty on the Non-Proliferation of Nuclear Weapons,[1]

Noting the provisions of article VIII, paragraph 3, of the Treaty regarding the convening of review conferences at five-year intervals,

Recalling its resolution 50/70 Q of 12 December 1995, in which the General Assembly noted that the States parties to the Treaty affirmed the need to continue to move with determination towards the full realization and effective implementation of the provisions of the Treaty, and accordingly adopted a set of principles and objectives,

Recalling also that, on 11 May 1995, the 1995 Review and Extension Conference of the Parties to the Treaty on the Non-Proliferation of Nuclear Weapons adopted three decisions on, respectively, strengthening the review process for the Treaty, principles and objectives for nuclear non-proliferation and disarmament, and extension of the Treaty,[2]

Reaffirming the resolution on the Middle East adopted on 11 May 1995 by the 1995 Review and Extension Conference,[2] in which the Conference reaffirmed the importance of the early realization of universal adherence to the Treaty and placement of nuclear facilities under full-scope International Atomic Energy Agency safeguards,

Reaffirming also its resolution 55/33 D of 20 November 2000, in which the General Assembly welcomed the adoption by consensus on 19 May 2000 of the Final Document of the 2000 Review Conference of the Parties to the

---

[1] See also United Nations, *Treaty Series*, vol. 729, No. 10485.
[2] See *1995 Review and Extension Conference of the Parties to the Treaty on the Non-Proliferation of Nuclear Weapons, Final Document, Part I* (NPT/CONF.1995/32 (Part I) and NPT/CONF.1995/32 (Part I)/Corr.2), annex.

Treaty on the Non-Proliferation of Nuclear Weapons,[3] including, in particular, the documents entitled "Review of the operation of the Treaty, taking into account the decisions and the resolution adopted by the 1995 Review and Extension Conference" and "Improving the effectiveness of the strengthened review process for the Treaty",[4]

Taking into consideration the unequivocal undertaking by the nuclear-weapon States, in the Final Document of the 2000 Review Conference, to accomplish the total elimination of their nuclear arsenals leading to nuclear disarmament, to which all States parties to the Treaty are committed under article VI of the Treaty,

Expressing concern that the ninth Review Conference of the Parties to the Treaty on the Non-Proliferation of Nuclear Weapons, held from 27 April to 22 May 2015, was not able to reach agreement on a substantive final document,

1. *Recalls* that the 2010 Review Conference of the Parties to the Treaty on the Non-Proliferation of Nuclear Weapons reaffirmed the continued validity of the practical steps agreed to in the Final Document of the 2000 Review Conference of the Parties to the Treaty on the Non-Proliferation of Nuclear Weapons;[5]

2. *Determines* to pursue practical steps for systematic and progressive efforts to implement article VI of the Treaty on the Non-Proliferation of Nuclear Weapons[1] and paragraphs 3 and 4 (c) of the decision on principles and objectives for nuclear non-proliferation and disarmament of the 1995 Review and Extension Conference of the Parties to the Treaty on the Non-Proliferation of Nuclear Weapons;[2]

3. *Calls for* practical steps, as agreed to at the 2000 Review Conference of the Parties to the Treaty on the Non-Proliferation of Nuclear Weapons, to be taken by all nuclear-weapon States, that would lead to nuclear disarmament in a way that promotes international stability and, based on the principle of undiminished security for all:

    (a) Further efforts to be made by the nuclear-weapon States to reduce their nuclear arsenals unilaterally;

    (b) Increased transparency by the nuclear-weapon States with regard to nuclear weapons capabilities and the implementation of agreements pursuant to article VI of the Treaty and as a voluntary confidence-building measure to support further progress in nuclear disarmament;

---

[3] *2000 Review Conference of the Parties to the Treaty on the Non-Proliferation of Nuclear Weapons, Final Document*, vols. I–III (NPT/CONF.2000/28 (Parts I and II), NPT/CONF.2000/28 (Part III) and NPT/CONF.2000/28 (Part IV)).

[4] Ibid., vol. I (NPT/CONF.2000/28 (Parts I and II)), part I.

[5] Ibid., section entitled "Article VI and eighth to twelfth preambular paragraphs", para. 15.

(c) The further reduction of non-strategic nuclear weapons, based on unilateral initiatives and as an integral part of the nuclear arms reduction and disarmament process;

(d) Concrete agreed measures to reduce further the operational status of nuclear weapons systems;

(e) A diminishing role for nuclear weapons in security policies so as to minimize the risk that these weapons will ever be used and to facilitate the process of their total elimination;

(f) The engagement, as soon as appropriate, of all the nuclear-weapon States in the process leading to the total elimination of their nuclear weapons;

4. *Notes* that the 2000 and 2010 Review Conferences agreed that legally binding security assurances by the five nuclear-weapon States to the non-nuclear-weapon States parties to the Treaty strengthen the nuclear non-proliferation regime;

5. *Urges* the States parties to the Treaty to follow up on the implementation of the nuclear disarmament obligations under the Treaty agreed to at the 1995, 2000 and 2010 Review Conferences within the framework of review conferences and their preparatory committees;

6. *Decides* to include in the provisional agenda of its seventy-fourth session, under the item entitled "General and complete disarmament", the sub-item entitled "Follow-up to nuclear disarmament obligations agreed to at the 1995, 2000 and 2010 Review Conferences of the Parties to the Treaty on the Non-Proliferation of Nuclear Weapons".

Action by the General Assembly

Date: 4 December 2017   Meeting: 62nd plenary meeting
Vote: 118-44-17   Report: A/72/409
     125-5-47, p.p. 6

Sponsors

Islamic Republic of Iran

Recorded vote

As a whole

In favour:
Afghanistan, Algeria, Angola, Antigua and Barbuda, Argentina, Azerbaijan, Bahamas, Bahrain, Bangladesh, Barbados, Belarus, Belize, Benin, Bhutan, Bolivia (Plurinational State of), Botswana, Brazil, Brunei Darussalam, Burkina Faso, Burundi, Cabo Verde, Cambodia, Chad, Chile, Colombia, Comoros, Congo, Costa Rica, Côte d'Ivoire, Cuba, Democratic Republic of the Congo, Djibouti, Dominican

Republic, Ecuador, Egypt, El Salvador, Equatorial Guinea, Eritrea, Ethiopia, Fiji, Gabon, Gambia, Ghana, Guatemala, Guinea, Guinea-Bissau, Guyana, Honduras, Indonesia, Iran (Islamic Republic of), Iraq, Jamaica, Jordan, Kazakhstan, Kenya, Kiribati, Kuwait, Kyrgyzstan, Lao People's Democratic Republic, Lebanon, Lesotho, Libya, Madagascar, Malawi, Malaysia, Maldives, Marshall Islands, Mauritania, Mauritius, Mexico, Mongolia, Morocco, Mozambique, Myanmar, Namibia, Nepal, Nicaragua, Nigeria, Oman, Panama, Papua New Guinea, Paraguay, Peru, Philippines, Qatar, Saint Kitts and Nevis, Saint Lucia, Saint Vincent and the Grenadines, Saudi Arabia, Senegal, Sierra Leone, Singapore, Solomon Islands, Somalia, South Africa, Sri Lanka, Sudan, Suriname, Swaziland, Syrian Arab Republic, Tajikistan, Thailand, Timor-Leste, Togo, Trinidad and Tobago, Tunisia, Turkmenistan, Uganda, United Arab Emirates, United Republic of Tanzania, Uruguay, Uzbekistan, Vanuatu, Venezuela (Bolivarian Republic of), Viet Nam, Yemen, Zambia, Zimbabwe

Against:

Albania, Andorra, Australia, Belgium, Bosnia and Herzegovina, Bulgaria, Canada, Croatia, Cyprus, Czech Republic, Denmark, Estonia, France, Germany, Greece, Hungary, Iceland, Ireland, Israel, Latvia, Lithuania, Luxembourg, Malta, Micronesia (Federated States of), Monaco, Montenegro, Netherlands, New Zealand, Norway, Poland, Portugal, Republic of Korea, Republic of Moldova, Romania, Russian Federation, Serbia, Slovakia, Slovenia, Spain, Sweden, the former Yugoslav Republic of Macedonia, Ukraine, United Kingdom, United States

Abstaining:

Armenia, Austria, China, Finland, Georgia, India, Italy, Japan, Liechtenstein, Mali, Pakistan, Rwanda, Samoa, San Marino, Switzerland, Tonga, Turkey

Sixth preambular paragraph

In favour:

Afghanistan, Algeria, Angola, Antigua and Barbuda, Argentina, Austria, Azerbaijan, Bahamas, Bahrain, Bangladesh, Barbados, Belarus, Belize, Benin, Bolivia (Plurinational State of), Botswana, Brazil, Brunei Darussalam, Burkina Faso, Burundi, Cabo Verde, Cambodia, Chad, Chile, Colombia, Comoros, Congo, Costa Rica, Côte d'Ivoire, Cuba, Democratic Republic of the Congo, Djibouti, Dominican Republic, Ecuador, Egypt, El Salvador, Equatorial Guinea, Eritrea, Ethiopia, Fiji, Gabon, Gambia, Ghana, Guatemala, Guinea, Guinea-Bissau, Guyana, Honduras, Indonesia, Iran (Islamic Republic of), Iraq, Jamaica, Japan, Jordan, Kazakhstan, Kenya, Kiribati, Kuwait, Kyrgyzstan, Lao People's

Democratic Republic, Lebanon, Lesotho, Liberia, Libya, Liechtenstein, Madagascar, Malawi, Malaysia, Maldives, Mauritania, Mauritius, Mexico, Mongolia, Morocco, Mozambique, Myanmar, Namibia, Nepal, New Zealand, Nicaragua, Nigeria, Oman, Panama, Papua New Guinea, Paraguay, Peru, Philippines, Qatar, Russian Federation, Rwanda, Saint Kitts and Nevis, Saint Lucia, Saint Vincent and the Grenadines, Saudi Arabia, Senegal, Sierra Leone, Singapore, Solomon Islands, Somalia, South Africa, Sri Lanka, Sudan, Suriname, Swaziland, Switzerland, Syrian Arab Republic, Tajikistan, Thailand, Timor-Leste, Togo, Trinidad and Tobago, Tunisia, Turkey, Turkmenistan, Uganda, United Arab Emirates, United Republic of Tanzania, Uruguay, Uzbekistan, Vanuatu, Venezuela (Bolivarian Republic of), Viet Nam, Yemen, Zambia, Zimbabwe

Against:

Canada, India, Israel, Micronesia (Federated States of), United States

Abstaining:

Albania, Andorra, Armenia, Australia, Belgium, Bhutan, Bosnia and Herzegovina, Bulgaria, Croatia, Cyprus, Czech Republic, Denmark, Estonia, Finland, France, Georgia, Germany, Greece, Hungary, Iceland, Ireland, Italy, Latvia, Lithuania, Luxembourg, Mali, Malta, Monaco, Montenegro, Netherlands, Norway, Pakistan, Poland, Portugal, Republic of Korea, Republic of Moldova, Romania, Samoa, San Marino, Serbia, Slovakia, Slovenia, Spain, Sweden, the former Yugoslav Republic of Macedonia, Ukraine, United Kingdom

Action by the First Committee

Date:	27 October 2017	Meeting:	24th meeting
Vote:	112-44-15	Draft resolution:	A/C.1/72/L.4
	115-5-47, p.p. 6		

Agenda item 99 (ee)

72/30   Humanitarian consequences of nuclear weapons

Text

The General Assembly,

Recalling its resolutions 70/47 of 7 December 2015 and 71/46 of 5 December 2016,

Reiterating the deep concern about the catastrophic consequences of nuclear weapons,

Stressing that the immense and uncontrollable destructive capability and indiscriminate nature of nuclear weapons cause unacceptable humanitarian consequences, as has been demonstrated through their past use and testing,

Recalling that concern about the humanitarian consequences of nuclear weapons has been reflected in numerous United Nations resolutions, including the first resolution adopted by the General Assembly, on 24 January 1946,

Recalling also that at the first special session of the General Assembly devoted to disarmament, in 1978, the Assembly stressed that nuclear weapons posed the greatest danger to mankind and to the survival of civilization,[1]

Welcoming the renewed interest and resolve of the international community, together with the International Committee of the Red Cross and international humanitarian organizations, to address the catastrophic consequences of nuclear weapons,

Recalling that the 2010 Review Conference of the Parties to the Treaty on the Non-Proliferation of Nuclear Weapons expressed deep concern at the catastrophic humanitarian consequences of any use of nuclear weapons,[2]

Noting the resolution of 26 November 2011 of the Council of Delegates of the International Red Cross and Red Crescent Movement entitled "Working towards the elimination of nuclear weapons",

Recalling the joint statements on the humanitarian consequences of nuclear weapons delivered to the General Assembly and during the 2010–2015 cycle of the review of the Treaty on the Non-Proliferation of Nuclear Weapons,[3]

Welcoming the facts-based discussions on the effects of a nuclear weapon detonation that were held at the conferences on the humanitarian impact of

---

[1] See resolution S-10/2.

[2] See *2010 Review Conference of the Parties to the Treaty on the Non-Proliferation of Nuclear Weapons, Final Document*, vol. I (NPT/CONF.2010/50 (Vol. I)), part I, *Conclusions and recommendations for follow-on actions*.

[3] United Nations, *Treaty Series*, vol. 729, No. 10485.

nuclear weapons, convened by Norway, on 4 and 5 March 2013, Mexico, on 13 and 14 February 2014, and Austria, on 8 and 9 December 2014,

Cognizant that a key message from experts and international organizations at those conferences was that no State or international body could address the immediate humanitarian emergency caused by a nuclear weapon detonation or provide adequate assistance to victims,

Firmly believing that it is in the interest of all States to engage in discussions on the humanitarian consequences of nuclear weapons with the aim of further broadening and deepening the understanding of this matter, and welcoming civil society's ongoing engagement,

Reaffirming the role of civil society, in partnership with Governments, in raising awareness about the unacceptable humanitarian consequences of nuclear weapons,

Emphasizing that the catastrophic consequences of nuclear weapons affect not only Governments but each and every citizen of our interconnected world and have deep implications for human survival, for the environment, for socioeconomic development, for our economies and for the health of future generations,

1.   *Stresses* that it is in the interest of the very survival of humanity that nuclear weapons never be used again, under any circumstances;

2.   *Emphasizes* that the only way to guarantee that nuclear weapons will never be used again is their total elimination;

3.   *Stresses* that the catastrophic effects of a nuclear weapon detonation, whether by accident, miscalculation or design, cannot be adequately addressed;

4.   *Expresses its firm belief* that awareness of the catastrophic consequences of nuclear weapons must underpin all approaches and efforts towards nuclear disarmament;

5.   *Calls upon* all States, in their shared responsibility, to prevent the use of nuclear weapons, to prevent their vertical and horizontal proliferation and to achieve nuclear disarmament;

6.   *Urges* States to exert all efforts to totally eliminate the threat of these weapons of mass destruction;

7.   *Decides* to include in the provisional agenda of its seventy-third session, under the item entitled "General and complete disarmament", the sub-item entitled "Humanitarian consequences of nuclear weapons".

Action by the General Assembly

Date: 4 December 2017	Meeting: 62nd plenary meeting
Vote: 141-15-27	Report: A/72/409

Sponsors

Algeria, Angola, **Austria**, Belize, Brazil, Cabo Verde, Chile, Costa Rica, Democratic Republic of the Congo, Dominican Republic, Egypt, Eritrea, Ghana, Guatemala, Indonesia, Ireland, Kazakhstan, Lebanon, Liechtenstein, Malawi, Malaysia, Malta, Mauritania, Mexico, Mongolia, Myanmar, Namibia, New Zealand, Nicaragua, Nigeria, Oman, Panama, Papua New Guinea, Peru, Samoa, Saudi Arabia, Senegal, South Africa, Sudan, Suriname, Swaziland, Sweden, Switzerland, Thailand, Togo, Trinidad and Tobago, Uruguay, Vanuatu, Venezuela (Bolivarian Republic of), Viet Nam, Zimbabwe

Co-sponsors

Andorra, Antigua and Barbuda, Bahamas, Bahrain, Benin, Bolivia (Plurinational State of), Burkina Faso, Central African Republic, Chad, Colombia, Côte d'Ivoire, Cyprus, El Salvador, Ethiopia, Guinea-Bissau, Guyana, Honduras, Kenya, Liberia, Libya, Madagascar, Maldives, Marshall Islands, Morocco, Mozambique, Paraguay, Philippines, San Marino, Sierra Leone, Singapore, the former Yugoslav Republic of Macedonia, Tunisia, Tuvalu, United Arab Emirates

Recorded vote

In favour:

Afghanistan, Algeria, Andorra, Angola, Antigua and Barbuda, Argentina, Austria, Azerbaijan, Bahamas, Bahrain, Bangladesh, Barbados, Belarus, Belize, Benin, Bhutan, Bolivia (Plurinational State of), Botswana, Brazil, Brunei Darussalam, Burkina Faso, Burundi, Cabo Verde, Cambodia, Chad, Chile, Colombia, Comoros, Congo, Costa Rica, Côte d'Ivoire, Cuba, Cyprus, Democratic Republic of the Congo, Djibouti, Dominican Republic, Ecuador, Egypt, El Salvador, Equatorial Guinea, Eritrea, Ethiopia, Fiji, Finland, Gabon, Gambia, Ghana, Greece, Guatemala, Guinea, Guinea-Bissau, Guyana, Haiti, Honduras, India, Indonesia, Iran (Islamic Republic of), Iraq, Ireland, Jamaica, Japan, Jordan, Kazakhstan, Kenya, Kiribati, Kuwait, Kyrgyzstan, Lao People's Democratic Republic, Lebanon, Lesotho, Liberia, Libya, Liechtenstein, Madagascar, Malawi, Malaysia, Maldives, Malta, Marshall Islands, Mauritania, Mauritius, Mexico, Mongolia, Morocco, Mozambique, Myanmar, Namibia, Nauru, Nepal, New Zealand, Nicaragua, Nigeria, Oman, Palau, Panama, Papua New Guinea, Paraguay, Peru, Philippines, Qatar, Republic of Moldova, Rwanda, Saint Kitts and Nevis, Saint Lucia, Samoa, San Marino, Saudi Arabia, Senegal, Serbia, Sierra Leone, Singapore, Solomon Islands, Somalia, South Africa, Sri Lanka, Sudan, Suriname, Swaziland, Sweden, Switzerland, Syrian Arab Republic, Tajikistan, Thailand, the former Yugoslav Republic of Macedonia, Timor-Leste, Togo, Tonga, Trinidad and Tobago, Tunisia, Tuvalu, Uganda, United Arab Emirates,

United Republic of Tanzania, Uruguay, Uzbekistan, Vanuatu, Venezuela (Bolivarian Republic of), Viet Nam, Yemen, Zambia, Zimbabwe

Against:

Czech Republic, Estonia, France, Hungary, Israel, Latvia, Lithuania, Monaco, Poland, Republic of Korea, Romania, Russian Federation, Turkey, United Kingdom, United States

Abstaining:

Albania, Armenia, Australia, Belgium, Bosnia and Herzegovina, Bulgaria, Canada, Central African Republic, China, Croatia, Democratic People's Republic of Korea, Denmark, Georgia, Germany, Iceland, Italy, Luxembourg, Mali, Montenegro, Netherlands, Norway, Pakistan, Portugal, Slovakia, Slovenia, Spain, Ukraine

Action by the First Committee

Date:	27 October 2017	Meeting:	24th meeting
Vote:	134-15-25	Draft resolution:	A/C.1/72/L.5

Agenda item 99 (bb)

72/31   Taking forward multilateral nuclear disarmament negotiations

Text

The General Assembly,

Recalling its resolutions 67/56 of 3 December 2012, 68/46 of 5 December 2013, 69/41 of 2 December 2014, 70/33 of 7 December 2015 and 71/258 of 23 December 2016 on taking forward multilateral nuclear disarmament negotiations for the achievement and maintenance of a world without nuclear weapons,

Deeply concerned about the catastrophic humanitarian consequences of any use of nuclear weapons,

Deeply concerned also about the risks related to the existence of nuclear weapons,

Recalling the Declaration of the Tenth Special Session of the General Assembly, the first special session devoted to disarmament,[1] in which it is stated, inter alia, that all the peoples of the world have a vital interest in the success of disarmament negotiations, and that all States have the right to participate in disarmament negotiations,

Reaffirming the role and functions of the Conference on Disarmament and the Disarmament Commission, as set out in the Final Document of the Tenth Special Session of the General Assembly,[2]

Recalling the United Nations Millennium Declaration,[3] in which it is stated, inter alia, that responsibility for managing worldwide economic and social development, as well as threats to international peace and security, must be shared among the nations of the world and should be exercised multilaterally and that, as the most universal and most representative organization in the world, the United Nations must play the central role,

Welcoming the efforts by Member States to secure progress in multilateral disarmament and the support of the Secretary-General for such efforts, and recalling in this regard the Secretary-General's five-point proposal on nuclear disarmament,

Recalling that the Treaty on the Non-Proliferation of Nuclear Weapons,[4] which serves as the cornerstone of the nuclear non-proliferation and disarmament regime, was negotiated considering the devastation that would

---

[1] Resolution S-10/2, sect. II.
[2] Ibid., sect. IV.
[3] Resolution 55/2.
[4] United Nations, *Treaty Series*, vol. 729, No. 10485.

be visited upon all mankind by a nuclear war and the consequent need to make every effort to avert the danger of such a war and to take measures to safeguard the security of peoples,

Stressing that the only way to guarantee that nuclear weapons are never used again is through their complete elimination and that a legally binding prohibition of nuclear weapons constitutes an essential contribution towards that end, as well as towards the implementation of article VI of the Treaty on the Non-Proliferation of Nuclear Weapons,

Recalling the obligations of States parties to the Treaty on the Non-Proliferation of Nuclear Weapons and their commitments as reflected in the outcome documents of the 1995 Review and Extension Conference of the Parties to the Treaty,[5] and of the 2000[6] and the 2010[7] Review Conferences of the Parties to the Treaty,

Stressing the importance of the full and effective implementation by the States parties to the Treaty on the Non-Proliferation of Nuclear Weapons of the various commitments made at the review conferences,

Reaffirming the absolute validity of multilateral diplomacy in the field of disarmament and non-proliferation, and determined to promote multilateralism as an essential way to develop arms regulation and disarmament negotiations,

Mindful of the obligation of States to engage in negotiations in good faith on effective measures towards nuclear disarmament,

Recognizing that the current international climate makes increased political attention to disarmament and non-proliferation issues, the promotion of multilateral disarmament and the achievement of a world without nuclear weapons all the more urgent,

Welcoming the high-level meeting of the General Assembly on nuclear disarmament, held on 26 September 2013 pursuant to its resolution 67/39 of 3 December 2012, which highlighted the wish of the international community for progress in this field, and noting its resolution 68/32 of 5 December 2013 as a follow-up to this meeting,

Welcoming also the report on the work of the Open-ended Working Group to develop proposals to take forward multilateral nuclear disarmament negotiations for the achievement and maintenance of a world without nuclear

---

[5] *1995 Review and Extension Conference of the Parties to the Treaty on the Non-Proliferation of Nuclear Weapons, Final Document,* Part I (NPT/CONF.1995/32 (Part I) and NPT/CONF.1995/32 (Part I)/Corr.2).

[6] *2000 Review Conference of the Parties to the Treaty on the Non-Proliferation of Nuclear Weapons, Final Document,* vols. I–III (NPT/CONF.2000/28 (Parts I and II), NPT/CONF.2000/28 (Part III) and NPT/CONF.2000/28 (Part IV)).

[7] *2010 Review Conference of the Parties to the Treaty on the Non-Proliferation of Nuclear Weapons, Final Document,* vols. I–III (NPT/CONF.2010/50 (Vol. I), NPT/CONF.2010/50 (Vol. II) and NPT/CONF.2010/50 (Vol. III)).

weapons, submitted pursuant to its resolution 67/56[8] and referenced in its resolution 68/46, and noting with appreciation the report of the Secretary-General submitted pursuant to its resolution 68/46,[9] containing the views of Member States on how to take forward multilateral nuclear disarmament negotiations, including the steps that Member States have already taken to that end,

Welcoming further the report of the Open-ended Working Group taking forward multilateral nuclear disarmament negotiations, established by the General Assembly by its resolution 70/33,[10] which met in Geneva during 2016,

Welcoming the efforts by all Member States, international organizations and civil society to continue to enrich the discussions on how to take forward multilateral nuclear disarmament negotiations in the United Nations bodies in which disarmament and peace and security are addressed,

Stressing the importance of inclusiveness, and encouraging the participation of all Member States in the efforts to achieve a nuclear-weapon-free world,

Emphasizing the importance and urgency of securing substantive progress on priority nuclear disarmament and non-proliferation issues,

Mindful of Article 11 of the Charter of the United Nations concerning the functions and powers of the General Assembly to consider and make recommendations with regard to, inter alia, disarmament,

1.　*Welcomes* the adoption on 7 July 2017 of the Treaty on the Prohibition of Nuclear Weapons by the United Nations conference to negotiate a legally binding instrument to prohibit nuclear weapons, leading towards their total elimination, convened pursuant to resolution 71/258;[11]

2.　*Also welcomes* the report of the conference;[12]

3.　*Notes* that the Treaty on the Prohibition of Nuclear Weapons was opened for signature at United Nations Headquarters in New York on 20 September 2017;

4.　*Calls upon* all States that have not yet done so to sign and, thereafter, ratify, accept or approve the Treaty on the Prohibition of Nuclear Weapons at the earliest possible date;

5.　*Reaffirms* that the Treaty on the Prohibition of Nuclear Weapons is an essential contribution towards nuclear disarmament;

---

[8]　A/68/514.
[9]　A/69/154 and A/69/154/Add.1.
[10]　A/71/371.
[11]　A/CONF.229/2017/8.
[12]　A/72/206.

6. *Reiterates* that additional measures, both practical and legally binding, for the irreversible, verifiable and transparent destruction of nuclear weapons would be needed in order to achieve and maintain a world without nuclear weapons, including the early entry into force of the Comprehensive Nuclear-Test-Ban Treaty[13] and the negotiation of a treaty on fissile material for nuclear weapons or other nuclear explosive devices;

7. *Recognizes* the value of the participation and contribution of international organizations and civil society to taking forward multilateral nuclear disarmament negotiations, including at the recently convened United Nations conference to negotiate a legally binding instrument to prohibit nuclear weapons, leading towards their total elimination;

8. *Reiterates* that the universal objective of taking forward multilateral nuclear disarmament negotiations remains the achievement and maintenance of a world without nuclear weapons, and emphasizes the importance of addressing issues related to nuclear weapons in a comprehensive, inclusive, interactive and constructive manner, for the advancement of multilateral nuclear disarmament negotiations;

9. *Reaffirms* the urgency of securing further substantive progress in multilateral nuclear disarmament negotiations;

10. *Recommends* that, consistent with the Treaty on the Prohibition of Nuclear Weapons, additional efforts can and should be pursued to elaborate concrete effective legal measures, legal provisions and norms that will need to be concluded to attain and maintain a world without nuclear weapons, and considers that the pursuit of any such measures, provisions and norms should complement and strengthen the nuclear disarmament and non-proliferation regime, including the three pillars of the Treaty on the Non-Proliferation of Nuclear Weapons;[4]

11. *Reaffirms* the importance of the Treaty on the Non-Proliferation of Nuclear Weapons;

12. *Recommends* that States consider implementing, as appropriate, the various measures suggested in the report of the Open-ended Working Group taking forward multilateral nuclear disarmament negotiations, established by the General Assembly by its resolution 70/33,[10] including but not limited to transparency measures related to the risks associated with existing nuclear weapons, measures to reduce and eliminate the risk of accidental, mistaken, unauthorized or intentional nuclear weapon detonations, additional measures to increase awareness and understanding of the complexity of and interrelationship between the wide range of humanitarian consequences that would result from any nuclear detonation, and other measures that could contribute to taking forward multilateral nuclear disarmament negotiations;

---

[13] See resolution 50/245 and A/50/1027.

13. *Looks forward* to the entry into force of the Treaty on the Prohibition of Nuclear Weapons and to the first meeting of States parties to be convened thereupon;

14. *Requests* the Secretary-General to render the necessary assistance and to provide such services as may be necessary to fulfil the tasks entrusted to him under the Treaty on the Prohibition of Nuclear Weapons;

15. *Decides* to include in the provisional agenda of its seventy-fourth session, under the item entitled "General and complete disarmament", the sub-item entitled "Taking forward multilateral nuclear disarmament negotiations";

16. *Also decides* to include in the provisional agenda of its seventy-third session, under the item entitled "General and complete disarmament", a sub-item entitled "Treaty on the Prohibition of Nuclear Weapons".

Action by the General Assembly

Date: 4 December 2017   Meeting: 62nd plenary meeting
Vote: 125-39-14   Report: A/72/409

Sponsors

Algeria, Angola, **Austria**, Belize, Brazil, Cabo Verde, Chile, Costa Rica, Democratic Republic of the Congo, Dominican Republic, Ecuador, Ghana, Guatemala, Indonesia, Ireland, Kazakhstan, Kenya, Liechtenstein, Malawi, Malaysia, Malta, Mexico, Namibia, New Zealand, Nicaragua, Nigeria, Panama, Peru, Philippines, Samoa, South Africa, Swaziland, Thailand, Togo, Trinidad and Tobago, Uruguay, Vanuatu, Venezuela (Bolivarian Republic of), Viet Nam, Zimbabwe

Co-sponsors

Antigua and Barbuda, Bangladesh, Bolivia (Plurinational State of), Chad, El Salvador, Fiji, Guinea-Bissau, Guyana, Honduras, Jamaica, Lesotho, Libya, Madagascar, Paraguay, Saint Lucia, San Marino, Sri Lanka, Tuvalu, Uganda

Recorded vote

In favour:

Afghanistan, Algeria, Angola, Antigua and Barbuda, Austria, Azerbaijan, Bahamas, Bahrain, Bangladesh, Barbados, Belize, Bhutan, Bolivia (Plurinational State of), Botswana, Brazil, Brunei Darussalam, Burkina Faso, Burundi, Cabo Verde, Cambodia, Chad, Chile, Colombia, Comoros, Congo, Costa Rica, Côte d'Ivoire, Cuba, Cyprus, Democratic Republic of the Congo, Djibouti, Dominican Republic, Ecuador, Egypt, El Salvador, Equatorial Guinea, Eritrea, Ethiopia, Fiji, Gabon, Gambia, Ghana, Guatemala, Guinea, Guinea-Bissau, Guyana, Honduras, Indonesia,

Iran (Islamic Republic of), Iraq, Ireland, Jamaica, Jordan, Kazakhstan, Kenya, Kiribati, Kuwait, Lao People's Democratic Republic, Lebanon, Lesotho, Liberia, Libya, Liechtenstein, Madagascar, Malawi, Malaysia, Maldives, Malta, Mauritania, Mauritius, Mexico, Mongolia, Morocco, Mozambique, Myanmar, Namibia, Nauru, Nepal, New Zealand, Nigeria, Oman, Palau, Panama, Papua New Guinea, Paraguay, Peru, Philippines, Qatar, Rwanda, Saint Kitts and Nevis, Saint Lucia, Saint Vincent and the Grenadines, Samoa, San Marino, Saudi Arabia, Senegal, Sierra Leone, Singapore, Solomon Islands, Somalia, South Africa, Sri Lanka, Sudan, Suriname, Swaziland, Sweden, Switzerland, Thailand, Timor-Leste, Togo, Tonga, Trinidad and Tobago, Tunisia, Turkmenistan, Tuvalu, Uganda, United Arab Emirates, United Republic of Tanzania, Uruguay, Vanuatu, Venezuela (Bolivarian Republic of), Viet Nam, Yemen, Zambia, Zimbabwe

Against:

Albania, Australia, Belgium, Bosnia and Herzegovina, Bulgaria, Canada, China, Croatia, Czech Republic, Denmark, Estonia, France, Germany, Greece, Hungary, Iceland, India, Israel, Italy, Japan, Latvia, Lithuania, Luxembourg, Monaco, Montenegro, Netherlands, Norway, Pakistan, Poland, Portugal, Republic of Korea, Romania, Russian Federation, Slovakia, Slovenia, Spain, Turkey, United Kingdom, United States

Abstaining:

Andorra, Argentina, Armenia, Belarus, Democratic People's Republic of Korea, Finland, Georgia, Kyrgyzstan, Mali, Nicaragua, Serbia, the former Yugoslav Republic of Macedonia, Ukraine, Uzbekistan

Action by the First Committee

Date: 27 October 2017   Meeting: 24th meeting
Vote: 118-39-11   Draft resolution: A/C.1/72/L.6

Agenda item 99 (aa)

72/32 Compliance with non-proliferation, arms limitation and disarmament agreements and commitments

Text

The General Assembly,

Recalling its resolution 69/59 of 2 December 2014 and other relevant resolutions on the question,

Recognizing the abiding concern of all Member States for ensuring respect for the rights and obligations arising from treaties to which they are parties and from other sources of international law,

Convinced that observance by Member States of the Charter of the United Nations and compliance with non-proliferation, arms limitation and disarmament agreements to which they are parties and with other agreed obligations are essential for regional and global peace, security and stability,

Stressing that failure by States parties to comply with such agreements and with other agreed obligations not only adversely affects the security of States parties but also can create security risks for other States relying on the constraints and commitments stipulated in those agreements,

Stressing also that the viability and effectiveness of non-proliferation, arms limitation and disarmament agreements and of other agreed obligations require that those agreements be fully complied with and enforced,

Concerned by non-compliance by some States with their respective obligations,

Noting that verification and compliance, and enforcement in a manner consistent with the Charter, are integrally related,

Recognizing the importance of and support for effective national, regional and international capacities for such verification, compliance and enforcement,

Recognizing also that full compliance by States with all their respective non-proliferation, arms limitation and disarmament agreements and with other agreed obligations they have undertaken contributes to efforts to prevent the development and proliferation, contrary to international obligations, of weapons of mass destruction, related technologies and means of delivery, as well as to efforts to deny non-State actors access to such capabilities,

1. *Underscores* the contribution that compliance with non-proliferation, arms limitation and disarmament agreements and with

other agreed obligations makes to enhancing confidence and to strengthening international security and stability;

2.   *Urges* all States to implement and to comply fully with their respective obligations;

3.   *Welcomes* efforts by all States to pursue additional areas of cooperation, as appropriate, that can increase confidence in compliance with existing non-proliferation, arms limitation and disarmament agreements and commitments and reduce the possibility of misinterpretation and misunderstanding;

4.   *Calls upon* all Member States to encourage and, for those States in a position to do so, to appropriately assist States which request assistance to increase their capacity to implement fully their obligations;

5.   *Calls upon* Member States to support efforts aimed at the resolution of compliance questions by means consistent with such agreements and with international law;

6.   *Welcomes* the role that the United Nations has played and continues to play in maintaining the integrity of certain arms limitation and disarmament and non-proliferation agreements and in addressing threats to international peace and security;

7.   *Calls upon* all concerned States to take concerted action, in a manner consistent with relevant international law, to encourage, through bilateral and multilateral means, the compliance by all States with their respective non-proliferation, arms limitation and disarmament agreements and with other agreed obligations, and to hold those not in compliance with such agreements accountable for their non-compliance in a manner consistent with the Charter of the United Nations;

8.   *Urges* those States not currently in compliance with their respective obligations and commitments to make the strategic decision to come back into compliance;

9.   *Encourages* efforts by all States, the United Nations and other international organizations, pursuant to their respective mandates, to take action, consistent with the Charter, to prevent serious damage to international security and stability arising from non-compliance by States with their existing non-proliferation, arms limitation and disarmament obligations;

10.   *Decides* to include in the provisional agenda of its seventy-fifth session, under the item entitled "General and complete disarmament", the sub-item entitled "Compliance with non-proliferation, arms limitation and disarmament agreements and commitments".

Action by the General Assembly

Date: 4 December 2017   Meeting: 62nd plenary meeting
Vote: 173-1-11   Report: A/72/409

Sponsors

Afghanistan, Albania, Andorra, Angola, Argentina, Australia, Belgium, Bosnia and Herzegovina, Bulgaria, Canada, Central African Republic, Croatia, Czech Republic, Dominican Republic, Estonia, Finland, France, Georgia, Germany, Greece, Guinea, Haiti, Hungary, Ireland, Israel, Italy, Japan, Latvia, Lithuania, Luxembourg, Malawi, Malta, Montenegro, Netherlands, New Zealand, Norway, Palau, Panama, Poland, Portugal, Republic of Korea, Republic of Moldova, Romania, Senegal, Slovakia, Slovenia, Spain, Swaziland, Sweden, the former Yugoslav Republic of Macedonia, Togo, Ukraine, United Kingdom, **United States**, Zambia

Co-sponsors

Austria, Benin, Burkina Faso, Cabo Verde, Chad, Colombia, Cyprus, Democratic Republic of the Congo, Denmark, El Salvador, Ghana, Guinea-Bissau, Guyana, Honduras, Iceland, Liberia, Liechtenstein, Madagascar, Maldives, Monaco, Myanmar, San Marino, Serbia, Seychelles, Sierra Leone, Timor-Leste, Trinidad and Tobago, Turkey, Uruguay

Recorded vote

In favour:

Afghanistan, Albania, Algeria, Andorra, Angola, Antigua and Barbuda, Argentina, Armenia, Australia, Austria, Azerbaijan, Bahamas, Bahrain, Bangladesh, Barbados, Belgium, Belize, Benin, Bhutan, Bolivia (Plurinational State of), Bosnia and Herzegovina, Botswana, Brazil, Brunei Darussalam, Bulgaria, Burkina Faso, Burundi, Cabo Verde, Cambodia, Canada, Chad, Chile, China, Colombia, Comoros, Congo, Costa Rica, Côte d'Ivoire, Croatia, Cyprus, Czech Republic, Democratic Republic of the Congo, Denmark, Djibouti, Dominican Republic, El Salvador, Eritrea, Estonia, Ethiopia, Fiji, Finland, France, Gabon, Gambia, Georgia, Germany, Ghana, Greece, Grenada, Guatemala, Guinea, Guinea-Bissau, Guyana, Haiti, Honduras, Hungary, Iceland, India, Indonesia, Iraq, Ireland, Israel, Italy, Jamaica, Japan, Jordan, Kazakhstan, Kenya, Kiribati, Kuwait, Kyrgyzstan, Lao People's Democratic Republic, Latvia, Lebanon, Lesotho, Liberia, Libya, Liechtenstein, Lithuania, Luxembourg, Madagascar, Malawi, Malaysia, Maldives, Malta, Marshall Islands, Mauritania, Mauritius, Mexico, Micronesia (Federated States of), Monaco, Mongolia, Montenegro, Morocco, Mozambique, Myanmar, Namibia, Nauru, Nepal, Netherlands, New Zealand, Nicaragua, Nigeria, Norway, Oman, Pakistan, Palau,

Panama, Papua New Guinea, Paraguay, Peru, Philippines, Poland, Portugal, Qatar, Republic of Korea, Republic of Moldova, Romania, Rwanda, Saint Kitts and Nevis, Saint Lucia, Saint Vincent and the Grenadines, Samoa, San Marino, Saudi Arabia, Senegal, Serbia, Sierra Leone, Singapore, Slovakia, Slovenia, Solomon Islands, Somalia, South Africa, Spain, Sri Lanka, Sudan, Suriname, Swaziland, Sweden, Switzerland, Tajikistan, Thailand, the former Yugoslav Republic of Macedonia, Timor-Leste, Togo, Tonga, Trinidad and Tobago, Tunisia, Turkey, Turkmenistan, Tuvalu, Uganda, Ukraine, United Arab Emirates, United Kingdom, United Republic of Tanzania, United States, Uruguay, Vanuatu, Viet Nam, Yemen, Zambia

Against:
Democratic People's Republic of Korea

Abstaining:
Belarus, Cuba, Ecuador, Egypt, Equatorial Guinea, Iran (Islamic Republic of), Mali, Russian Federation, Syrian Arab Republic, Venezuela (Bolivarian Republic of), Zimbabwe

Action by the First Committee

Date: 31 October 2017	Meeting:	26th meeting
Vote: 165-1-11	Draft resolution:	A/C.1/72/L.7

Agenda item 99 (t)

72/33 Confidence-building measures in the regional and subregional context

Text

The General Assembly,

Guided by the purposes and principles enshrined in the Charter of the United Nations,

Recalling its resolutions 58/43 of 8 December 2003, 59/87 of 3 December 2004, 60/64 of 8 December 2005, 61/81 of 6 December 2006, 62/45 of 5 December 2007, 63/45 of 2 December 2008, 64/43 of 2 December 2009, 65/47 of 8 December 2010, 66/38 of 2 December 2011, 67/61 of 3 December 2012, 68/55 of 5 December 2013, 69/46 of 2 December 2014, 70/42 of 7 December 2015 and 71/39 of 5 December 2016 on confidence-building measures in the regional and subregional context,

Recalling also its resolution 57/337 of 3 July 2003 on the prevention of armed conflict, in which the General Assembly calls upon Member States to settle their disputes by peaceful means, as set out in Chapter VI of the Charter, inter alia, by any procedures adopted by the parties,

Recalling further the resolutions and guidelines adopted by consensus by the General Assembly and the Disarmament Commission relating to confidence-building measures and their implementation at the global, regional and subregional levels,

Considering the importance and effectiveness of confidence-building measures taken at the initiative and with the agreement of all States concerned, and taking into account the specific characteristics of each region, since such measures can contribute to regional stability,

Convinced that resources released by disarmament, including regional disarmament, can be devoted to economic and social development and to the protection of the environment for the benefit of all peoples, in particular those of the developing countries,

Recognizing the need for meaningful dialogue among States concerned to avert conflict,

Welcoming the peace processes already initiated by States concerned to resolve their disputes through peaceful means bilaterally or through mediation, inter alia, by third parties, regional organizations or the United Nations,

Recognizing that States in some regions have already taken steps towards confidence-building measures at the bilateral, subregional and regional levels in the political and military fields, including arms control and disarmament, and noting that such confidence-building measures have improved peace and security in those regions and contributed to progress in the socioeconomic conditions of their people,

Concerned that the continuation of disputes among States, particularly in the absence of an effective mechanism to resolve them through peaceful means, may contribute to the arms race and endanger the maintenance of international peace and security and the efforts of the international community to promote arms control and disarmament,

1.   *Calls upon* Member States to refrain from the use or threat of use of force in accordance with the purposes and principles of the Charter of the United Nations;

2.   *Reaffirms its commitment* to the peaceful settlement of disputes under Chapter VI of the Charter, in particular Article 33, which provides for a solution by negotiation, enquiry, mediation, conciliation, arbitration, judicial settlement, resort to regional agencies or arrangements or other peaceful means chosen by the parties;

3.   *Reaffirms* the ways and means regarding confidence- and security-building measures set out in the report of the Disarmament Commission on its 1993 session;[1]

4.   *Calls upon* Member States to pursue these ways and means through sustained consultations and dialogue, while at the same time avoiding actions that may hinder or impair such a dialogue;

5.   *Urges* States to comply strictly with all bilateral, regional and international agreements, including arms control and disarmament agreements, to which they are party;

6.   *Emphasizes* that the objective of confidence-building measures should be to help to strengthen international peace and security and to be consistent with the principle of undiminished security at the lowest level of armaments;

7.   *Encourages* the promotion of bilateral and regional confidence-building measures, with the consent and participation of the parties concerned, to avoid conflict and prevent the unintended and accidental outbreak of hostilities;

8.   *Requests* the Secretary-General to submit a report to the General Assembly at its seventy-third session containing the views of Member States on confidence-building measures in the regional and subregional context;

9.   *Decides* to include in the provisional agenda of its seventy-third session, under the item entitled "General and complete disarmament",

---

[1] *Official Records of the General Assembly, Forty-eighth Session, Supplement No. 42* (A/48/42), annex II, sect. III.A.

the sub-item entitled "Confidence-building measures in the regional and subregional context".

Action by the General Assembly

Date: 4 December 2017   Meeting: 62nd plenary meeting
Vote: Adopted without a vote   Report: A/72/409

Sponsors

Ecuador, Egypt, Eritrea, **Pakistan**, Syrian Arab Republic, Ukraine, Uruguay, Zambia

Co-sponsors

Bangladesh, Kazakhstan, Lebanon, Maldives, the former Yugoslav Republic of Macedonia

Action by the First Committee

Date: 1 November 2017   Meeting: 27th meeting
Vote: Adopted without a vote   Draft resolution: A/C.1/72/L.11

Agenda item 99 (f)

72/34   Regional disarmament

Text

The General Assembly,

Recalling its resolutions 45/58 P of 4 December 1990, 46/36 I of 6 December 1991, 47/52 J of 9 December 1992, 48/75 I of 16 December 1993, 49/75 N of 15 December 1994, 50/70 K of 12 December 1995, 51/45 K of 10 December 1996, 52/38 P of 9 December 1997, 53/77 O of 4 December 1998, 54/54 N of 1 December 1999, 55/33 O of 20 November 2000, 56/24 H of 29 November 2001, 57/76 of 22 November 2002, 58/38 of 8 December 2003, 59/89 of 3 December 2004, 60/63 of 8 December 2005, 61/80 of 6 December 2006, 62/38 of 5 December 2007, 63/43 of 2 December 2008, 64/41 of 2 December 2009, 65/45 of 8 December 2010, 66/36 of 2 December 2011, 67/57 of 3 December 2012, 68/54 of 5 December 2013, 69/45 of 2 December 2014, 70/43 of 7 December 2015 and 71/40 of 5 December 2016 on regional disarmament,

Believing that the efforts of the international community to move towards the ideal of general and complete disarmament are guided by the inherent human desire for genuine peace and security, the elimination of the danger of war and the release of economic, intellectual and other resources for peaceful pursuits,

Affirming the abiding commitment of all States to the purposes and principles enshrined in the Charter of the United Nations in the conduct of their international relations,

Noting that essential guidelines for progress towards general and complete disarmament were adopted at the tenth special session of the General Assembly,[1]

Taking note of the guidelines and recommendations for regional approaches to disarmament within the context of global security adopted by the Disarmament Commission at its 1993 substantive session,[2]

Welcoming the prospects of genuine progress in the field of disarmament engendered in recent years as a result of negotiations between the two super-Powers,

Taking note of the recent proposals for disarmament at the regional and subregional levels,

---

[1] Resolution S-10/2.

[2] *Official Records of the General Assembly, Forty-eighth Session, Supplement No. 42* (A/48/42), annex II.

Recognizing the importance of confidence-building measures for regional and international peace and security,

Convinced that endeavours by countries to promote regional disarmament, taking into account the specific characteristics of each region and in accordance with the principle of undiminished security at the lowest level of armaments, would enhance the security of all States and would thus contribute to international peace and security by reducing the risk of regional conflicts,

1. *Stresses* that sustained efforts are needed, within the framework of the Conference on Disarmament and under the umbrella of the United Nations, to make progress on the entire range of disarmament issues;

2. *Affirms* that global and regional approaches to disarmament complement each other and should therefore be pursued simultaneously to promote regional and international peace and security;

3. *Calls upon* States to conclude agreements, wherever possible, for nuclear non-proliferation, disarmament and confidence-building measures at the regional and subregional levels;

4. *Welcomes* the initiatives towards disarmament, nuclear non-proliferation and security undertaken by some countries at the regional and subregional levels;

5. *Supports and encourages* efforts aimed at promoting confidence-building measures at the regional and subregional levels to ease regional tensions and to further disarmament and nuclear non-proliferation measures at the regional and subregional levels;

6. *Decides* to include in the provisional agenda of its seventy-third session, under the item entitled "General and complete disarmament", the sub-item entitled "Regional disarmament".

Action by the General Assembly

    Date: 4 December 2017   Meeting: 62nd plenary meeting
    Vote: Adopted without a vote   Report: A/72/409

Sponsors

    Ecuador, Egypt, Eritrea, Iraq, Nigeria, **Pakistan**, Peru, Saudi Arabia

Co-sponsors

    Bangladesh, Jordan, Maldives, Nepal, Sri Lanka, Turkey

Action by the First Committee

    Date: 1 November 2017   Meeting: 27th meeting
    Vote: Adopted without a vote   Draft resolution: A/C.1/72/L.12

Agenda item 99 (g)

72/35 Conventional arms control at the regional and subregional levels

Text

The General Assembly,

Recalling its resolutions 48/75 J of 16 December 1993, 49/75 O of 15 December 1994, 50/70 L of 12 December 1995, 51/45 Q of 10 December 1996, 52/38 Q of 9 December 1997, 53/77 P of 4 December 1998, 54/54 M of 1 December 1999, 55/33 P of 20 November 2000, 56/24 I of 29 November 2001, 57/77 of 22 November 2002, 58/39 of 8 December 2003, 59/88 of 3 December 2004, 60/75 of 8 December 2005, 61/82 of 6 December 2006, 62/44 of 5 December 2007, 63/44 of 2 December 2008, 64/42 of 2 December 2009, 65/46 of 8 December 2010, 66/37 of 2 December 2011, 67/62 of 3 December 2012, 68/56 of 5 December 2013, 69/47 of 2 December 2014, 70/44 of 7 December 2015 and 71/41 of 5 December 2016,

Recognizing the crucial role of conventional arms control in promoting regional and international peace and security,

Convinced that conventional arms control needs to be pursued primarily in the regional and subregional contexts since most threats to peace and security in the post-cold-war era arise mainly among States located in the same region or subregion,

Aware that the preservation of a balance in the defence capabilities of States at the lowest level of armaments would contribute to peace and stability and should be a prime objective of conventional arms control,

Desirous of promoting agreements to strengthen regional peace and security at the lowest possible level of armaments and military forces,

Noting with particular interest the initiatives taken in this regard in different regions of the world, in particular the commencement of consultations among a number of Latin American countries and the proposals for conventional arms control made in the context of South Asia, and recognizing, in the context of this subject, the relevance and value of the Treaty on Conventional Armed Forces in Europe,[1] which is a cornerstone of European security,

Believing that militarily significant States and States with larger military capabilities have a special responsibility in promoting such agreements for regional security,

---

[1] See CD/1064.

Believing also that an important objective of conventional arms control in regions of tension should be to prevent the possibility of military attack launched by surprise and to avoid aggression,

1. *Decides* to give urgent consideration to the issues involved in conventional arms control at the regional and subregional levels;

2. *Requests* the Conference on Disarmament to consider the formulation of principles that can serve as a framework for regional agreements on conventional arms control, and looks forward to a report of the Conference on this subject;

3. *Requests* the Secretary-General, in the meantime, to seek the views of Member States on the subject and to submit a report to the General Assembly at its seventy-third session;

4. *Decides* to include in the provisional agenda of its seventy-third session, under the item entitled "General and complete disarmament", the sub-item entitled "Conventional arms control at the regional and subregional levels".

Action by the General Assembly

Date: 4 December 2017	Meeting: 62nd plenary meeting
Vote: 184-1-2	Report: A/72/409
140-1-39, o.p. 2	

Sponsors

Ecuador, Eritrea, Italy, **Pakistan**, Peru, Syrian Arab Republic, Ukraine, Zambia

Co-sponsors

Bangladesh, Belarus, Egypt

Recorded vote

As a whole

In favour:

Afghanistan, Albania, Algeria, Andorra, Angola, Antigua and Barbuda, Argentina, Armenia, Australia, Austria, Azerbaijan, Bahamas, Bahrain, Bangladesh, Barbados, Belarus, Belgium, Belize, Benin, Bolivia (Plurinational State of), Bosnia and Herzegovina, Botswana, Brazil, Brunei Darussalam, Bulgaria, Burkina Faso, Burundi, Cabo Verde, Cambodia, Cameroon, Canada, Central African Republic, Chad, Chile, China, Colombia, Comoros, Congo, Costa Rica, Côte d'Ivoire, Croatia, Cuba, Cyprus, Czech Republic, Democratic People's Republic of Korea, Democratic Republic of the Congo, Denmark, Djibouti, Dominican Republic, Ecuador, Egypt, El Salvador, Equatorial Guinea, Eritrea,

Estonia, Ethiopia, Fiji, Finland, France, Gabon, Gambia, Georgia, Germany, Ghana, Greece, Guatemala, Guinea, Guinea-Bissau, Guyana, Haiti, Honduras, Hungary, Iceland, Indonesia, Iran (Islamic Republic of), Iraq, Ireland, Israel, Italy, Jamaica, Japan, Jordan, Kazakhstan, Kenya, Kiribati, Kuwait, Kyrgyzstan, Lao People's Democratic Republic, Latvia, Lebanon, Lesotho, Liberia, Libya, Liechtenstein, Lithuania, Luxembourg, Madagascar, Malawi, Malaysia, Maldives, Mali, Malta, Marshall Islands, Mauritania, Mauritius, Mexico, Micronesia (Federated States of), Monaco, Mongolia, Montenegro, Morocco, Mozambique, Myanmar, Namibia, Nauru, Nepal, Netherlands, New Zealand, Nicaragua, Nigeria, Norway, Oman, Pakistan, Palau, Panama, Papua New Guinea, Paraguay, Peru, Philippines, Poland, Portugal, Qatar, Republic of Korea, Republic of Moldova, Romania, Rwanda, Saint Kitts and Nevis, Saint Lucia, Saint Vincent and the Grenadines, Samoa, San Marino, Saudi Arabia, Senegal, Serbia, Sierra Leone, Singapore, Slovakia, Slovenia, Solomon Islands, Somalia, South Africa, Spain, Sri Lanka, Sudan, Suriname, Swaziland, Sweden, Switzerland, Syrian Arab Republic, Tajikistan, Thailand, the former Yugoslav Republic of Macedonia, Timor-Leste, Togo, Tonga, Trinidad and Tobago, Tunisia, Turkey, Turkmenistan, Tuvalu, Uganda, Ukraine, United Arab Emirates, United Kingdom, United Republic of Tanzania, United States, Uruguay, Uzbekistan, Vanuatu, Venezuela (Bolivarian Republic of), Viet Nam, Yemen, Zambia, Zimbabwe

Against:
India

Abstaining:
Bhutan, Russian Federation

Operative paragraph 2

In favour:
Afghanistan, Algeria, Angola, Antigua and Barbuda, Argentina, Azerbaijan, Bahamas, Bahrain, Bangladesh, Barbados, Belarus, Belgium, Belize, Benin, Bolivia (Plurinational State of), Bosnia and Herzegovina, Botswana, Brazil, Brunei Darussalam, Bulgaria, Burkina Faso, Burundi, Cabo Verde, Cambodia, Canada, Chad, Chile, China, Colombia, Comoros, Congo, Costa Rica, Côte d'Ivoire, Cuba, Democratic People's Republic of Korea, Democratic Republic of the Congo, Djibouti, Dominican Republic, Ecuador, Egypt, El Salvador, Equatorial Guinea, Eritrea, Ethiopia, Fiji, Gabon, Gambia, Ghana, Guatemala, Guinea, Guinea-Bissau, Guyana, Haiti, Honduras, Iceland, Indonesia, Iran (Islamic Republic of), Iraq, Italy, Jamaica, Japan, Jordan, Kazakhstan, Kenya, Kiribati, Kuwait, Kyrgyzstan, Lao People's Democratic Republic, Lebanon, Lesotho, Liberia, Libya, Luxembourg, Madagascar,

Malawi, Malaysia, Maldives, Mali, Mauritania, Mauritius, Mongolia, Morocco, Mozambique, Myanmar, Namibia, Nepal, Nicaragua, Nigeria, Oman, Pakistan, Palau, Panama, Papua New Guinea, Paraguay, Peru, Philippines, Portugal, Qatar, Republic of Korea, Republic of Moldova, Romania, Rwanda, Saint Kitts and Nevis, Saint Lucia, Saint Vincent and the Grenadines, Samoa, Saudi Arabia, Senegal, Serbia, Sierra Leone, Singapore, Solomon Islands, Somalia, Sri Lanka, Sudan, Suriname, Swaziland, Syrian Arab Republic, Tajikistan, Thailand, Timor-Leste, Togo, Trinidad and Tobago, Tunisia, Turkey, Turkmenistan, Tuvalu, Uganda, Ukraine, United Arab Emirates, United Republic of Tanzania, United States, Uruguay, Uzbekistan, Vanuatu, Venezuela (Bolivarian Republic of), Viet Nam, Yemen, Zambia, Zimbabwe

Against:

India

Abstaining:

Albania, Andorra, Australia, Austria, Bhutan, Croatia, Cyprus, Czech Republic, Denmark, Estonia, Finland, France, Georgia, Germany, Greece, Hungary, Ireland, Israel, Latvia, Liechtenstein, Lithuania, Malta, Mexico, Monaco, Montenegro, Netherlands, New Zealand, Norway, Poland, Russian Federation, San Marino, Slovakia, Slovenia, South Africa, Spain, Sweden, Switzerland, the former Yugoslav Republic of Macedonia, United Kingdom

Action by the First Committee

Date:	1 November 2017	Meeting:	27th meeting
Vote:	174-1-2	Draft resolution:	A/C.1/72/L.13/Rev.1
	131-1-38, o.p. 2		

Agenda item 99 (dd)

72/36   Countering the threat posed by improvised explosive devices

Text

The General Assembly,

Recalling its resolutions 70/46 of 7 December 2015 and 71/72 of 5 December 2016,

Expressing grave concern over the devastation caused by the increasing use of improvised explosive devices by illegal armed groups, terrorists and other unauthorized recipients,[1] which has affected a large number of countries and has resulted in thousands of casualties, both civilian and military, and, in this regard, stressing the need for all actors to comply with applicable international law at all times,

Expressing profound concern at the indiscriminate use and effects of improvised explosive devices and at the increasing humanitarian impact of such attacks on civilian populations worldwide, in particular through the perpetration of terrorist acts, and noting the need for a comprehensive approach in addressing this concern,

Expressing concern at the serious harm that such improvised explosive device attacks have caused to United Nations staff and peacekeepers, and to humanitarian workers, by threatening their lives, increasing the cost of their activities, limiting their freedom of movement and affecting their ability to effectively deliver on their mandates,

Expressing concern also about the negative impact of these attacks on socioeconomic development, infrastructure and freedom of movement, and on the security and stability of States, and thus underlining the need to address this issue in order to achieve relevant goals and targets under the 2030 Agenda for Sustainable Development,[2] in particular target 16.1 on significantly reducing all forms of violence and related death rates everywhere,

Urging Member States to ensure that any measures taken or means employed to implement the present resolution comply with international law, in particular the Charter of the United Nations, applicable international humanitarian law and human rights law,

Recognizing the importance of full involvement and equal opportunities for participation for both women and men in countering the threat posed by improvised explosive devices,

---

[1] See resolution 69/51, A/CONF.192/BMS/2014/2, A/71/187 and Security Council resolution 2370 (2017).

[2] Resolution 70/1.

Recognizing also that the wide spectrum of materials that can be used for the manufacture of improvised explosive devices, including those sourced from the military and civilian industry, contributes to their diverse nature and their deployment methods, which thus requires an appropriate approach to the formulation of measures to counter them,

Noting that the impact of improvised explosive devices spans a wide array of policy areas and that, owing to the extent of the cross-cutting nature of the issue, a whole-of-government approach focusing on the capacity of Governments to effectively bring together several policy strands for comprehensive action is essential,

Underlining the important role that States can play in raising awareness among private sector and other entities about the possible theft, diversion and misuse of their products to make improvised explosive devices, with a view to enabling those entities to develop effective strategies to counter the threat of improvised explosive devices,[3] including to prevent the adverse impact of the diversion of materials and the potential loss of revenue and risk to reputation, either in a partnership with governmental authorities, or through business-to-business processes or activities,

Noting existing industry-led initiatives that seek to increase industry oversight and accountability along the supply chain for precursor components, and encouraging States to engage, as appropriate, with private sector industry actors in supporting such initiatives,

Noting also the contribution of good governance, the promotion of human rights, the rule of law, adherence to the principles of the Charter and sustained and inclusive socioeconomic growth, including through effective measures and mechanisms for persons belonging to vulnerable groups, as important elements in comprehensively addressing the issue of improvised explosive devices, in particular in post-conflict situations,

Stressing the paramount need to prevent illegal armed groups, terrorists and other unauthorized recipients from, and identify the networks that support them in, obtaining, handling, financing, storing, using or seeking access to all types of explosives, whether military or civilian, as well as other military or civilian materials and components that can be used to manufacture improvised explosive devices, including detonators, detonating cords and chemical components, while at the same time avoiding any undue restrictions on the legitimate use of those materials,

Recalling, in this context, relevant resolutions on the prevention of the acquisition of weapons by terrorists, including improvised explosive device

---

[3] See the Guiding Principles on Business and Human Rights: Implementing the United Nations "Protect, Respect and Remedy" Framework (A/HRC/17/31, annex).

components, and their transfer to and between terrorists, associated groups and other illegal armed groups and criminals,[4]

Stressing the importance of effectively securing conventional ammunition stockpiles in order to mitigate the risk of their diversion to illicit use as materials for improvised explosive devices,

Stressing also the importance of engagement by all Member States in a comprehensive and coordinated community of action to counter the global threat posed by improvised explosive devices in the hands of illegal armed groups, terrorists and other unauthorized recipients, taking into account national capacities,

Noting that, at the global level, organizations across many sectors have expertise that can contribute to a useful set of measures for the mitigation of improvised explosive devices, and noting also the value of considered and coordinated efforts by various stakeholders, including intergovernmental and regional organizations and industry associations, with a view to investing effectively in coordination and information exchange,

Noting also the discussions on the issue of improvised explosive devices by the informal group of experts under the Protocol on Prohibitions or Restrictions on the Use of Mines, Booby Traps and Other Devices as amended on 3 May 1996 (Amended Protocol II)[5] and on the technical annex to the Protocol on Explosive Remnants of War (Protocol V)[6] to the Convention on Prohibitions or Restrictions on the Use of Certain Conventional Weapons Which May Be Deemed to Be Excessively Injurious or to Have Indiscriminate Effects,[7] and further noting that, in the view of the States parties thereto, improvised anti-personnel mines also fall within the scope of the Convention on the Prohibition of the Use, Stockpiling, Production and Transfer of Anti-Personnel Mines and on Their Destruction,[8]

Noting further the multilateral efforts to counter improvised explosive devices of the Programme Global Shield, led by the World Customs Organization and assisted by the International Criminal Police Organization (INTERPOL) and the United Nations Office on Drugs and Crime, to prevent the smuggling and illicit diversion of precursor chemicals that could be used to build improvised explosive devices, the network of regional and multilateral communities of action established by States to counter improvised explosive devices, the research on those devices undertaken by the United Nations Institute for Disarmament Research and the work undertaken by the Mine Action Service of the United Nations to mitigate the threat posed by those

---

[4] See Security Council resolution 2370 (2017).
[5] United Nations, *Treaty Series*, vol. 2048, No. 22495.
[6] Ibid., vol. 2399, No. 22495.
[7] Ibid., vol. 1342, No. 22495.
[8] Ibid., vol. 2056, No. 35597.

devices to civilians, United Nations staff, peacekeepers and humanitarian personnel, in particular in the field,

Taking note of the International Convention for the Suppression of Terrorist Bombings[9] and the United Nations Global Counter-Terrorism Strategy[10] and the efforts undertaken to strengthen the capability of the United Nations system to assist Member States in implementing the Strategy, including through the establishment of the Office of Counter-Terrorism,[11]

Reaffirming the inherent right of Member States to individual or collective self-defence in accordance with Article 51 of the Charter,

1.   *Notes* the continued value of the report of the Secretary-General submitted pursuant to resolution 70/46,[12] including the recommendations contained therein;

2.   *Recognizes* that existing approaches in multilateral arms regulation, while valuable, do not fully address the issue of improvised explosive devices, and therefore strongly urges States to develop and implement, where appropriate, all national measures, including outreach and partnerships with relevant actors, including the private sector, necessary to promote awareness, vigilance and good practices among their nationals, persons subject to their jurisdiction and firms incorporated in their territory or subject to their jurisdiction that are involved in the production, sale, supply, purchase, transfer and/or storage of precursor components and materials that could be used to make improvised explosive devices;

3.   *Strongly encourages* States, where appropriate, to develop and adopt their own national policy to counter improvised explosive devices that includes civilian-military cooperation, to strengthen their countermeasure capability, to prevent their territory from being used for terrorist purposes and to combat illegal armed groups, terrorists and other unauthorized recipients in their use of improvised explosive devices, while bearing in mind their obligations under applicable international law, and notes that the policy could include measures to support international and regional efforts to prevent, protect against, respond to, recover from and mitigate attacks using improvised explosive devices and their widespread consequences;

4.   *Urges* all States, in particular those that have the capacity to do so, as well as the United Nations system and other relevant organizations and institutions supporting affected States, to provide support to reduce the risks posed by improvised explosive devices in a manner which takes into consideration the different needs of women, girls, boys and men;

---

[9] Ibid., vol. 2149, No. 37517.
[10] Resolution 60/288.
[11] See resolution 71/291.
[12] A/71/187.

5. *Stresses* the need for States to take appropriate measures to strengthen the management of their national ammunition stockpiles to prevent the diversion of materials for making improvised explosive devices to illicit markets, illegal armed groups, terrorists and other unauthorized recipients, and encourages the application of the International Ammunition Technical Guidelines for the safer and more secure management of ammunition stockpiles, while also recognizing the importance of capacity-building, through both technical and financial assistance, in this regard, as well as the contributions made by various United Nations entities to that end;[13]

6. *Underlines* that, for the issue of improvised explosive devices to be effectively addressed, it is essential to comprehend the importance of action needed at the local and community levels, through activities ranging from awareness-raising of the threat posed by such devices and of possible threat mitigation measures, in conjunction with distributors and local retailers, and intelligence-gathering, to establishing deradicalization programmes, and the need for Governments to engage continuously with local authorities and groups, and encourages States in a position to do so to support initiatives and efforts to that end;

7. *Encourages* States to enhance, as appropriate, international and regional cooperation, including the sharing of information on good practices as appropriate and where relevant, in cooperation with the International Criminal Police Organization (INTERPOL), the United Nations Office on Drugs and Crime and the World Customs Organization, in order to address the theft, diversion, loss and illicit use of materials for making improvised explosive devices, while ensuring the security of sensitive information that is shared;

8. *Also encourages* States to take measures to stem the transfer of knowledge of improvised explosive devices and their construction and use by illegal armed groups, terrorists and other unauthorized recipients, as well as measures to stem the illicit acquisition of components over the Internet;

9. *Further encourages* States to take measures, including awareness raising and support for research, to combat illicit procurement of components, explosives and materials for the construction of improvised explosive devices, including through the use of the "dark web";[14]

10. *Encourages* States to participate, in accordance with their obligations and commitments, in the ongoing work on improvised explosive

---

[13] The General Assembly, in its resolution 66/42, welcomed the completion of the International Ammunition Technical Guidelines and the establishment of the "Safer Guard" knowledge resource management programme for the stockpile management of conventional ammunition.

[14] Content of the dark web exists on overlay networks which use the Internet but require specific software, configurations or authorizations that are not indexed by search engines.

devices by the informal group of experts under the Protocol on Prohibitions or Restrictions on the Use of Mines, Booby Traps and Other Devices as amended on 3 May 1996 (Amended Protocol II)[5] to the Convention on Prohibitions or Restrictions on the Use of Certain Conventional Weapons Which May Be Deemed to Be Excessively Injurious or to Have Indiscriminate Effects,[7] while recognizing the role of international organizations in providing technical support and insight for these discussions;

11. *Also encourages* States to participate, as appropriate, in a comprehensive and coordinated community of action to counter improvised explosive devices in accordance with their respective international obligations and commitments, and to consider supporting the Programme Global Shield of the World Customs Organization and other multilateral and regional efforts;

12. *Encourages* States and international, regional and other organizations with relevant expertise that are in a position to do so to render to interested States, upon their request, technical, financial and material assistance aimed at strengthening the capacity of such States to counter the threat of improvised explosive devices, including through assistance for the development of good practices for the protection of civilians from attacks using such devices and for the development of standards to ensure the safety of personnel involved in the disposal of improvised explosive devices, and to provide appropriate assistance to the victims of such attacks;

13. *Encourages* States to respond to the needs of today's peacekeepers to operate in new threat environments involving improvised explosive devices, including by providing, in consultation with the Department of Peacekeeping Operations of the Secretariat, the appropriate training, capabilities, information and knowledge management and technology required to counter improvised explosive devices, and to ensure that adequate financial resources are allocated to meet such needs, takes note of the Guidelines on Improvised Explosive Device Threat Mitigation in Mission Settings developed by the Department of Peacekeeping Operations and the Department of Field Support of the Secretariat,[15] and encourages the full implementation of the Guidelines in all peacekeeping operations;

14. *Recognizes* that improvised explosive devices are being increasingly used in terrorist activities, takes note of the work of the Counter-Terrorism Committee Executive Directorate and the Office of Counter-Terrorism related to the prevention of the acquisition of weapons by terrorists, and encourages all relevant entities of the United Nations system to continue to address the issue of improvised explosive devices, as appropriate and in line with their respective mandates, and to coordinate their activities to that end;

15. *Urges* Member States to comply fully with all relevant United Nations resolutions, including those related to preventing terrorist groups from

---

[15] Available from www.un.org/disarmament/convarms/ieds.

using and accessing materials that can be used in the making of improvised explosive devices;[16]

16. *Encourages* States and relevant international and regional organizations and non-governmental organizations, including international industry associations, to continue to build upon existing awareness and risk education campaigns regarding the urgent threat of improvised explosive devices and to disseminate threat mitigation measures;

17. *Encourages* States and relevant international and regional organizations to engage, as appropriate, with private sector entities in discussions and initiatives on countering improvised explosive devices, including on issues such as accountability throughout the supply chain for dual-use components, traceability procedures, improving the regulation of explosive precursors, where possible and as appropriate, strengthening security for the transport and storage of explosives and of precursors, as well as enhancing the vetting procedures for personnel with access to explosives or to precursors useful to the manufacture of explosives, while avoiding undue restrictions on the legitimate use of and access to such materials;

18. *Notes* the relevant research undertaken by the United Nations Institute for Disarmament Research, and encourages States in a position to do so to continue to support its work in this area;[17]

19. *Strongly encourages* States to share information, on a voluntary basis, on the diversion of commercial-grade explosives and commercially available detonators to the illicit trade and transfers to illegal armed groups, terrorists and other unauthorized recipients, through relevant channels, including the INTERPOL Chemical Anti-Smuggling Enforcement and Chemical Risk Identification and Mitigation programmes and the Programme Global Shield of the World Customs Organization;

20. *Takes into account* the existing initiatives at the international, regional and national levels to counter improvised explosive devices, and encourages the engagement by States in an open and inclusive dialogue on steps forward to harmonize diverse ongoing efforts;

21. *Urges* States in a position to do so to contribute funding to the diverse areas of work needed to effectively address the issue of improvised explosive devices, including research, clearance, ammunition stockpile management, preventing violent extremism as and when conducive to terrorism, awareness-raising, capacity-building, information management and victim assistance, through existing trust funds and arrangements, including

---

[16] Including Security Council resolutions 1373 (2001), 2160 (2014), 2161 (2014), 2199 (2015), 2253 (2015), 2255 (2015) and 2370 (2017).

[17] See www.unidir.org/programmes/conventionalweapons/examining-the-roles-responsibilities-and-potentialcontributions-of-private-sector-industry-actors-in-stemming-the-flow-of-improvised-explosive-devices-and-related-materials.

those of the Office of Counter-Terrorism, the United Nations Institute for Disarmament Research and the Office for Disarmament Affairs of the Secretariat and the voluntary trust fund for assistance in mine action, efforts undertaken under relevant conventions[18] or through regional or national programmes;

22. *Welcomes* the establishment by the Office for Disarmament Affairs, in coordination with other relevant entities, of an online hub providing impartial, authoritative information relevant to addressing the issue of improvised explosive devices in a comprehensive manner, and encourages States to utilize the hub to access existing initiatives, policies, documents and tools relevant to countering the threat posed by improvised explosive devices;[15]

23. *Takes note* of the ongoing elaboration of United Nations Improvised Explosive Device Disposal Standards coordinated by the Mine Action Service of the United Nations in cooperation with national technical experts, including consideration of their place within the International Mine Action Standards and the broader mine action framework, mindful of the need to avoid duplication;

24. *Notes* that the updated United Nations Policy on Victim Assistance in Mine Action highlights the significance of integrating victim assistance efforts into broader international and national frameworks, as well as the importance of sustained services and support to victims, including the victims of improvised explosive devices;

25. *Encourages* States in a position to do so to support the United Nations Institute for Disarmament Research, in consultation with relevant bodies of the United Nations system, in developing a voluntary self-assessment tool to assist States in identifying gaps and challenges in their national regulation and preparedness regarding improvised explosive devices;

26. *Recognizes* the important contribution of civil society to addressing the issue of improvised explosive devices, including in clearance, awareness-raising, risk education, victim assistance and preventing violent extremism as and when conducive to terrorism, in particular at the local and community levels;

27. *Requests* the Secretary-General to report to the General Assembly at its seventy-third session on the implementation of the present resolution, acknowledging and taking into account existing efforts, both inside and outside the United Nations, and seeking the views of Member States;

---

[18] Convention on Prohibitions or Restrictions on the Use of Certain Conventional Weapons Which May Be Deemed to Be Excessively Injurious or to Have Indiscriminate Effects and Convention on the Prohibition of the Use, Stockpiling, Production and Transfer of Anti-Personnel Mines and on Their Destruction.

28. *Encourages* States to continue to hold open, informal consultations, where appropriate, before the seventy-third session of the General Assembly, focusing on matters of coordination within the United Nations system and beyond, with information provided by States, international and regional organizations as well as experts from non-governmental organizations, including relevant private sector stakeholders, on efforts to prevent, counter and mitigate the threat posed by improvised explosive devices, which could assist the Assembly in maintaining a comprehensive overview of relevant global activities;

29. *Decides* to include in the provisional agenda of its seventy-third session, under the item entitled "General and complete disarmament", the sub-item entitled "Countering the threat posed by improvised explosive devices".

Action by the General Assembly

Date: 4 December 2017   Meeting: 62nd plenary meeting
Vote: Adopted without a vote   Report: A/72/409

Sponsors

Afghanistan, Angola, Australia, Belgium, Bulgaria, Croatia, Czech Republic, Denmark, Eritrea, Estonia, Finland, France, Germany, Greece, Hungary, Iraq, Italy, Kazakhstan, Latvia, Luxembourg, Mali, Monaco, Montenegro, Netherlands, Poland, Portugal, Romania, Slovakia, Slovenia, Spain, Sudan, Sweden, Ukraine, United Kingdom

Co-sponsors

Azerbaijan, Bangladesh, Canada, Georgia, Ghana, Haiti, India, Lithuania, Maldives, Niger, Nigeria, Norway, Senegal, Tajikistan, Turkey, Turkmenistan, United States, Uzbekistan

Action by the First Committee

Date: 31 October 2017   Meeting: 26th meeting
Vote: Adopted without a vote Draft resolution: A/C.1/72/L.15/Rev.1

Agenda item 99 (gg)

72/37   Ethical imperatives for a nuclear-weapon-free world

Text

The General Assembly,

Recalling its resolution 70/50 of 7 December 2015, adopted on the occasion of the seventieth anniversary of the United Nations, which was established to save succeeding generations from the untold suffering of the scourge of war, and its resolution 71/55 of 5 December 2016,

Recalling also that the United Nations emerged at the time of the immense trail of death and destruction resulting from the Second World War, 72 years ago,

Recalling further the noble principles of the Charter of the United Nations, which enjoin the international community, individually and collectively, to spare no effort in promoting the ethical imperative of "in larger freedom", so that all peoples may enjoy freedom from want, freedom from fear and the freedom to live in dignity,

Convinced that, given the catastrophic humanitarian consequences and risks associated with a nuclear weapon detonation, Member States have long envisaged nuclear disarmament and nuclear non-proliferation as urgent and interlinked ethical imperatives in achieving the objectives of the Charter, which is reflected in the first resolution, resolution 1 (I), adopted by the General Assembly on 24 January 1946, aimed at the elimination from national armaments of atomic weapons and of all other major weapons adaptable to mass destruction,

Acknowledging, in this connection, the ethical imperatives outlined in the provisions of its resolutions and reports and those of other related international initiatives on the catastrophic humanitarian consequences and risks posed by a nuclear weapon detonation, including the declaration that the use of nuclear weapons would cause indiscriminate suffering and as such is a violation of the Charter and the laws of humanity and international law,[1] the condemnation of nuclear war as contrary to human conscience and a violation of the fundamental right to life,[2] the threat to the very survival of humankind posed by the existence of nuclear weapons,[3] the detrimental environmental effects of the use of nuclear weapons,[4] and the disquiet that was expressed

---

[1] See resolution 1653 (XVI).
[2] See resolution 38/75.
[3] See resolution S-10/2.
[4] See resolution 50/70 M.

at the continued spending on the development and maintenance of nuclear arsenals,[5]

Acknowledging also the preamble to and article VI of the Treaty on the Non-Proliferation of Nuclear Weapons[6] and the advisory opinion of the International Court of Justice on the legality of the threat or use of nuclear weapons,[7] in which the Court unanimously concluded that there exists an obligation to pursue in good faith and bring to a conclusion negotiations leading to nuclear disarmament in all its aspects under strict and effective international control,

Acknowledging further the United Nations Millennium Declaration,[8] in which Heads of State and Government resolved to strive for the elimination of weapons of mass destruction, particularly nuclear weapons, and to keep all options open for achieving that aim, including the possibility of convening an international conference to identify ways of eliminating nuclear dangers,

Concerned that, despite the long-standing recognition it has accorded to these ethical imperatives and while much effort has been directed to addressing nuclear non-proliferation, limited progress has been made in meeting the nuclear disarmament obligations required to achieve and maintain the nuclear-weapon-free world that the international community demands,

Disappointed at the continued absence of progress towards multilateral negotiations on nuclear disarmament in the Conference on Disarmament, despite unrelenting efforts of Member States towards this end,

Noting with satisfaction the increasing awareness, renewed attention and growing momentum that has been generated by Member States and the international community since 2010 regarding the catastrophic humanitarian consequences and risks associated with nuclear weapons, which underpin the ethical imperatives for nuclear disarmament and the urgency of achieving and maintaining a nuclear-weapon-free world, together with all related international initiatives,

Welcoming the adoption on 7 July 2017 of the Treaty on the Prohibition of Nuclear Weapons,[9] in which the ethical imperatives for nuclear disarmament are acknowledged,

Conscious of the absolute validity of multilateral diplomacy in relation to nuclear disarmament, and determined to promote multilateralism as essential to nuclear disarmament negotiations,

---

[5] See A/59/119.
[6] United Nations, *Treaty Series*, vol. 729, No. 10485.
[7] A/51/218, annex.
[8] Resolution 55/2.
[9] A/CONF.229/2017/8.

1. *Calls upon* all States to acknowledge the catastrophic humanitarian consequences and risks posed by a nuclear weapon detonation, whether by accident, miscalculation or design;

2. *Acknowledges* the ethical imperatives for nuclear disarmament and the urgency of achieving and maintaining a nuclear-weapon-free world, which is a "global public good of the highest order", serving both national and collective security interests;

3. *Declares*:

(a) The global threat posed by nuclear weapons must urgently be eliminated;

(b) Discussions, decisions and actions on nuclear weapons must focus on the effects of these weapons on human beings and the environment and must be guided by the unspeakable suffering and unacceptable harm that they cause;

(c) Greater attention must be given to the impact of a nuclear weapon detonation on women and the importance of their participation in discussions, decisions and actions on nuclear weapons;

(d) Nuclear weapons serve to undermine collective security, heighten the risk of nuclear catastrophe, aggravate international tension and make conflict more dangerous;

(e) Arguments in favour of the retention of nuclear weapons have a negative impact on the credibility of the nuclear disarmament and non-proliferation regime;

(f) The long-term plans for the modernization of nuclear weapons arsenals run contrary to commitments and obligations to nuclear disarmament and engender perceptions of the indefinite possession of these weapons;

(g) In a world where basic human needs have not yet been met, the vast resources allocated to the modernization of nuclear weapons arsenals could instead be redirected to meeting the Sustainable Development Goals;

(h) Given the humanitarian impact of nuclear weapons, it is inconceivable that any use of nuclear weapons, irrespective of the cause, would be compatible with the requirements of international humanitarian law or international law, or the laws of morality, or the dictates of public conscience;

(i) Given their indiscriminate nature and potential to annihilate humanity, nuclear weapons are inherently immoral;

4. *Notes* that all responsible States have a solemn duty to take decisions that serve to protect their people and each other from the ravages of a nuclear weapon detonation, and that the only way for States to do so is through the total elimination of nuclear weapons;

5.   *Stresses* that all States share an ethical responsibility to act with urgency and determination, with the support of all relevant stakeholders, to take the effective measures, including legally binding measures, necessary to eliminate and prohibit all nuclear weapons, given their catastrophic humanitarian consequences and associated risks;

6.   *Decides* to include in the provisional agenda of its seventy-third session, under the item entitled "General and complete disarmament", the sub-item entitled "Ethical imperatives for a nuclear-weapon-free world".

Action by the General Assembly

Date: 4 December 2017   Meeting: 62nd plenary meeting
Vote: 130-36-15   Report: A/72/409
      125-37-13, p.p. 11

Sponsors

Algeria, Angola, Austria, Brazil, Cabo Verde, Costa Rica, Ecuador, El Salvador, Ghana, Guatemala, Ireland, Kazakhstan, Kenya, Malawi, Mexico, Namibia, Nigeria, Panama, Peru, Samoa, Senegal, **South Africa**, Swaziland, Thailand, Trinidad and Tobago, Uruguay, Viet Nam, Zambia

Co-sponsors

Benin, Chile, Lesotho, Philippines, Togo

Recorded vote

As a whole

In favour:

Afghanistan, Algeria, Angola, Antigua and Barbuda, Argentina, Austria, Azerbaijan, Bahamas, Bahrain, Bangladesh, Barbados, Belarus, Belize, Benin, Bhutan, Bolivia (Plurinational State of), Botswana, Brazil, Brunei Darussalam, Burkina Faso, Burundi, Cabo Verde, Cambodia, Central African Republic, Chad, Chile, Colombia, Comoros, Congo, Costa Rica, Côte d'Ivoire, Cuba, Democratic Republic of the Congo, Djibouti, Dominican Republic, Ecuador, Egypt, El Salvador, Equatorial Guinea, Eritrea, Ethiopia, Fiji, Gabon, Gambia, Ghana, Guatemala, Guinea-Bissau, Guyana, Honduras, Indonesia, Iran (Islamic Republic of), Iraq, Ireland, Jamaica, Jordan, Kazakhstan, Kenya, Kiribati, Kuwait, Kyrgyzstan, Lao People's Democratic Republic, Lebanon, Lesotho, Liberia, Libya, Liechtenstein, Madagascar, Malawi, Malaysia, Maldives, Malta, Mauritania, Mauritius, Mexico, Mongolia, Morocco, Mozambique, Myanmar, Namibia, Nauru, Nepal, New Zealand, Nicaragua, Nigeria, Oman, Palau, Panama, Papua New Guinea, Paraguay, Peru, Philippines, Qatar, Republic of Moldova, Rwanda, Saint

Kitts and Nevis, Saint Lucia, Saint Vincent and the Grenadines, Samoa, San Marino, Saudi Arabia, Senegal, Sierra Leone, Singapore, Solomon Islands, Somalia, South Africa, Sri Lanka, Sudan, Suriname, Swaziland, Syrian Arab Republic, Tajikistan, Thailand, Timor-Leste, Togo, Tonga, Trinidad and Tobago, Tunisia, Tuvalu, Uganda, United Arab Emirates, United Republic of Tanzania, Uruguay, Uzbekistan, Vanuatu, Venezuela (Bolivarian Republic of), Viet Nam, Yemen, Zambia, Zimbabwe

Against:

Albania, Australia, Belgium, Bulgaria, Canada, Croatia, Czech Republic, Denmark, Estonia, Finland, France, Germany, Greece, Hungary, Iceland, Israel, Italy, Latvia, Lithuania, Luxembourg, Monaco, Montenegro, Netherlands, Norway, Poland, Portugal, Republic of Korea, Romania, Russian Federation, Slovakia, Slovenia, Spain, Turkey, Ukraine, United Kingdom, United States

Abstaining:

Andorra, Armenia, Bosnia and Herzegovina, China, Cyprus, Democratic People's Republic of Korea, Georgia, India, Japan, Mali, Pakistan, Serbia, Sweden, Switzerland, the former Yugoslav Republic of Macedonia

Eleventh preambular paragraph

In favour:

Afghanistan, Algeria, Angola, Antigua and Barbuda, Argentina, Austria, Azerbaijan, Bahamas, Bahrain, Bangladesh, Barbados, Belize, Benin, Bhutan, Bolivia (Plurinational State of), Botswana, Brazil, Brunei Darussalam, Burkina Faso, Burundi, Cabo Verde, Cambodia, Chad, Chile, Colombia, Comoros, Congo, Costa Rica, Côte d'Ivoire, Cuba, Cyprus, Democratic Republic of the Congo, Djibouti, Dominican Republic, Ecuador, Egypt, El Salvador, Equatorial Guinea, Eritrea, Ethiopia, Fiji, Gabon, Gambia, Ghana, Guatemala, Guinea-Bissau, Guyana, Honduras, Indonesia, Iran (Islamic Republic of), Iraq, Ireland, Jamaica, Jordan, Kazakhstan, Kenya, Kuwait, Kyrgyzstan, Lao People's Democratic Republic, Lebanon, Lesotho, Liberia, Libya, Liechtenstein, Madagascar, Malawi, Malaysia, Maldives, Malta, Mauritania, Mauritius, Mexico, Mongolia, Morocco, Mozambique, Myanmar, Namibia, Nepal, New Zealand, Nicaragua, Nigeria, Oman, Palau, Panama, Papua New Guinea, Paraguay, Peru, Philippines, Qatar, Republic of Moldova, Rwanda, Saint Kitts and Nevis, Saint Lucia, Saint Vincent and the Grenadines, Samoa, San Marino, Saudi Arabia, Senegal, Sierra Leone, Singapore, Solomon Islands, Somalia, South Africa, Sri Lanka, Sudan, Suriname, Swaziland, Sweden, Switzerland, Thailand, Timor-Leste, Togo, Trinidad and Tobago, Tunisia, Tuvalu, Uganda, United Arab

Emirates, United Republic of Tanzania, Uruguay, Vanuatu, Venezuela (Bolivarian Republic of), Viet Nam, Yemen, Zambia, Zimbabwe

Against:

Albania, Australia, Belgium, Bosnia and Herzegovina, Bulgaria, Canada, China, Croatia, Czech Republic, Denmark, Estonia, France, Germany, Greece, Hungary, Iceland, Israel, Italy, Latvia, Lithuania, Luxembourg, Monaco, Montenegro, Netherlands, Norway, Poland, Portugal, Republic of Korea, Romania, Russian Federation, Slovakia, Slovenia, Spain, Turkey, Ukraine, United Kingdom, United States

Abstaining:

Andorra, Armenia, Belarus, Democratic People's Republic of Korea, Finland, Georgia, India, Japan, Kiribati, Mali, Pakistan, Serbia, the former Yugoslav Republic of Macedonia

Action by the First Committee

Date: 27 October 2017
Vote: 122-36-14
     118-37-11, p.p. 11

Meeting: 24th meeting
Draft resolution: A/C.1/72/L.17

Agenda item 99 (b)

72/38   Nuclear disarmament

Text

The General Assembly,

Recalling its resolution 49/75 E of 15 December 1994 on a step-by-step reduction of the nuclear threat, and its resolutions 50/70 P of 12 December 1995, 51/45 O of 10 December 1996, 52/38 L of 9 December 1997, 53/77 X of 4 December 1998, 54/54 P of 1 December 1999, 55/33 T of 20 November 2000, 56/24 R of 29 November 2001, 57/79 of 22 November 2002, 58/56 of 8 December 2003, 59/77 of 3 December 2004, 60/70 of 8 December 2005, 61/78 of 6 December 2006, 62/42 of 5 December 2007, 63/46 of 2 December 2008, 64/53 of 2 December 2009, 65/56 of 8 December 2010, 66/51 of 2 December 2011, 67/60 of 3 December 2012, 68/47 of 5 December 2013, 69/48 of 2 December 2014, 70/52 of 7 December 2015 and 71/63 of 5 December 2016 on nuclear disarmament,

Reaffirming the commitment of the international community to the goal of the total elimination of nuclear weapons and the establishment of a nuclear-weapon-free world,

Bearing in mind that the Convention on the Prohibition of the Development, Production and Stockpiling of Bacteriological (Biological) and Toxin Weapons and on Their Destruction of 1972[1] and the Convention on the Prohibition of the Development, Production, Stockpiling and Use of Chemical Weapons and on Their Destruction of 1993[2] have already established legal regimes on the complete prohibition of biological and chemical weapons, respectively, and determined to achieve a comprehensive nuclear weapons convention on the prohibition of the development, testing, production, stockpiling, loan, transfer, use and threat of use of nuclear weapons and on their destruction, and to conclude such an international convention at an early date,

Recognizing the urgent need to take concrete practical steps towards achieving the establishment of a world free of nuclear weapons,

Bearing in mind paragraph 50 of the Final Document of the Tenth Special Session of the General Assembly, the first special session devoted to disarmament,[3] calling for the urgent negotiation of agreements for the cessation of the qualitative improvement and development of nuclear-weapon systems and for a comprehensive and phased programme with agreed time frames, wherever feasible, for the progressive and balanced reduction of

---

[1] United Nations, *Treaty Series*, vol. 1015, No. 14860.
[2] Ibid., vol. 1974, No. 33757.
[3] Resolution S-10/2.

nuclear weapons and their means of delivery, leading to their ultimate and complete elimination at the earliest possible time,

Reaffirming the conviction of the States parties to the Treaty on the Non-Proliferation of Nuclear Weapons[4] that the Treaty is a cornerstone of nuclear non-proliferation and nuclear disarmament, and the importance of the decision on strengthening the review process for the Treaty, the decision on principles and objectives for nuclear non-proliferation and disarmament, the decision on the extension of the Treaty and the resolution on the Middle East, adopted by the 1995 Review and Extension Conference of the Parties to the Treaty on the Non-Proliferation of Nuclear Weapons,[5]

Stressing the importance of the 13 steps for the systematic and progressive efforts to achieve the objective of nuclear disarmament leading to the total elimination of nuclear weapons, as agreed to by the States parties in the Final Document of the 2000 Review Conference of the Parties to the Treaty on the Non-Proliferation of Nuclear Weapons,[6]

Recognizing the important work done at the 2010 Review Conference of the Parties to the Treaty on the Non-Proliferation of Nuclear Weapons,[7] and affirming its 22-point action plan on nuclear disarmament as an impetus to intensify work aimed at beginning negotiations for a nuclear weapons convention,

Expressing deep concern that the 2015 Review Conference of the Parties to the Treaty on the Non-Proliferation of Nuclear Weapons, held from 27 April to 22 May 2015, did not reach agreement on a substantive final document,

Reaffirming the continued validity of agreements reached at the 1995 Review and Extension Conference and the 2000 and 2010 Review Conferences until all their objectives are achieved, and calling for their full and immediate fulfilment, including the action plan on nuclear disarmament adopted at the 2010 Review Conference,

Reiterating the highest priority accorded to nuclear disarmament in the Final Document of the Tenth Special Session of the General Assembly and by the international community,

---

[4] United Nations, *Treaty Series*, vol. 729, No. 10485.

[5] See *1995 Review and Extension Conference of the Parties to the Treaty on the Non-Proliferation of Nuclear Weapons, Final Document, Part I* (NPT/CONF.1995/32 (Part I) and NPT/CONF.1995/32 (Part I)/Corr.2), annex.

[6] *2000 Review Conference of the Parties to the Treaty on the Non-Proliferation of Nuclear Weapons, Final Document*, vol. I (NPT/CONF.2000/28 (Parts I and II)), part I, section entitled "Article VI and eighth to twelfth preambular paragraphs", para. 15.

[7] *2010 Review Conference of the Parties to the Treaty on the Non-Proliferation of Nuclear Weapons, Final Document*, vols. I–III (NPT/CONF.2010/50 (Vol. I), NPT/CONF.2010/50 (Vol. II) and NPT/CONF.2010/50 (Vol. III)).

Reiterating its call for an early entry into force of the Comprehensive Nuclear-Test-Ban Treaty,[8]

Noting the new strategic arms reduction treaty between the Russian Federation and the United States of America, in order to achieve further cuts in their deployed and non-deployed strategic nuclear weapons, and stressing that such cuts should be irreversible, verifiable and transparent,

Noting also the statements by nuclear-weapon States of their intention to pursue actions in achieving a world free of nuclear weapons, as well as the steps taken to reduce the role and number of nuclear weapons, and urging nuclear-weapon States to take further measures for progress on nuclear disarmament within a specified framework of time,

Recognizing the complementarity of bilateral, plurilateral and multilateral negotiations on nuclear disarmament, and that bilateral negotiations can never replace multilateral negotiations in this respect,

Noting the support expressed in the Conference on Disarmament and in the General Assembly for the elaboration of an international convention to assure non-nuclear-weapon States, without exception or discrimination, against the use or threat of use of nuclear weapons under any circumstances, and the multilateral efforts in the Conference to reach agreement on such an international convention at an early date,

Recalling the advisory opinion of the International Court of Justice on the legality of the threat or use of nuclear weapons, issued on 8 July 1996,[9] and welcoming the unanimous reaffirmation by all judges of the Court that there exists an obligation for all States to pursue in good faith and bring to a conclusion negotiations leading to nuclear disarmament in all its aspects under strict and effective international control,

Recalling also paragraph 176 of the Final Document of the Seventeenth Conference of Heads of State or Government of Non-Aligned Countries, held on Margarita Island, Bolivarian Republic of Venezuela, from 13 to 18 September 2016, in which the Conference on Disarmament was called upon to agree on a balanced and comprehensive programme of work by, inter alia, establishing an ad hoc committee on nuclear disarmament as soon as possible and as the highest priority, while the necessity was emphasized of starting negotiations in the Conference on Disarmament, without further delay, on a comprehensive nuclear weapons convention that sets, inter alia, a phased programme for the complete elimination of nuclear weapons within a specified framework of time,

---

[8] See resolution 50/245 and A/50/1027.

[9] A/51/218, annex.

Noting the adoption of the programme of work for the 2009 session by the Conference on Disarmament on 29 May 2009,[10] after years of stalemate, and regretting that, despite substantive informal consultations in the working group on the way ahead on all items on the agenda of the Conference on Disarmament, as mandated by the decision of the Conference of 17 February 2017,[11] and intensive consultations by the relevant Presidents of the Conference with a view to agreeing on a programme of work,[12] the Conference did not succeed in reaching consensus on a programme of work for its 2017 session,

Welcoming the proposals submitted by the States members of the Conference on Disarmament that are members of the Group of 21 on the follow-up to the 2013 high-level meeting of the General Assembly on nuclear disarmament, pursuant to Assembly resolution 68/32 of 5 December 2013, as contained in documents of the Conference,[13]

Reaffirming the importance and validity of the Conference on Disarmament as the sole multilateral disarmament negotiating forum, and expressing the need to adopt and implement a balanced and comprehensive programme of work on the basis of its agenda and dealing with, inter alia, four core issues, in accordance with the rules of procedure,[14] and by taking into consideration the security concerns of all States,

Reaffirming also the specific mandate conferred upon the Disarmament Commission by the General Assembly, in its decision 52/492 of 8 September 1998, to discuss the subject of nuclear disarmament as one of its main substantive agenda items,

Recalling the United Nations Millennium Declaration,[15] in which Heads of State and Government resolved to strive for the elimination of weapons of mass destruction, in particular nuclear weapons, and to keep all options open for achieving that aim, including the possibility of convening an international conference to identify ways of eliminating nuclear dangers,

Underlining the importance of implementing its decision in resolution 68/32 to convene, no later than 2018, a United Nations high-level international conference on nuclear disarmament to review the progress made in this regard,

Recalling the high-level meeting of the General Assembly on nuclear disarmament held on 26 September 2013, and the strong support for nuclear disarmament expressed therein,

---

[10] See *Official Records of the General Assembly, Sixty-fourth Session, Supplement No. 27* (A/64/27), para. 18.
[11] Ibid., *Seventy-second Session, Supplement No. 27* (A/72/27), para. 15.
[12] Ibid., para. 20.
[13] See CD/1999 and CD/2067.
[14] CD/8/Rev.9.
[15] Resolution 55/2.

Welcoming the commemoration of 26 September as the International Day for the Total Elimination of Nuclear Weapons, devoted to furthering this objective, as declared by the General Assembly in its resolution 68/32 and subsequently welcomed in its resolutions 69/58 of 2 December 2014, 70/34 of 7 December 2015 and 71/71 of 5 December 2016,

Taking note of the declaration of the States members of the Agency for the Prohibition of Nuclear Weapons in Latin America and the Caribbean on the International Day for the Total Elimination of Nuclear Weapons, in Mexico City on 26 September 2017,[16]

Expressing deep concern about the catastrophic humanitarian consequences of any use of nuclear weapons,

Noting the successful convening of the first, second and third Conferences on the Humanitarian Impact of Nuclear Weapons, in Oslo on 4 and 5 March 2013, in Nayarit, Mexico, on 13 and 14 February 2014, and in Vienna on 8 and 9 December 2014, and noting also that 127 nations have formally endorsed the Humanitarian Pledge issued following the Third Conference,[17]

Welcoming the signing by the nuclear-weapon States, namely, China, France, the Russian Federation, the United Kingdom of Great Britain and Northern Ireland and the United States of America, of the Protocol to the Treaty on a Nuclear-Weapon-Free Zone in Central Asia, in New York on 6 May 2014,

Welcoming also the proclamation of Latin America and the Caribbean as a Zone of Peace on 29 January 2014 during the Second Summit of the Community of Latin American and Caribbean States, held in Havana on 28 and 29 January 2014,

Welcoming further the successful adoption of the Treaty on the Prohibition of Nuclear Weapons on 7 July 2017,[18]

Reaffirming that, in accordance with the Charter of the United Nations, States should refrain from the use or threat of use of nuclear weapons in settling their disputes in international relations,

Seized of the danger of the use of weapons of mass destruction, particularly nuclear weapons, in terrorist acts and the urgent need for concerted international efforts to control and overcome it,

1. *Urges* all nuclear-weapon States to take effective disarmament measures to achieve the total elimination of all nuclear weapons at the earliest possible time;

---

[16] See A/C.1/72/2.
[17] See CD/2039.
[18] A/CONF.229/2017/8.

2.   *Reaffirms* that nuclear disarmament and nuclear non-proliferation are substantively interrelated and mutually reinforcing, that the two processes must go hand in hand and that there is a genuine need for a systematic and progressive process of nuclear disarmament;

3.   *Welcomes and encourages* the efforts to establish new nuclear-weapon-free zones in different parts of the world, including the establishment of a Middle East zone free of nuclear weapons, on the basis of agreements or arrangements freely arrived at among the States of the regions concerned, which is an effective measure for limiting the further spread of nuclear weapons geographically and contributes to the cause of nuclear disarmament;

4.   *Encourages* States parties to the Treaty on the South-East Asia Nuclear-Weapon-Free Zone[19] and the nuclear-weapon States to intensify ongoing efforts to resolve all outstanding issues, in accordance with the objectives and principles of the Treaty, pertaining to the signing and ratifying of the Protocol to the Treaty;

5.   *Recognizes* that there is a genuine need to diminish the role of nuclear weapons in strategic doctrines and security policies to minimize the risk that these weapons will ever be used and to facilitate the process of their total elimination;

6.   *Urges* the nuclear-weapon States to stop immediately the qualitative improvement, development, production and stockpiling of nuclear warheads and their delivery systems;

7.   *Also urges* the nuclear-weapon States, as an interim measure, to de-alert and deactivate immediately their nuclear weapons and to take other concrete measures to reduce further the operational status of their nuclear-weapon systems, while stressing that reductions in deployments and in operational status cannot substitute for irreversible cuts in and the total elimination of nuclear weapons;

8.   *Reiterates its call upon* the nuclear-weapon States to carry out effective nuclear disarmament measures with a view to achieving the total elimination of nuclear weapons within a specified framework of time;

9.   *Calls upon* the nuclear-weapon States, pending the achievement of the total elimination of nuclear weapons, to agree on an internationally and legally binding instrument on a joint undertaking not to be the first to use nuclear weapons;

10. *Urges* the nuclear-weapon States to commence plurilateral negotiations among themselves at an appropriate stage on further deep reductions of their nuclear weapons, in an irreversible, verifiable and transparent manner, as an effective measure of nuclear disarmament;

---

[19] United Nations, *Treaty Series*, vol. 1981, No. 33873.

11. *Underlines* the importance of applying the principles of transparency, irreversibility and verifiability to the process of nuclear disarmament;

12. *Also underlines* the importance of the unequivocal undertaking by the nuclear-weapon States, in the Final Document of the 2000 Review Conference of the Parties to the Treaty on the Non-Proliferation of Nuclear Weapons, to accomplish the total elimination of their nuclear arsenals leading to nuclear disarmament, to which all States parties are committed under article VI of the Treaty,[6] and the reaffirmation by the States parties that the total elimination of nuclear weapons is the only absolute guarantee against the use or threat of use of nuclear weapons;[20]

13. *Calls for* the full and effective implementation of the 13 practical steps for nuclear disarmament contained in the Final Document of the 2000 Review Conference;[6]

14. *Also calls for* the full implementation of the action plan as set out in the conclusions and recommendations for follow-on actions of the Final Document of the 2010 Review Conference of the Parties to the Treaty on the Non-Proliferation of Nuclear Weapons, particularly the 22-point action plan on nuclear disarmament;[7]

15. *Urges* the nuclear-weapon States to carry out further reductions of non-strategic nuclear weapons, including on unilateral initiatives and as an integral part of the nuclear arms reduction and disarmament process;

16. *Calls for* the immediate commencement of negotiations in the Conference on Disarmament, in the context of an agreed, comprehensive and balanced programme of work, on a non-discriminatory, multilateral and internationally and effectively verifiable treaty banning the production of fissile material for nuclear weapons or other nuclear explosive devices on the basis of the report of the Special Coordinator[21] and the mandate contained therein;

17. *Urges* the Conference on Disarmament to commence as early as possible its substantive work during its 2018 session, on the basis of a comprehensive and balanced programme of work that takes into consideration all the real and existing priorities in the field of disarmament and arms control, including the immediate commencement of negotiations on a comprehensive nuclear weapons convention;

---

[20] *2000 Review Conference of the Parties to the Treaty on the Non-Proliferation of Nuclear Weapons, Final Document*, vol. I (NPT/CONF.2000/28 (Parts I and II)), part I, section entitled "Article VII and the security of non-nuclear-weapon States", para. 2.

[21] CD/1299.

18. *Calls for* the conclusion of an international legal instrument on unconditional security assurances to non-nuclear-weapon States against the threat or use of nuclear weapons under any circumstances;

19. *Also calls for* the early entry into force, universalization and strict observance of the Comprehensive Nuclear-Test-Ban Treaty[8] as a contribution to nuclear disarmament, while welcoming the latest ratifications of the Treaty, by Myanmar and Swaziland, on 21 September 2016;

20. *Reiterates its call upon* the Conference on Disarmament to establish, as soon as possible and as the highest priority, an ad hoc committee on nuclear disarmament in 2018 and to commence negotiations on a phased programme of nuclear disarmament leading to the total elimination of nuclear weapons within a specified framework of time;

21. *Calls for* the convening, no later than 2018, of a United Nations high-level international conference on nuclear disarmament to review the progress made in this regard;

22. *Requests* the Secretary-General to submit to the General Assembly at its seventy-third session a report on the implementation of the present resolution;

23. *Decides* to include in the provisional agenda of its seventy-third session, under the item entitled "General and complete disarmament", the sub-item entitled "Nuclear disarmament".

Action by the General Assembly

Date: 4 December 2017   Meeting: 62nd plenary meeting
Vote: 119-41-20   Report: A/72/409
      123-38-11, p.p. 32
      172-1-5, o.p. 16

Sponsors

Angola, Cuba, Ecuador, Eritrea, Indonesia, Kenya, Lao People's Democratic Republic, Malawi, Mongolia, **Myanmar**, Namibia, Nepal, Nicaragua, Philippines, Samoa, Sierra Leone, Swaziland, Thailand, Tonga, Venezuela (Bolivarian Republic of), Viet Nam, Zambia, Zimbabwe

Co-sponsors

Belize, Bhutan, Bolivia (Plurinational State of), Brazil, Brunei Darussalam, Burkina Faso, Cambodia, Fiji, Ghana, Guinea-Bissau, Honduras, Malaysia, Mozambique, Nigeria, Panama, Senegal, Sri Lanka, Timor-Leste

Recorded vote

As a whole

In favour:

Afghanistan, Algeria, Angola, Antigua and Barbuda, Argentina, Azerbaijan, Bahamas, Bahrain, Bangladesh, Barbados, Belize, Benin, Bhutan, Bolivia (Plurinational State of), Botswana, Brazil, Brunei Darussalam, Burkina Faso, Burundi, Cabo Verde, Cambodia, Central African Republic, Chad, Chile, China, Colombia, Comoros, Congo, Costa Rica, Côte d'Ivoire, Cuba, Democratic Republic of the Congo, Djibouti, Dominican Republic, Ecuador, Egypt, El Salvador, Equatorial Guinea, Eritrea, Ethiopia, Fiji, Gabon, Gambia, Ghana, Guatemala, Guinea-Bissau, Guyana, Honduras, Indonesia, Iran (Islamic Republic of), Iraq, Jamaica, Jordan, Kazakhstan, Kenya, Kiribati, Kuwait, Kyrgyzstan, Lao People's Democratic Republic, Lebanon, Lesotho, Liberia, Libya, Madagascar, Malawi, Malaysia, Maldives, Mauritania, Mauritius, Mexico, Mongolia, Morocco, Mozambique, Myanmar, Namibia, Nepal, Nicaragua, Nigeria, Oman, Palau, Panama, Papua New Guinea, Paraguay, Peru, Philippines, Qatar, Rwanda, Saint Kitts and Nevis, Saint Lucia, Saint Vincent and the Grenadines, Samoa, Saudi Arabia, Senegal, Sierra Leone, Singapore, Solomon Islands, Somalia, Sri Lanka, Sudan, Suriname, Swaziland, Syrian Arab Republic, Tajikistan, Thailand, Timor-Leste, Togo, Tonga, Trinidad and Tobago, Tunisia, Uganda, United Arab Emirates, United Republic of Tanzania, Uruguay, Vanuatu, Venezuela (Bolivarian Republic of), Viet Nam, Yemen, Zambia, Zimbabwe

Against:

Albania, Andorra, Australia, Belgium, Bosnia and Herzegovina, Bulgaria, Canada, Croatia, Czech Republic, Denmark, Estonia, Finland, France, Germany, Greece, Hungary, Iceland, Israel, Italy, Latvia, Lithuania, Luxembourg, Micronesia (Federated States of), Monaco, Montenegro, Netherlands, Norway, Poland, Portugal, Republic of Korea, Romania, Russian Federation, Slovakia, Slovenia, Spain, Switzerland, the former Yugoslav Republic of Macedonia, Turkey, Ukraine, United Kingdom, United States

Abstaining:

Armenia, Austria, Belarus, Cyprus, Democratic People's Republic of Korea, India, Ireland, Japan, Liechtenstein, Mali, Malta, Marshall Islands, New Zealand, Pakistan, Republic of Moldova, San Marino, Serbia, South Africa, Sweden, Uzbekistan

Thirty-second preambular paragraph

In favour:

Afghanistan, Algeria, Angola, Antigua and Barbuda, Argentina, Austria, Azerbaijan, Bahamas, Bahrain, Bangladesh, Barbados, Belize, Benin, Bhutan, Bolivia (Plurinational State of), Botswana, Brazil, Brunei Darussalam, Burkina Faso, Burundi, Cabo Verde, Cambodia, Chad, Chile, Colombia, Comoros, Congo, Costa Rica, Côte d'Ivoire, Cuba, Cyprus, Democratic Republic of the Congo, Djibouti, Dominican Republic, Ecuador, Egypt, El Salvador, Equatorial Guinea, Eritrea, Ethiopia, Fiji, Gabon, Gambia, Ghana, Guatemala, Guinea-Bissau, Guyana, Honduras, Indonesia, Iran (Islamic Republic of), Iraq, Ireland, Jamaica, Jordan, Kazakhstan, Kenya, Kiribati, Kuwait, Lao People's Democratic Republic, Lebanon, Lesotho, Liberia, Libya, Liechtenstein, Madagascar, Malawi, Malaysia, Maldives, Malta, Mauritania, Mexico, Mongolia, Morocco, Mozambique, Myanmar, Namibia, Nepal, New Zealand, Nicaragua, Nigeria, Oman, Palau, Panama, Papua New Guinea, Paraguay, Peru, Philippines, Qatar, Republic of Moldova, Rwanda, Saint Kitts and Nevis, Saint Lucia, Saint Vincent and the Grenadines, Samoa, San Marino, Saudi Arabia, Senegal, Sierra Leone, Singapore, Solomon Islands, Somalia, South Africa, Sri Lanka, Sudan, Suriname, Swaziland, Sweden, Switzerland, Thailand, Timor-Leste, Togo, Trinidad and Tobago, Tunisia, Uganda, United Arab Emirates, United Republic of Tanzania, Uruguay, Vanuatu, Venezuela (Bolivarian Republic of), Viet Nam, Yemen, Zambia, Zimbabwe

Against:

Albania, Australia, Belgium, Bosnia and Herzegovina, Bulgaria, Canada, China, Croatia, Czech Republic, Denmark, Estonia, Finland, France, Germany, Greece, Hungary, Iceland, Israel, Italy, Latvia, Lithuania, Luxembourg, Monaco, Montenegro, Netherlands, Norway, Poland, Portugal, Republic of Korea, Romania, Russian Federation, Slovakia, Slovenia, Spain, Turkey, Ukraine, United Kingdom, United States

Abstaining:

Andorra, Armenia, Belarus, Democratic People's Republic of Korea, India, Japan, Mali, Mauritius, Pakistan, Serbia, the former Yugoslav Republic of Macedonia

Operative paragraph 16*

In favour:

Afghanistan, Albania, Algeria, Andorra, Angola, Antigua and Barbuda, Argentina, Armenia, Australia, Austria, Azerbaijan, Bahamas, Bahrain,

---

* Subsequently, the delegation of the United States informed the Secretariat that it had intended to abstain. The voting tally above does not reflect this information.

Bangladesh, Barbados, Belarus, Belgium, Belize, Benin, Bhutan, Bolivia (Plurinational State of), Bosnia and Herzegovina, Botswana, Brazil, Brunei Darussalam, Bulgaria, Burkina Faso, Burundi, Cabo Verde, Cambodia, Canada, Chad, Chile, China, Colombia, Comoros, Congo, Costa Rica, Côte d'Ivoire, Croatia, Cuba, Cyprus, Czech Republic, Democratic Republic of the Congo, Denmark, Djibouti, Dominican Republic, Ecuador, Egypt, El Salvador, Equatorial Guinea, Eritrea, Estonia, Ethiopia, Fiji, Finland, Gabon, Gambia, Germany, Ghana, Greece, Guatemala, Guinea, Guinea-Bissau, Guyana, Honduras, Hungary, Iceland, India, Indonesia, Iran (Islamic Republic of), Iraq, Ireland, Italy, Jamaica, Japan, Jordan, Kazakhstan, Kenya, Kiribati, Kuwait, Kyrgyzstan, Lao People's Democratic Republic, Latvia, Lebanon, Lesotho, Liberia, Libya, Liechtenstein, Lithuania, Luxembourg, Madagascar, Malawi, Malaysia, Maldives, Mali, Malta, Marshall Islands, Mauritania, Mauritius, Mexico, Micronesia (Federated States of), Monaco, Mongolia, Montenegro, Morocco, Mozambique, Myanmar, Namibia, Nepal, Netherlands, New Zealand, Nicaragua, Nigeria, Norway, Oman, Palau, Panama, Papua New Guinea, Paraguay, Peru, Philippines, Poland, Portugal, Qatar, Republic of Korea, Republic of Moldova, Romania, Rwanda, Saint Kitts and Nevis, Saint Lucia, Saint Vincent and the Grenadines, Samoa, San Marino, Saudi Arabia, Senegal, Serbia, Sierra Leone, Singapore, Slovakia, Slovenia, Solomon Islands, Somalia, South Africa, Spain, Sri Lanka, Sudan, Suriname, Swaziland, Sweden, Switzerland, Syrian Arab Republic, Tajikistan, Thailand, the former Yugoslav Republic of Macedonia, Timor-Leste, Togo, Trinidad and Tobago, Tunisia, Turkey, Uganda, Ukraine, United Arab Emirates, United Republic of Tanzania, United States, Uruguay, Vanuatu, Venezuela (Bolivarian Republic of), Viet Nam, Yemen, Zambia, Zimbabwe

Against:
Pakistan

Abstaining:
Democratic People's Republic of Korea, France, Israel, Russian Federation, United Kingdom

Action by the First Committee

Date: 1 November 2017   Meeting: 27th meeting
Vote: 110-41-18   Draft resolution: A/C.1/72/L.18
      114-37-11, p.p. 32
      159-1-6, o.p. 16

Agenda item 99 (q)

72/39 Towards a nuclear-weapon-free world: accelerating the implementation of nuclear disarmament commitments

Text

The General Assembly,

Recalling its resolutions 1 (I) of 24 January 1946, 70/51 of 7 December 2015 and 71/54 of 5 December 2016,

Reiterating its grave concern at the danger to humanity posed by nuclear weapons, which should inform all deliberations, decisions and actions relating to nuclear disarmament and nuclear non-proliferation,

Recalling the expression of deep concern by the 2010 Review Conference of the Parties to the Treaty on the Non-Proliferation of Nuclear Weapons at the catastrophic humanitarian consequences of any use of nuclear weapons, and its resolve to seek a safer world for all and to achieve the peace and security of a world without nuclear weapons,[1]

Noting with satisfaction the renewed attention to the catastrophic humanitarian consequences and risks associated with nuclear weapons that has been generated by the international community since 2010 and the growing awareness that these concerns should underpin the need for nuclear disarmament and the urgency of achieving and maintaining a nuclear-weapon-free world, and noting with satisfaction also the prominence accorded to the humanitarian impact of nuclear weapons in multilateral disarmament forums,

Recalling the discussions held at the Conferences on the Humanitarian Impact of Nuclear Weapons, hosted by Norway, on 4 and 5 March 2013, Mexico, on 13 and 14 February 2014, and Austria, on 8 and 9 December 2014, aimed at understanding and developing a greater awareness of the catastrophic consequences of nuclear weapon detonations which further reinforce the urgency of nuclear disarmament,

Emphasizing the compelling evidence, including that presented at the Conferences on the Humanitarian Impact of Nuclear Weapons, that has detailed the catastrophic consequences that would result from a nuclear weapon detonation, reaching well beyond national borders and also imperilling the achievement of the Sustainable Development Goals, the lack of capacity of States and international organizations to deal with the aftermath

---

[1] See *2010 Review Conference of the Parties to the Treaty on the Non-Proliferation of Nuclear Weapons, Final Document*, vol. I (NPT/CONF.2010/50 (Vol. I)), part I, *Conclusions and recommendations for follow-on actions.*

and the risk of an occurrence, due to an accident, systems failure or human error,

Noting the research findings presented to the Vienna Conference regarding the strongly disproportionate and gendered impact of exposure to ionizing radiation for women and girls,

Recalling the convening, on 26 September 2013, of the high-level meeting of the General Assembly on nuclear disarmament and its resolution 70/34 of 7 December 2015 on the follow-up to that meeting and the decisions contained therein, and taking note of the report of the Secretary-General submitted pursuant to that resolution,[2]

Welcoming the commemoration and promotion of 26 September as the International Day for the Total Elimination of Nuclear Weapons,

Welcoming also the adoption on 7 July 2017 of the Treaty on the Prohibition of Nuclear Weapons, negotiated by the United Nations conference to negotiate a legally binding instrument to prohibit nuclear weapons, leading towards their total elimination, pursuant to resolution 71/258 of 23 December 2016,[3]

Underlining the importance of nuclear disarmament and non-proliferation education,

Reaffirming that transparency, verifiability and irreversibility are cardinal principles applying to nuclear disarmament and nuclear non-proliferation, which are mutually reinforcing processes,

Recalling the decisions and the resolution adopted at the 1995 Review and Extension Conference of the Parties to the Treaty on the Non-Proliferation of Nuclear Weapons,[4] the basis upon which the Treaty was indefinitely extended, and the Final Documents of the 2000[5] and the 2010[6] Review Conferences of the Parties to the Treaty on the Non-Proliferation of Nuclear Weapons, and in particular the unequivocal undertaking by the nuclear-weapon States to accomplish the total elimination of their nuclear arsenals, leading to nuclear disarmament, in accordance with commitments made under article VI of the Treaty on the Non-Proliferation of Nuclear Weapons,[7]

---

[2] A/71/131.

[3] A/CONF.229/2017/8.

[4] See *1995 Review and Extension Conference of the Parties to the Treaty on the Non-Proliferation of Nuclear Weapons, Final Document, Part I* (NPT/CONF.1995/32 (Part I) and NPT/CONF.1995/32 (Part I)/Corr.2), annex.

[5] *2000 Review Conference of the Parties to the Treaty on the Non-Proliferation of Nuclear Weapons, Final Document*, vols. I–III (NPT/CONF.2000/28 (Parts I and II), NPT/CONF.2000/28 (Part III) and NPT/CONF.2000/28 (Part IV)).

[6] *2010 Review Conference of the Parties to the Treaty on the Non-Proliferation of Nuclear Weapons, Final Document*, vols. I–III (NPT/CONF.2010/50 (Vol. I), NPT/CONF.2010/50 (Vol. II) and NPT/CONF.2010/50 (Vol. III)).

[7] United Nations, *Treaty Series*, vol. 729, No. 10485.

Reaffirming the commitment of all States parties to the Treaty on the Non-Proliferation of Nuclear Weapons to applying the principles of irreversibility, verifiability and transparency in relation to the implementation of their treaty obligations,

Recognizing the continued vital importance of the entry into force of the Comprehensive Nuclear-Test-Ban Treaty[8] to the advancement of nuclear disarmament and nuclear non-proliferation objectives,

Recalling that the total elimination of nuclear weapons is the only absolute guarantee against the use or threat of use of nuclear weapons and the legitimate interest of non-nuclear-weapon States in receiving unequivocal and legally binding negative security assurances from nuclear-weapon States pending the total elimination of nuclear weapons,

Reaffirming the conviction that, pending the total elimination of nuclear weapons, the establishment and maintenance of nuclear-weapon-free zones enhances global and regional peace and security, strengthens the nuclear non-proliferation regime and contributes towards realizing the objectives of nuclear disarmament, and welcoming the Conferences of States Parties and Signatories to Treaties that Establish Nuclear-Weapon-Free Zones and Mongolia,

Urging States to continue to make real progress towards strengthening all existing nuclear-weapon-free zones, inter alia, through the ratification of existing treaties and relevant protocols and the withdrawal or revision of any reservations or interpretative declarations contrary to the object and purpose of the treaties establishing such zones,

Recalling the encouragement expressed at the 2010 Review Conference for the establishment of further nuclear-weapon-free zones, on the basis of arrangements freely arrived at among the States of the region concerned, reaffirming the expectation that this will be followed by concerted international efforts to create such zones in areas where they do not currently exist, especially in the Middle East, in this context noting with deep disappointment the non-fulfilment of the agreement at the 2010 Review Conference on practical steps to fully implement the 1995 resolution on the Middle East, and disappointed that no agreement could be reached at the 2015 Review Conference of the Parties to the Treaty on the Non-Proliferation of Nuclear Weapons on this issue,

Deeply disappointed at the continued absence of progress towards multilateral nuclear disarmament at the Conference on Disarmament, which has been unable for the past 21 years to agree upon and implement a programme of work, and disappointed that the Disarmament Commission has not produced a substantive outcome on nuclear disarmament since 1999,

---

[8] See resolution 50/245 and A/50/1027.

Deeply regretting the lack of any substantive outcome of the 2015 Review Conference,

Disappointed that the 2015 Review Conference missed an opportunity to strengthen the Treaty on the Non-Proliferation of Nuclear Weapons, enhance progress towards its full implementation and universality and monitor the implementation of commitments made and actions agreed upon at the 1995, 2000 and 2010 Review Conferences, and deeply concerned about the impact of this failure on the Treaty and the balance between its three pillars,

Welcoming the discussions that took place at the first session of the Preparatory Committee for the 2020 Review Conference of the Parties to the Treaty on the Non-Proliferation of Nuclear Weapons, held in Vienna from 2 to 12 May 2017,

Encouraging efforts towards the full implementation of the Treaty between the Russian Federation and the United States of America on Measures for the Further Reduction and Limitation of Strategic Offensive Arms, while re-emphasizing the encouragement of the 2010 Review Conference to both States to continue discussions on follow-on measures in order to achieve deeper reductions in their nuclear arsenals,

Underlining the importance of multilateralism in relation to nuclear disarmament, while recognizing the value of unilateral, bilateral and regional initiatives and the importance of compliance with the terms of these initiatives,

1.   *Reiterates* that each article of the Treaty on the Non-Proliferation of Nuclear Weapons[7] is binding on the States parties at all times and in all circumstances and that all States parties should be held fully accountable with respect to strict compliance with their obligations under the Treaty, and calls upon all States parties to comply fully with all decisions, resolutions and commitments made at the 1995, 2000 and 2010 Review Conferences;

2.   *Also reiterates* the deep concern expressed by the 2010 Review Conference of the Parties to the Treaty on the Non-Proliferation of Nuclear Weapons at the catastrophic humanitarian consequences of any use of nuclear weapons, and the need for all States at all times to comply with applicable international law, including international humanitarian law;[1]

3.   *Acknowledges* the evidence presented at the Conferences on the Humanitarian Impact of Nuclear Weapons, and calls upon Member States, in their relevant decisions and actions, to give due prominence to the humanitarian imperatives that underpin nuclear disarmament and to the urgency of achieving this goal;

4.   *Recalls* the reaffirmation of the continued validity of the practical steps agreed to in the Final Document of the 2000 Review Conference of the

Parties to the Treaty on the Non-Proliferation of Nuclear Weapons,[9] including the specific reaffirmation of the unequivocal undertaking of the nuclear-weapon States to accomplish the total elimination of their nuclear arsenals leading to nuclear disarmament, to which all States parties are committed under article VI of the Treaty, recalls the commitment of the nuclear-weapon States to accelerating concrete progress on the steps leading to nuclear disarmament, and calls upon the nuclear-weapon States to take all steps necessary to accelerate the fulfilment of their commitments;

5.   *Calls upon* the nuclear-weapon States to fulfil their commitment to undertaking further efforts to reduce and ultimately eliminate all types of nuclear weapons, deployed and non-deployed, including through unilateral, bilateral, regional and multilateral measures;

6.   *Urges* all States possessing nuclear weapons to decrease the operational readiness of nuclear-weapon systems in a verifiable and transparent manner with a view to ensuring that all nuclear weapons are removed from high alert status;

7.   *Encourages* the nuclear-weapon States to make concrete reductions in the role and significance of nuclear weapons in all military and security concepts, doctrines and policies, pending their total elimination;

8.   *Encourages* all States that are part of regional alliances that include nuclear-weapon States to diminish the role of nuclear weapons in their collective security doctrines, pending their total elimination;

9.   *Underlines* the recognition by States parties to the Treaty on the Non-Proliferation of Nuclear Weapons of the legitimate interest of non-nuclear-weapon States in the constraining by the nuclear-weapon States of the development and qualitative improvement of nuclear weapons and their ending the development of advanced new types of nuclear weapons, and calls upon the nuclear-weapon States to take steps in this regard;

10.   *Encourages* further steps by all nuclear-weapon States, in accordance with the previous obligations and commitments on nuclear disarmament, to ensure the irreversible removal of all fissile material designated by each nuclear-weapon State as no longer required for military purposes, and calls upon all States to support, within the context of the International Atomic Energy Agency, the development of appropriate nuclear disarmament verification capabilities and legally binding verification arrangements, thereby ensuring that such material remains permanently outside military programmes in a verifiable manner;

---

[9] *2000 Review Conference of the Parties to the Treaty on the Non-Proliferation of Nuclear Weapons, Final Document*, vol. I (NPT/CONF.2000/28 (Parts I and II)), part I, section entitled "Article VI and eighth to twelfth preambular paragraphs", para. 15.

11. *Calls upon* all States parties to the Treaty on the Non-Proliferation of Nuclear Weapons to work towards the full implementation of the resolution on the Middle East adopted at the 1995 Review and Extension Conference of the Parties to the Treaty on the Non-Proliferation of Nuclear Weapons,[4] which is inextricably linked to the indefinite extension of the Treaty, and expresses disappointment and deep concern at the lack of a substantive outcome of the 2015 Review Conference of the Parties to the Treaty on the Non-Proliferation of Nuclear Weapons, including on the process to establish a Middle East zone free of nuclear weapons and all other weapons of mass destruction as contained in the 1995 resolution on the Middle East, which remains valid until fully implemented;

12. *Urges* the co-sponsors of the 1995 resolution on the Middle East to present proposals and exert their utmost efforts with a view to ensuring the early establishment of a Middle East zone free of nuclear weapons and all other weapons of mass destruction as contained in the 1995 resolution on the Middle East;

13. *Stresses* the fundamental role of the Treaty on the Non-Proliferation of Nuclear Weapons in achieving nuclear disarmament and nuclear non-proliferation, and looks forward to the second session of the Preparatory Committee for the 2020 Review Conference of the Parties to the Treaty on the Non-Proliferation of Nuclear Weapons, to be held in Geneva from 23 April to 4 May 2018;

14. *Calls upon* all States parties to spare no effort to achieve the universality of the Treaty on the Non-Proliferation of Nuclear Weapons, and in this regard urges India, Israel and Pakistan to accede to the Treaty as non-nuclear-weapon States promptly and without conditions, and to place all their nuclear facilities under International Atomic Energy Agency safeguards;

15. *Urges* the Democratic People's Republic of Korea to fulfil its commitments under the Six-Party Talks, including those in the September 2005 joint statement, to abandon all nuclear weapons and existing nuclear programmes, to return, at an early date, to the Treaty on the Non-Proliferation of Nuclear Weapons and to adhere to its International Atomic Energy Agency safeguards agreement,[10] with a view to achieving the denuclearization of the Korean Peninsula in a peaceful manner, and reaffirms its firm support for the Six-Party Talks;

16. *Urges* all States to work together to overcome obstacles within the international disarmament machinery that are inhibiting efforts to advance the cause of nuclear disarmament in a multilateral context, and urges the Conference on Disarmament once again to commence, without delay, substantive work that advances the agenda of nuclear disarmament, particularly through multilateral negotiations;

---

[10] United Nations, *Treaty Series*, vol. 1677, No. 28986.

17. *Urges* all States parties to the Treaty on the Non-Proliferation of Nuclear Weapons to fully implement without delay their obligations and commitments under the Treaty and as agreed to at the 1995, 2000 and 2010 Review Conferences;

18. *Urges* the nuclear-weapon States to implement their nuclear disarmament obligations and commitments, both qualitative and quantitative, in a manner that enables the States parties to regularly monitor progress, including through a standard detailed reporting format, thereby enhancing confidence and trust not only among the nuclear-weapon States but also between the nuclear-weapon States and the non-nuclear-weapon States and contributing to nuclear disarmament;

19. *Also urges* the nuclear-weapon States to include in their reports to be submitted throughout the 2020 review cycle of the Treaty on the Non-Proliferation of Nuclear Weapons concrete and detailed information concerning the implementation of their obligations and commitments on nuclear disarmament;

20. *Encourages* States parties to the Treaty on the Non-Proliferation of Nuclear Weapons to discuss options, including tools such as a set of benchmarks or similar criteria, to improve the measurability of the implementation of nuclear disarmament obligations and commitments, in order to ensure and facilitate the objective evaluation of progress;[11]

21. *Urges* Member States to pursue multilateral negotiations without delay in good faith on effective measures for the achievement and maintenance of a nuclear-weapon-free world, in keeping with the spirit and purpose of General Assembly resolution 1 (I) and article VI of the Treaty on the Non-Proliferation of Nuclear Weapons;

22. *Calls upon* Member States to continue to support efforts to identify, elaborate, negotiate and implement further effective legally binding measures for nuclear disarmament, and welcomes in this regard the adoption on 7 July 2017 of the Treaty on the Prohibition of Nuclear Weapons;[3]

23. *Recommends* that measures be taken to increase awareness among civil society of the risks and catastrophic impact of any nuclear detonation, including through disarmament education;

24. *Decides* to include in the provisional agenda of its seventy-third session, under the item entitled "General and complete disarmament", the sub-item entitled "Towards a nuclear-weapon-free world: accelerating the implementation of nuclear disarmament commitments" and to review the implementation of the present resolution at that session.

---

[11] See NPT/CONF.2020/PC.I/WP.13.

Action by the General Assembly

Date: 4 December 2017   Meeting: 62nd plenary meeting
Vote: 137-31-16   Report: A/72/409
      127-37-11, p.p. 10
      169-4-6, o.p. 14
      128-37-11, o.p. 22

Sponsors

Angola, Austria, Brazil, Ecuador, Egypt, Ireland, Liechtenstein, **Mexico**, New Zealand, South Africa, Thailand, Trinidad and Tobago

Co-sponsors

Belize, Ghana, Namibia, Nigeria, Philippines, Samoa, State of Palestine

Recorded vote

As a whole

In favour:

Afghanistan, Algeria, Angola, Antigua and Barbuda, Argentina, Armenia, Austria, Azerbaijan, Bahamas, Bahrain, Bangladesh, Barbados, Belarus, Belize, Benin, Bhutan, Bolivia (Plurinational State of), Botswana, Brazil, Brunei Darussalam, Burkina Faso, Burundi, Cabo Verde, Cambodia, Central African Republic, Chad, Chile, Colombia, Comoros, Congo, Costa Rica, Côte d'Ivoire, Cuba, Cyprus, Democratic Republic of the Congo, Djibouti, Dominican Republic, Ecuador, Egypt, El Salvador, Equatorial Guinea, Eritrea, Ethiopia, Fiji, Gabon, Gambia, Ghana, Grenada, Guatemala, Guinea-Bissau, Guyana, Honduras, Indonesia, Iran (Islamic Republic of), Iraq, Ireland, Jamaica, Jordan, Kazakhstan, Kenya, Kiribati, Kuwait, Kyrgyzstan, Lao People's Democratic Republic, Lebanon, Lesotho, Liberia, Libya, Liechtenstein, Madagascar, Malawi, Malaysia, Maldives, Mali, Malta, Mauritania, Mauritius, Mexico, Mongolia, Morocco, Mozambique, Myanmar, Namibia, Nauru, Nepal, New Zealand, Nicaragua, Nigeria, Oman, Palau, Panama, Papua New Guinea, Paraguay, Peru, Philippines, Qatar, Republic of Moldova, Rwanda, Saint Kitts and Nevis, Saint Lucia, Saint Vincent and the Grenadines, Samoa, San Marino, Saudi Arabia, Senegal, Sierra Leone, Singapore, Solomon Islands, Somalia, South Africa, Sri Lanka, Sudan, Suriname, Swaziland, Sweden, Switzerland, Syrian Arab Republic, Tajikistan, Thailand, Timor-Leste, Togo, Tonga, Trinidad and Tobago, Tunisia, Turkmenistan, Tuvalu, Uganda, United Arab Emirates, United Republic of Tanzania, Uruguay, Uzbekistan, Vanuatu, Venezuela (Bolivarian Republic of), Viet Nam, Yemen, Zambia, Zimbabwe

Against:

Albania, Belgium, Bulgaria, China, Croatia, Czech Republic, Democratic People's Republic of Korea, Denmark, Estonia, France, Germany, Greece, Hungary, India, Israel, Italy, Latvia, Lithuania, Luxembourg, Monaco, Montenegro, Poland, Portugal, Romania, Russian Federation, Slovakia, Slovenia, Spain, Turkey, United Kingdom, United States

Abstaining:

Andorra, Australia, Bosnia and Herzegovina, Canada, Finland, Georgia, Iceland, Japan, Micronesia (Federated States of), Netherlands, Norway, Pakistan, Republic of Korea, Serbia, the former Yugoslav Republic of Macedonia, Ukraine

Tenth preambular paragraph

In favour:

Afghanistan, Algeria, Angola, Antigua and Barbuda, Argentina, Austria, Azerbaijan, Bahamas, Bahrain, Bangladesh, Barbados, Belize, Benin, Bhutan, Bolivia (Plurinational State of), Botswana, Brazil, Brunei Darussalam, Burkina Faso, Burundi, Cabo Verde, Cambodia, Chad, Chile, Colombia, Comoros, Congo, Costa Rica, Côte d'Ivoire, Cuba, Cyprus, Democratic Republic of the Congo, Djibouti, Dominican Republic, Ecuador, Egypt, El Salvador, Equatorial Guinea, Eritrea, Ethiopia, Fiji, Gabon, Gambia, Ghana, Grenada, Guatemala, Guinea-Bissau, Guyana, Honduras, Indonesia, Iran (Islamic Republic of), Iraq, Ireland, Jamaica, Jordan, Kazakhstan, Kenya, Kiribati, Kuwait, Lao People's Democratic Republic, Lebanon, Lesotho, Liberia, Libya, Liechtenstein, Madagascar, Malawi, Malaysia, Maldives, Mali, Malta, Mauritania, Mauritius, Mexico, Mongolia, Morocco, Mozambique, Myanmar, Namibia, Nepal, New Zealand, Nicaragua, Nigeria, Oman, Panama, Papua New Guinea, Paraguay, Peru, Philippines, Qatar, Republic of Moldova, Rwanda, Saint Kitts and Nevis, Saint Lucia, Saint Vincent and the Grenadines, Samoa, San Marino, Saudi Arabia, Senegal, Sierra Leone, Singapore, Solomon Islands, Somalia, South Africa, Sri Lanka, Sudan, Suriname, Swaziland, Sweden, Switzerland, Thailand, Timor-Leste, Togo, Trinidad and Tobago, Tunisia, Turkmenistan, Tuvalu, Uganda, United Arab Emirates, United Republic of Tanzania, Uruguay, Vanuatu, Venezuela (Bolivarian Republic of), Viet Nam, Yemen, Zambia, Zimbabwe

Against:

Albania, Australia, Belgium, Bosnia and Herzegovina, Bulgaria, Canada, China, Croatia, Czech Republic, Denmark, Estonia, France, Germany, Greece, Hungary, Iceland, Israel, Italy, Latvia, Lithuania, Luxembourg, Monaco, Montenegro, Netherlands, Norway, Poland, Portugal, Republic of Korea, Romania, Russian Federation, Slovakia, Slovenia, Spain, Turkey, Ukraine, United Kingdom, United States

Abstaining:

Andorra, Armenia, Belarus, Democratic People's Republic of Korea, Finland, Georgia, India, Japan, Pakistan, Serbia, the former Yugoslav Republic of Macedonia

Operative paragraph 14

In favour:

Afghanistan, Albania, Algeria, Andorra, Angola, Antigua and Barbuda, Argentina, Armenia, Australia, Austria, Azerbaijan, Bahamas, Bahrain, Bangladesh, Barbados, Belarus, Belgium, Belize, Benin, Bolivia (Plurinational State of), Bosnia and Herzegovina, Botswana, Brazil, Brunei Darussalam, Bulgaria, Burkina Faso, Burundi, Cabo Verde, Cambodia, Canada, Central African Republic, Chad, Chile, China, Colombia, Comoros, Congo, Costa Rica, Côte d'Ivoire, Croatia, Cuba, Cyprus, Czech Republic, Democratic Republic of the Congo, Denmark, Djibouti, Dominican Republic, Ecuador, Egypt, El Salvador, Equatorial Guinea, Eritrea, Estonia, Ethiopia, Fiji, Finland, Gabon, Gambia, Ghana, Greece, Grenada, Guatemala, Guinea, Guinea-Bissau, Guyana, Honduras, Iceland, Indonesia, Iran (Islamic Republic of), Iraq, Ireland, Italy, Jamaica, Japan, Jordan, Kazakhstan, Kenya, Kiribati, Kuwait, Kyrgyzstan, Lao People's Democratic Republic, Latvia, Lebanon, Lesotho, Liberia, Libya, Liechtenstein, Lithuania, Luxembourg, Madagascar, Malawi, Malaysia, Maldives, Mali, Malta, Mauritania, Mauritius, Mexico, Mongolia, Montenegro, Morocco, Mozambique, Myanmar, Namibia, Nepal, Netherlands, New Zealand, Nicaragua, Nigeria, Norway, Oman, Panama, Papua New Guinea, Paraguay, Peru, Philippines, Poland, Portugal, Qatar, Republic of Korea, Republic of Moldova, Romania, Russian Federation, Rwanda, Saint Kitts and Nevis, Saint Lucia, Saint Vincent and the Grenadines, Samoa, San Marino, Saudi Arabia, Senegal, Serbia, Sierra Leone, Singapore, Slovakia, Slovenia, Solomon Islands, Somalia, South Africa, Spain, Sri Lanka, Sudan, Suriname, Swaziland, Sweden, Switzerland, Syrian Arab Republic, Tajikistan, Thailand, the former Yugoslav Republic of Macedonia, Timor-Leste, Togo, Trinidad and Tobago, Tunisia, Turkey, Turkmenistan, Tuvalu, Uganda, Ukraine, United Arab Emirates, United Republic of Tanzania, Uruguay, Uzbekistan, Vanuatu, Venezuela (Bolivarian Republic of), Viet Nam, Yemen, Zambia, Zimbabwe

Against:

India, Israel, Pakistan, United States

Abstaining:

Bhutan, France, Georgia, Germany, Hungary, United Kingdom

Operative paragraph 22

In favour:

Afghanistan, Algeria, Angola, Antigua and Barbuda, Argentina, Austria, Azerbaijan, Bahamas, Bahrain, Bangladesh, Barbados, Belize, Benin, Bhutan, Bolivia (Plurinational State of), Botswana, Brazil, Brunei Darussalam, Burkina Faso, Burundi, Cabo Verde, Cambodia, Chad, Chile, Colombia, Comoros, Congo, Costa Rica, Côte d'Ivoire, Cuba, Cyprus, Democratic Republic of the Congo, Djibouti, Dominican Republic, Ecuador, Egypt, El Salvador, Equatorial Guinea, Eritrea, Ethiopia, Fiji, Gabon, Gambia, Ghana, Grenada, Guatemala, Guinea-Bissau, Guyana, Honduras, Indonesia, Iran (Islamic Republic of), Iraq, Ireland, Jamaica, Jordan, Kazakhstan, Kenya, Kiribati, Kuwait, Lao People's Democratic Republic, Lebanon, Lesotho, Liberia, Libya, Liechtenstein, Madagascar, Malawi, Malaysia, Maldives, Mali, Malta, Mauritania, Mauritius, Mexico, Mongolia, Morocco, Mozambique, Myanmar, Namibia, Nepal, New Zealand, Nicaragua, Nigeria, Oman, Panama, Papua New Guinea, Paraguay, Peru, Philippines, Qatar, Republic of Moldova, Rwanda, Saint Kitts and Nevis, Saint Lucia, Saint Vincent and the Grenadines, Samoa, San Marino, Saudi Arabia, Senegal, Sierra Leone, Singapore, Solomon Islands, Somalia, South Africa, Sri Lanka, Sudan, Suriname, Swaziland, Sweden, Switzerland, Syrian Arab Republic, Thailand, Timor-Leste, Togo, Trinidad and Tobago, Tunisia, Turkmenistan, Tuvalu, Uganda, United Arab Emirates, United Republic of Tanzania, Uruguay, Vanuatu, Venezuela (Bolivarian Republic of), Viet Nam, Yemen, Zambia, Zimbabwe

Against:

Albania, Australia, Belgium, Bosnia and Herzegovina, Bulgaria, Canada, China, Croatia, Czech Republic, Denmark, Estonia, France, Germany, Greece, Hungary, Iceland, Israel, Italy, Latvia, Lithuania, Luxembourg, Monaco, Montenegro, Netherlands, Norway, Poland, Portugal, Republic of Korea, Romania, Russian Federation, Slovakia, Slovenia, Spain, Turkey, Ukraine, United Kingdom, United States

Abstaining:

Andorra, Armenia, Belarus, Democratic People's Republic of Korea, Finland, Georgia, India, Japan, Pakistan, Serbia, the former Yugoslav Republic of Macedonia

Action by the First Committee

Date: 27 October 2017   Meeting: 24th meeting
Vote: 127-32-14   Draft resolution: A/C.1/72/L.19
     118-37-10, p.p. 10
     157-4-6, o.p. 14
     121-37-10, o.p. 22

Agenda item 99 (n)

72/40 Assistance to States for curbing the illicit traffic in small arms and light weapons and collecting them

Text

The General Assembly,

Recalling its resolution 71/52 of 5 December 2016 on assistance to States for curbing the illicit traffic in small arms and light weapons and collecting them,

Deeply concerned by the magnitude of human casualty and suffering, especially among children, caused by the illicit proliferation and use of small arms and light weapons,

Concerned by the negative impact that the illicit proliferation and use of those weapons continue to have on the efforts of States in the Sahelo-Saharan subregion in the areas of poverty eradication, sustainable development and the maintenance of peace, security and stability,

Bearing in mind the Bamako Declaration on an African Common Position on the Illicit Proliferation, Circulation and Trafficking of Small Arms and Light Weapons, adopted in Bamako on 1 December 2000,[1]

Recalling the report of the Secretary-General entitled "In larger freedom: towards development, security and human rights for all",[2] in which he emphasized that States must strive just as hard to eliminate the threat of small arms and light weapons as they do to eliminate the threat of weapons of mass destruction,

Recalling also the International Instrument to Enable States to Identify and Trace, in a Timely and Reliable Manner, Illicit Small Arms and Light Weapons, adopted on 8 December 2005,[3]

Recalling further the expression of support in the 2005 World Summit Outcome for the implementation of the Programme of Action to Prevent, Combat and Eradicate the Illicit Trade in Small Arms and Light Weapons in All Its Aspects,[4]

Recalling the adoption, on 14 June 2006 in Abuja at the thirtieth ordinary summit of the Economic Community of West African States, of the Convention on Small Arms and Light Weapons, Their Ammunition and Other Related Materials, in replacement of the moratorium on the importation, exportation and manufacture of small arms and light weapons in West Africa,

---

[1] A/CONF.192/PC/23, annex.
[2] A/59/2005.
[3] See decision 60/519 and A/60/88 and A/60/88/Corr.2, annex.
[4] Resolution 60/1, para. 94.

Recalling also the entry into force of the Convention on 29 September 2009,

Recalling further the decision taken by the Economic Community to establish the Small Arms Unit, responsible for advocating appropriate policies and developing and implementing programmes, as well as the establishment of the Economic Community's Small Arms Control Programme, launched on 6 June 2006 in Bamako, in replacement of the Programme for Coordination and Assistance for Security and Development,

Taking note of the latest report of the Secretary-General on the illicit trade in small arms and light weapons in all its aspects and assistance to States for curbing the illicit traffic in small arms and light weapons and collecting them,[5]

Recalling, in that regard, the decision of the European Union to significantly support the Economic Community in its efforts to combat the illicit proliferation of small arms and light weapons,

Recognizing the important role that civil society organizations play, by raising public awareness, in efforts to curb the illicit traffic in small arms and light weapons,

Recalling the report of the Sixth Biennial Meeting of States to Consider the Implementation of the Programme of Action to Prevent, Combat and Eradicate the Illicit Trade in Small Arms and Light Weapons in All Its Aspects, held in New York from 6 to 10 June 2016,[6]

Welcoming the inclusion of small arms and light weapons in the scope of the Arms Trade Treaty,[7] as well as the inclusion of international assistance in its provisions,

1. *Commends* the United Nations and international, regional and other organizations for their assistance to States for curbing the illicit traffic in small arms and light weapons and collecting them;

2. *Encourages* the Secretary-General to pursue his efforts in the context of the implementation of General Assembly resolution 49/75 G of 15 December 1994 and the recommendations of the United Nations advisory missions aimed at curbing the illicit circulation of small arms and light weapons and collecting them in the affected States that so request, with the support of the United Nations Regional Centre for Peace and Disarmament in Africa and in close cooperation with the African Union;

3. *Encourages* the international community to support the implementation of the Economic Community of West African States

---

[5] A/72/122.
[6] A/CONF.192/BMS/2016/2.
[7] See resolution 67/234 B.

Convention on Small Arms and Light Weapons, Their Ammunition and Other Related Materials;

4. *Encourages* the countries of the Sahelo-Saharan subregion to facilitate the effective functioning of national commissions to combat the illicit proliferation of small arms and light weapons, and in that regard invites the international community to lend its support wherever possible;

5. *Encourages* the collaboration of civil society organizations and associations in the efforts of the national commissions to combat the illicit traffic in small arms and light weapons and in the implementation of the Programme of Action to Prevent, Combat and Eradicate the Illicit Trade in Small Arms and Light Weapons in All Its Aspects;[8]

6. *Encourages* cooperation among State organs, international organizations and civil society in support of programmes and projects aimed at combating the illicit traffic in small arms and light weapons and collecting them;

7. *Calls upon* the international community to provide technical and financial support to strengthen the capacity of civil society organizations to take action to help to combat the illicit trade in small arms and light weapons;

8. *Invites* the Secretary-General and those States and organizations that are in a position to do so to continue to provide assistance to States for curbing the illicit traffic in small arms and light weapons and collecting them;

9. *Requests* the Secretary-General to continue to consider the matter and to report to the General Assembly at its seventy-third session on the implementation of the present resolution;

10. *Decides* to include in the provisional agenda of its seventy-third session, under the item entitled "General and complete disarmament", the sub-item entitled "Assistance to States for curbing the illicit traffic in small arms and light weapons and collecting them".

Action by the General Assembly

Date: 4 December 2017   Meeting: 62nd plenary meeting
Vote: Adopted without a vote   Report: A/72/409

Sponsors

Albania, Algeria, Angola, Australia, Belgium, Bosnia and Herzegovina, Bulgaria, Canada, Croatia, Czech Republic, Eritrea, Estonia, Finland, France, Germany, Greece, Hungary, Iceland, Ireland, Italy, Kazakhstan, Latvia, Lithuania, Luxembourg, Madagascar, Malawi, **Mali** (on behalf

---

[8] *Report of the United Nations Conference on the Illicit Trade in Small Arms and Light Weapons in All Its Aspects, New York, 9–20 July 2001* (A/CONF.192/15), chap. IV, para. 24.

of the States Members of the United Nations that are members of the Economic Community of West African States), Malta, Mauritania, Netherlands, Norway, Poland, Portugal, Republic of Moldova, Romania, Serbia, Slovakia, Slovenia, Spain, Sudan, Swaziland, Sweden, Thailand, United Kingdom, Zimbabwe

Co-sponsors

Andorra, Austria, Chad, Colombia, Cyprus, Denmark, Djibouti, Dominican Republic, Georgia, Guyana, Liechtenstein, Maldives, Monaco, Montenegro, Mozambique, New Zealand, San Marino, the former Yugoslav Republic of Macedonia, Trinidad and Tobago, Turkey, Uganda

Action by the First Committee

Date:	31 October 2017	Meeting:	26th meeting
Vote:	Adopted without a vote	Draft resolution:	A/C.1/72/L.21

Agenda item 99 (o)

72/41 Reducing nuclear danger

Text

The General Assembly,

Bearing in mind that the use of nuclear weapons poses the most serious threat to mankind and to the survival of civilization,

Reaffirming that any use or threat of use of nuclear weapons would constitute a violation of the Charter of the United Nations,

Convinced that the proliferation of nuclear weapons in all its aspects would seriously enhance the danger of nuclear war,

Convinced also that nuclear disarmament and the complete elimination of nuclear weapons are essential to remove the danger of nuclear war,

Considering that, until nuclear weapons cease to exist, it is imperative on the part of the nuclear-weapon States to adopt measures that assure non-nuclear-weapon States against the use or threat of use of nuclear weapons,

Considering also that the hair-trigger alert of nuclear weapons carries unacceptable risks of unintentional or accidental use of nuclear weapons, which would have catastrophic consequences for all mankind,

Emphasizing the need to adopt measures to avoid accidental, unauthorized or unexplained incidents arising from computer anomalies or other technical malfunctions,

Conscious that limited steps relating to de-alerting and de-targeting have been taken by the nuclear-weapon States and that further practical, realistic and mutually reinforcing steps are necessary to contribute to the improvement in the international climate for negotiations leading to the elimination of nuclear weapons,

Mindful that a diminishing role for nuclear weapons in the security policies of nuclear-weapon States would have a positive impact on international peace and security and improve the conditions for the further reduction and the elimination of nuclear weapons,

Reiterating the highest priority accorded to nuclear disarmament in the Final Document of the Tenth Special Session of the General Assembly[1] and by the international community,

Recalling the advisory opinion of the International Court of Justice on the legality of the threat or use of nuclear weapons[2] that there exists an obligation for all States to pursue in good faith and bring to a conclusion

---

[1] Resolution S-10/2.
[2] A/51/218, annex.

negotiations leading to nuclear disarmament in all its aspects under strict and effective international control,

Recalling also the call, in the United Nations Millennium Declaration,[3] to seek to eliminate the dangers posed by weapons of mass destruction and the resolve to strive for the elimination of weapons of mass destruction, particularly nuclear weapons, including the possibility of convening an international conference to identify ways of eliminating nuclear dangers,

1. *Calls for* a review of nuclear doctrines and, in this context, immediate and urgent steps to reduce the risks of unintentional and accidental use of nuclear weapons, including through de-alerting and de-targeting nuclear weapons;

2. *Requests* the five nuclear-weapon States to take measures towards the implementation of paragraph 1 above;

3. *Calls upon* Member States to take the measures necessary to prevent the proliferation of nuclear weapons in all its aspects and to promote nuclear disarmament, with the objective of eliminating nuclear weapons;

4. *Takes note* of the report of the Secretary-General submitted pursuant to paragraph 5 of its resolution 71/37 of 5 December 2016;[4]

5. *Requests* the Secretary-General to intensify efforts and support initiatives that would contribute to the full implementation of the seven recommendations identified in the report of the Advisory Board on Disarmament Matters that would significantly reduce the risk of nuclear war,[5] and also to continue to encourage Member States to consider the convening of an international conference, as proposed in the United Nations Millennium Declaration,[3] to identify ways of eliminating nuclear dangers, and to report thereon to the General Assembly at its seventy-third session;

6. *Decides* to include in the provisional agenda of its seventy-third session, under the item entitled "General and complete disarmament", the sub-item entitled "Reducing nuclear danger".

Action by the General Assembly

Date: 4 December 2017   Meeting: 62nd plenary meeting
Vote: 124-49-11   Report: A/72/409

Sponsors

Afghanistan, Angola, Bhutan, Cuba, Ecuador, **India**, Indonesia, Mauritius, Myanmar, Nicaragua, Samoa, Venezuela (Bolivarian Republic of), Viet Nam

---

[3] Resolution 55/2.
[4] A/72/321.
[5] A/56/400, para. 3.

Co-sponsors

> Bangladesh, Bolivia (Plurinational State of), Jordan, Malawi, Malaysia, Maldives, Nepal, Sri Lanka

Recorded vote

In favour:

> Afghanistan, Algeria, Angola, Antigua and Barbuda, Azerbaijan, Bahamas, Bahrain, Bangladesh, Barbados, Belize, Benin, Bhutan, Bolivia (Plurinational State of), Botswana, Brazil, Brunei Darussalam, Burkina Faso, Burundi, Cabo Verde, Cambodia, Central African Republic, Chad, Chile, Colombia, Comoros, Congo, Costa Rica, Côte d'Ivoire, Cuba, Democratic Republic of the Congo, Djibouti, Dominican Republic, Ecuador, Egypt, El Salvador, Equatorial Guinea, Eritrea, Ethiopia, Fiji, Gabon, Gambia, Ghana, Grenada, Guatemala, Guinea-Bissau, Guyana, Honduras, India, Indonesia, Iran (Islamic Republic of), Iraq, Jamaica, Jordan, Kazakhstan, Kenya, Kiribati, Kuwait, Kyrgyzstan, Lao People's Democratic Republic, Lebanon, Lesotho, Liberia, Libya, Madagascar, Malawi, Malaysia, Maldives, Mali, Mauritania, Mauritius, Mexico, Mongolia, Morocco, Mozambique, Myanmar, Namibia, Nauru, Nepal, Nicaragua, Nigeria, Oman, Pakistan, Palau, Panama, Papua New Guinea, Paraguay, Peru, Philippines, Qatar, Rwanda, Saint Kitts and Nevis, Saint Lucia, Saint Vincent and the Grenadines, Samoa, Saudi Arabia, Senegal, Sierra Leone, Singapore, Solomon Islands, Somalia, South Africa, Sri Lanka, Sudan, Suriname, Swaziland, Syrian Arab Republic, Tajikistan, Thailand, Timor-Leste, Togo, Tonga, Trinidad and Tobago, Tunisia, Turkmenistan, Tuvalu, Uganda, United Arab Emirates, United Republic of Tanzania, Uruguay, Vanuatu, Venezuela (Bolivarian Republic of), Viet Nam, Yemen, Zambia

Against:

> Albania, Andorra, Australia, Austria, Belgium, Bosnia and Herzegovina, Bulgaria, Canada, Croatia, Cyprus, Czech Republic, Denmark, Estonia, Finland, France, Germany, Greece, Hungary, Iceland, Ireland, Israel, Italy, Latvia, Liechtenstein, Lithuania, Luxembourg, Malta, Micronesia (Federated States of), Monaco, Montenegro, Netherlands, New Zealand, Norway, Poland, Portugal, Republic of Korea, Republic of Moldova, Romania, San Marino, Slovakia, Slovenia, Spain, Sweden, Switzerland, the former Yugoslav Republic of Macedonia, Turkey, Ukraine, United Kingdom, United States

Abstaining:

> Argentina, Armenia, Belarus, China, Democratic People's Republic of Korea, Georgia, Japan, Marshall Islands, Russian Federation, Serbia, Uzbekistan

Action by the First Committee

Date: 27 October 2017	Meeting:	24th meeting
Vote: 116-49-10	Draft resolution:	A/C.1/72/L.22

Agenda item 99 (s)

72/42   Measures to prevent terrorists from acquiring weapons of mass destruction

Text

The General Assembly,

Recalling its resolution 71/38 of 5 December 2016,

Recognizing the determination of the international community to combat terrorism, as evidenced in relevant General Assembly and Security Council resolutions,

Deeply concerned by the growing risk of linkages between terrorism and weapons of mass destruction, and in particular by the fact that terrorists may seek to acquire weapons of mass destruction,

Cognizant of the steps taken by States to implement Security Council resolution 1540 (2004) of 28 April 2004 on the non-proliferation of weapons of mass destruction,

Taking note of Security Council resolution 2325 (2016) of 15 December 2016 on the non-proliferation of weapons of mass destruction,

Welcoming the entry into force on 7 July 2007 of the International Convention for the Suppression of Acts of Nuclear Terrorism,[1]

Welcoming also the adoption, by consensus, of amendments to strengthen the Convention on the Physical Protection of Nuclear Material[2] by the International Atomic Energy Agency on 8 July 2005, and their entry into force on 8 May 2016,

Noting the support expressed in the Final Document of the Seventeenth Conference of Heads of State or Government of Non-Aligned Countries, held on Margarita Island, Bolivarian Republic of Venezuela, from 13 to 18 September 2016, for measures to prevent terrorists from acquiring weapons of mass destruction,

Noting also that the Group of Eight, the European Union, the Regional Forum of the Association of Southeast Asian Nations and others have taken into account in their deliberations the dangers posed by the likely acquisition by terrorists of weapons of mass destruction and the need for international cooperation in combating it, and that the Global Initiative to Combat Nuclear Terrorism has been launched jointly by the Russian Federation and the United States of America,

---

[1] United Nations, *Treaty Series*, vol. 2445, No. 44004.

[2] Ibid., vol. 1456, No. 24631.

Noting further the holding of the Nuclear Security Summit on 12 and 13 April 2010 in Washington, D.C., on 26 and 27 March 2012 in Seoul, on 24 and 25 March 2014 in The Hague and on 31 March and 1 April 2016 in Washington, D.C.,

Noting the holding of the high-level meeting on countering nuclear terrorism, with a focus on strengthening the legal framework, in New York on 28 September 2012,

Acknowledging the consideration of issues relating to terrorism and weapons of mass destruction by the Advisory Board on Disarmament Matters,[3]

Taking note of the holding by the International Atomic Energy Agency of the International Conference on Nuclear Security: Commitments and Actions, in Vienna in December 2016, and the first International Conference on Nuclear Security: Enhancing Global Efforts, in Vienna in July 2013, and the relevant resolutions adopted by the General Conference of the Agency at its sixty-first regular session,

Taking note also of the Code of Conduct on the Safety and Security of Radioactive Sources, approved by the Board of Governors of the International Atomic Energy Agency on 8 September 2003, and the supplementary Guidance on the Management of Disused Radioactive Sources, approved by the Board of Governors of the Agency on 11 September 2017,

Taking note further of the 2005 World Summit Outcome adopted at the high-level plenary meeting of the General Assembly on 16 September 2005[4] and the adoption of the United Nations Global Counter-Terrorism Strategy[5] on 8 September 2006,

Taking note of the report of the Secretary-General submitted pursuant to paragraph 5 of resolution 71/38,[6]

Mindful of the urgent need for addressing, within the United Nations framework and through international cooperation, this threat to humanity,

Emphasizing that progress is urgently needed in the area of disarmament and non-proliferation in order to maintain international peace and security and to contribute to global efforts against terrorism,

1.   *Calls upon* all Member States to support international efforts to prevent terrorists from acquiring weapons of mass destruction and their means of delivery;

2.   *Appeals* to all Member States to consider early accession to and ratification of the International Convention for the Suppression of Acts of

---

[3] See A/59/361.
[4] Resolution 60/1.
[5] Resolution 60/288.
[6] A/72/344.

Nuclear Terrorism,[1] and encourages States parties to the Convention to review its implementation;

3.   *Urges* all Member States to take and strengthen national measures, as appropriate, to prevent terrorists from acquiring weapons of mass destruction, their means of delivery and materials and technologies related to their manufacture;

4.   *Encourages* cooperation among and between Member States and relevant regional and international organizations for strengthening national capacities in this regard;

5.   *Requests* the Secretary-General to compile a report on measures already taken by international organizations on issues relating to the linkage between the fight against terrorism and the proliferation of weapons of mass destruction and to seek the views of Member States on additional relevant measures, including national measures, for tackling the global threat posed by the acquisition by terrorists of weapons of mass destruction and to report to the General Assembly at its seventy-third session;

6.   *Decides* to include in the provisional agenda of its seventy-third session, under the item entitled "General and complete disarmament", the sub-item entitled "Measures to prevent terrorists from acquiring weapons of mass destruction".

Action by the General Assembly

Date: 4 December 2017   Meeting: 62nd plenary meeting
Vote: Adopted without a vote   Report: A/72/409

Sponsors

Afghanistan, Albania, Angola, Argentina, Australia, Austria, Azerbaijan, Belgium, Bhutan, Bosnia and Herzegovina, Bulgaria, Canada, Costa Rica, Croatia, Czech Republic, Estonia, Finland, Germany, Ghana, Greece, Hungary, Iceland, **India**, Iraq, Ireland, Italy, Kazakhstan, Kenya, Latvia, Lithuania, Luxembourg, Mali, Malta, Mauritius, Mongolia, Montenegro, Myanmar, Netherlands, Norway, Poland, Portugal, Republic of Korea, Republic of Moldova, Samoa, Serbia, Singapore, Slovakia, Slovenia, Sweden, Thailand

Co-sponsors

Armenia, Bangladesh, Benin, Chile, Cyprus, Democratic Republic of the Congo, Denmark, France, Georgia, Guatemala, Guinea-Bissau, Guyana, Haiti, Honduras, Jamaica, Kyrgyzstan, Liechtenstein, Madagascar, Malawi, Maldives, Monaco, Nepal, New Zealand, Nigeria, Papua New Guinea, Paraguay, Philippines, Romania, Russian Federation, San Marino, Senegal, Spain, Sri Lanka, the former Yugoslav Republic of

Macedonia, Togo, Tunisia, Turkey, Uganda, Ukraine, United Kingdom, United States, Zimbabwe

Action by the First Committee

Date: 30 October 2017   Meeting: 25th meeting
Vote: Adopted without a vote   Draft resolution: A/C.1/72/L.23

Agenda item 99 (I)

72/43 Implementation of the Convention on the Prohibition of the Development, Production, Stockpiling and Use of Chemical Weapons and on Their Destruction

Text

The General Assembly,

Recalling its previous resolutions on the subject of chemical weapons, in particular resolution 71/69 of 5 December 2016,

Determined to achieve the effective prohibition of the development, production, acquisition, transfer, stockpiling and use of chemical weapons and their destruction,

Reaffirming its strong support for the Convention on the Prohibition of the Development, Production, Stockpiling and Use of Chemical Weapons and on Their Destruction[1] and for the Organisation for the Prohibition of Chemical Weapons on the twentieth anniversary of the entry into force of the Convention and its deep appreciation of the Organisation, which was awarded the Nobel Peace Prize for 2013 for its extensive efforts to eliminate chemical weapons,

Re-emphasizing its unequivocal support for the decision of the Director General of the Organisation for the Prohibition of Chemical Weapons to continue the mission to establish the facts surrounding the allegations of the use of chemical weapons, including toxic chemicals, for hostile purposes in the Syrian Arab Republic, while stressing that the safety and security of mission personnel remains the top priority, and recalling the continuation of the work, pursuant to Security Council resolutions 2235 (2015) of 7 August 2015 and 2319 (2016) of 17 November 2016, of the Joint Investigative Mechanism of the Organisation for the Prohibition of Chemical Weapons and the United Nations, which was established to identify to the greatest extent feasible individuals, entities, groups or Governments that were perpetrators, organizers, sponsors or otherwise involved in the use of chemicals as weapons, including chlorine or any other toxic chemical, in the Syrian Arab Republic, where the fact-finding mission of the Organisation for the Prohibition of Chemical Weapons determined that a specific incident in the Syrian Arab Republic involved or likely involved the use of chemicals as weapons,

Reaffirming the importance of the outcome of the Third Special Session of the Conference of the States Parties to Review the Operation of the Chemical Weapons Convention, held in The Hague from 8 to 19 April 2013

---

[1] United Nations, *Treaty Series*, vol. 1974, No. 33757.

(the Third Review Conference), including its consensus final report, in which the Conference addressed all aspects of the Convention and made important recommendations on its continued implementation,

Emphasizing that the Third Review Conference welcomed the fact that the Convention is a unique multilateral agreement banning an entire category of weapons of mass destruction in a non-discriminatory and verifiable manner under strict and effective international control and noted with satisfaction that the Convention continues to be a remarkable success and an example of effective multilateralism,

Convinced that the Convention, 20 years after its entry into force, has reinforced its role as the international norm against chemical weapons, and that it constitutes a major contribution to:

(a)   International peace and security,

(b)   Eliminating chemical weapons and preventing their re-emergence,

(c)   The ultimate objective of general and complete disarmament under strict and effective international control,

(d)   Excluding completely, for the sake of all mankind, the possibility of the use of chemical weapons,

(e)   Promoting international cooperation and exchange in scientific and technical information in the field of chemical activities among States parties for peaceful purposes in order to enhance the economic and technological development of all States parties,

1.   *Reaffirms its condemnation in the strongest possible terms* of the use of chemical weapons by anyone under any circumstances, emphasizing that any use of chemical weapons anywhere, at any time, by anyone, under any circumstances is unacceptable and is and would be a violation of international law and expressing its strong conviction that those individuals responsible for the use of chemical weapons must and should be held accountable;

2.   *Condemns in the strongest possible terms* the use of chemical weapons as reported by the Joint Investigative Mechanism of the Organisation for the Prohibition of Chemical Weapons and the United Nations in:

(a)   Its reports of 24 August 2016[2] and 21 October 2016,[3] which concluded that there was sufficient information to determine that the Syrian Arab Armed Forces were responsible for the attacks which released toxic substances in Talmenes, Syrian Arab Republic, on 21 April 2014, in Sarmin, Syrian Arab Republic, on 16 March 2015, and in Qmenas, Syrian Arab Republic, also on 16 March 2015, and that the so-called "Islamic State in

---

[2]   See S/2016/738/Rev.1.
[3]   See S/2016/888.

Iraq and the Levant" used sulfur mustard in Marea, Syrian Arab Republic, on 21 August 2015; and

(b) Its report of 26 October 2017,[4] which concluded that there was sufficient information to be confident that Islamic State in Iraq and the Levant was responsible for the use of sulfur mustard at Umm Hawsh on 15 and 16 September 2016 and that the Syrian Arab Republic was responsible for the release of sarin at Khan Shaykhun on 4 April 2017;

and demands that the perpetrators immediately desist from any further use of chemical weapons;

3. *Reiterates* the grave concern expressed by the Executive Council of the Organisation for the Prohibition of Chemical Weapons in its decision EC-84/DEC.8 of 9 March 2017 that, according to statements by the Government of Malaysia, a chemical weapon – the Schedule 1 nerve agent VX – was used in a fatal incident on 13 February 2017 at Kuala Lumpur International Airport 2;

4. *Emphasizes* that the universality of the Convention on the Prohibition of the Development, Production, Stockpiling and Use of Chemical Weapons and on Their Destruction[1] is essential to achieving its object and purpose and to enhancing the security of States parties, as well as to international peace and security, underlines the fact that the objectives of the Convention will not be fully realized as long as there remains even a single State not party to the Convention that could possess or acquire such weapons, and calls upon all States that have not yet done so to become parties to the Convention without delay;

5. *Underlines* the fact that the full, effective and non-discriminatory implementation of all articles of the Convention makes a major contribution to international peace and security through the elimination of existing stockpiles of chemical weapons and the prohibition of their acquisition and use, and provides for assistance and protection in the event of use or threat of use of chemical weapons and for international cooperation for peaceful purposes in the field of chemical activities;

6. *Notes* the impact of scientific and technological progress on the effective implementation of the Convention and the importance for the Organisation for the Prohibition of Chemical Weapons and its policymaking organs of taking due account of such developments;

7. *Reaffirms* that the obligation of the States parties to complete the destruction of chemical weapons stockpiles and the destruction or conversion of chemical weapons production facilities in accordance with the provisions of the Convention and the Annex on Implementation and Verification (Verification Annex) and under the verification of the Technical Secretariat of

---

[4] See S/2017/904.

the Organisation for the Prohibition of Chemical Weapons is essential for the realization of the object and purpose of the Convention;

8. *Stresses* the importance to the Convention that all possessors of chemical weapons, chemical weapons production facilities or chemical weapons development facilities, including previously declared possessor States, should be among the States parties to the Convention, and welcomes progress to that end;

9. *Recalls* that the Third Special Session of the Conference of the States Parties to Review the Operation of the Chemical Weapons Convention expressed concern regarding the statement made by the Director General of the Organisation for the Prohibition of Chemical Weapons in his report to the Executive Council of the Organisation at its sixty-eighth session, provided in accordance with paragraph 2 of decision C-16/DEC.11 of 1 December 2011 adopted by the Conference of the States Parties at its sixteenth session, that three possessor States parties, namely, Libya, the Russian Federation and the United States of America, had been unable to fully meet the final extended deadline of 29 April 2012 for the destruction of their chemical weapons stockpiles, and also expressed determination that the destruction of all categories of chemical weapons should be completed in the shortest time possible in accordance with the provisions of the Convention and the Verification Annex, and with the full application of the relevant decisions that have been taken;

10. *Welcomes* the confirmation by the Director General of the Organisation for the Prohibition of Chemical Weapons expressed in his report of 5 October 2017,[5] based upon information received from the Russian Federation and independent information received from the inspectors of the Organisation, regarding the completion of the full destruction of chemical weapons declared by the Russian Federation;

11. *Also welcomes* the ongoing progress related to the destruction of Libya's remaining category 2 chemical weapons outside the territory of Libya in line with the relevant Executive Council decisions;

12. *Notes with concern* that, along with the threat of the possible production, acquisition and use of chemical weapons by States, the international community also faces the danger of the production, acquisition and use of chemical weapons by non-State actors, including terrorists, concerns which have highlighted the necessity of achieving universal adherence to the Convention, as well as the high level of readiness of the Organisation for the Prohibition of Chemical Weapons, and stresses that the full and effective implementation of all provisions of the Convention, including those on national implementation (article VII) and assistance and protection (article X), constitutes an important contribution to the efforts of

---

[5] EC-86/DG.31.

the United Nations in the global fight against terrorism in all its forms and manifestations;

13.　*Notes* that the effective application of the verification system builds confidence in compliance with the Convention by States parties;

14.　*Stresses* the importance of the Organisation for the Prohibition of Chemical Weapons in verifying compliance with the provisions of the Convention as well as in promoting the timely and efficient accomplishment of all its objectives;

15.　*Expresses grave concern* that the Technical Secretariat, as reported by the Director General in his report of 4 October 2017,[6] is not able to resolve all identified gaps, inconsistencies and discrepancies in the declaration of the Syrian Arab Republic and, therefore, cannot fully verify that the Syrian Arab Republic has submitted a declaration that can be considered accurate and complete in accordance with the Convention or Executive Council decision EC-M33/DEC.1, and underscores the importance of such full verification;

16.　*Urges* all States parties to the Convention to meet in full and on time their obligations under the Convention and to support the Organisation for the Prohibition of Chemical Weapons in its implementation activities;

17.　*Welcomes* the progress made in the national implementation of article VII obligations, commends the States parties and the Technical Secretariat for assisting other States parties, on request, with the implementation of the follow-up to the plan of action regarding article VII obligations, and urges States parties that have not fulfilled their obligations under article VII to do so without further delay, in accordance with their constitutional processes;

18.　*Emphasizes* the continuing relevance and importance of the provisions of article X of the Convention, welcomes the activities of the Organisation for the Prohibition of Chemical Weapons in relation to assistance and protection against chemical weapons, supports further efforts by both States parties and the Technical Secretariat to promote a high level of readiness to respond to chemical weapons threats as articulated in article X, and welcomes the effectiveness and efficiency of the increased focus on making full use of regional and subregional capacities and expertise, including taking advantage of established training centres;

19.　*Reaffirms* that the provisions of the Convention shall be implemented in a manner that avoids hampering the economic or technological development of States parties and international cooperation in the field of chemical activities for purposes not prohibited under the Convention, including the international exchange of scientific and technical

---

[6] EC-86/DG.30.

information, and chemicals and equipment for the production, processing or use of chemicals for purposes not prohibited under the Convention;

20. *Emphasizes* the importance of the provisions of article XI of the Convention relating to the economic and technological development of States parties, recalls that the full, effective and non-discriminatory implementation of those provisions contributes to universality, and reaffirms the undertaking of the States parties to foster international cooperation for peaceful purposes in the field of chemical activities of the States parties and the importance of that cooperation and its contribution to the promotion of the Convention as a whole;

21. *Notes with appreciation* the ongoing work of the Organisation for the Prohibition of Chemical Weapons to achieve the object and purpose of the Convention, to ensure the full implementation of its provisions, including those for international verification of compliance with it, and to provide a forum for consultation and cooperation among States parties;

22. *Stresses* the importance of the preparatory work related to the Fourth Special Session of the Conference of the States Parties to Review the Operation of the Chemical Weapons Convention;

23. *Welcomes* the cooperation between the United Nations and the Organisation for the Prohibition of Chemical Weapons within the framework of the relationship agreement between the United Nations and the Organisation,[7] in accordance with the provisions of the Convention;

24. *Decides* to include in the provisional agenda of its seventy-third session, under the item entitled "General and complete disarmament", the sub-item entitled "Implementation of the Convention on the Prohibition of the Development, Production, Stockpiling and Use of Chemical Weapons and on Their Destruction".

Action by the General Assembly

Date:	4 December 2017	Meeting:	62nd plenary meeting
Vote:	159-7-14	Report:	A/72/409
	142-9-23, p.p. 4		
	133-12-25, o.p. 2		
	138-10-26, o.p. 15		

Sponsors

Poland

---

[7] United Nations, *Treaty Series*, vol. 2160, No. 1240.

Recorded vote

As a whole

In favour:

Afghanistan, Albania, Algeria, Andorra, Antigua and Barbuda, Argentina, Australia, Austria, Azerbaijan, Bahamas, Bahrain, Bangladesh, Barbados, Belgium, Belize, Benin, Bhutan, Bosnia and Herzegovina, Botswana, Brazil, Brunei Darussalam, Bulgaria, Burkina Faso, Cabo Verde, Cambodia, Cameroon, Canada, Central African Republic, Chad, Chile, Colombia, Comoros, Congo, Costa Rica, Côte d'Ivoire, Croatia, Cyprus, Czech Republic, Denmark, Djibouti, Dominican Republic, Ecuador, Egypt, El Salvador, Equatorial Guinea, Eritrea, Estonia, Ethiopia, Fiji, Finland, France, Gabon, Gambia, Georgia, Germany, Ghana, Greece, Guatemala, Guinea, Guinea-Bissau, Guyana, Haiti, Honduras, Hungary, Iceland, India, Indonesia, Iraq, Ireland, Israel, Italy, Jamaica, Japan, Jordan, Kazakhstan, Kiribati, Kuwait, Lao People's Democratic Republic, Latvia, Lesotho, Liberia, Libya, Liechtenstein, Lithuania, Luxembourg, Madagascar, Malawi, Malaysia, Maldives, Malta, Marshall Islands, Mauritania, Mauritius, Mexico, Micronesia (Federated States of), Monaco, Mongolia, Montenegro, Morocco, Mozambique, Myanmar, Namibia, Nepal, Netherlands, New Zealand, Nigeria, Norway, Oman, Pakistan, Palau, Panama, Papua New Guinea, Paraguay, Peru, Philippines, Poland, Portugal, Qatar, Republic of Korea, Republic of Moldova, Romania, Saint Kitts and Nevis, Saint Lucia, Saint Vincent and the Grenadines, Samoa, San Marino, Saudi Arabia, Senegal, Sierra Leone, Singapore, Slovakia, Slovenia, Solomon Islands, Somalia, South Africa, Spain, Sri Lanka, Sudan, Swaziland, Sweden, Switzerland, Tajikistan, Thailand, the former Yugoslav Republic of Macedonia, Timor-Leste, Togo, Trinidad and Tobago, Tunisia, Turkey, Ukraine, United Arab Emirates, United Kingdom, United States, Uruguay, Uzbekistan, Vanuatu, Viet Nam, Yemen, Zambia

Against:

Burundi, China, Democratic People's Republic of Korea, Iran (Islamic Republic of), Russian Federation, Syrian Arab Republic, Zimbabwe

Abstaining:

Angola, Armenia, Belarus, Bolivia (Plurinational State of), Cuba, Kenya, Kyrgyzstan, Lebanon, Mali, Nicaragua, Rwanda, Uganda, United Republic of Tanzania, Venezuela (Bolivarian Republic of)

Fourth preambular paragraph

In favour:

Afghanistan, Albania, Andorra, Antigua and Barbuda, Argentina, Australia, Austria, Bahamas, Bahrain, Bangladesh, Barbados, Belgium,

Belize, Bhutan, Bosnia and Herzegovina, Botswana, Brazil, Brunei Darussalam, Bulgaria, Burkina Faso, Cabo Verde, Cambodia, Canada, Chad, Chile, Colombia, Comoros, Costa Rica, Côte d'Ivoire, Croatia, Cyprus, Czech Republic, Denmark, Djibouti, Dominican Republic, Egypt, El Salvador, Equatorial Guinea, Estonia, Ethiopia, Fiji, Finland, France, Gabon, Gambia, Georgia, Germany, Ghana, Greece, Guatemala, Guinea, Guinea-Bissau, Guyana, Haiti, Honduras, Hungary, Iceland, India, Indonesia, Ireland, Israel, Italy, Jamaica, Japan, Jordan, Kiribati, Kuwait, Latvia, Lesotho, Liberia, Libya, Liechtenstein, Lithuania, Luxembourg, Madagascar, Malawi, Malaysia, Maldives, Malta, Marshall Islands, Mauritania, Mexico, Micronesia (Federated States of), Monaco, Mongolia, Montenegro, Morocco, Mozambique, Myanmar, Nepal, Netherlands, New Zealand, Norway, Pakistan, Palau, Panama, Papua New Guinea, Paraguay, Peru, Philippines, Poland, Portugal, Qatar, Republic of Korea, Republic of Moldova, Romania, Rwanda, Saint Kitts and Nevis, Saint Lucia, Saint Vincent and the Grenadines, Samoa, San Marino, Saudi Arabia, Senegal, Sierra Leone, Singapore, Slovakia, Slovenia, Solomon Islands, Somalia, South Africa, Spain, Sri Lanka, Swaziland, Sweden, Switzerland, Thailand, the former Yugoslav Republic of Macedonia, Timor-Leste, Togo, Trinidad and Tobago, Tunisia, Turkey, Ukraine, United Arab Emirates, United Kingdom, United States, Uruguay, Vanuatu, Viet Nam, Yemen, Zambia

Against:

Belarus, Burundi, Congo, Democratic People's Republic of Korea, Iran (Islamic Republic of), Nicaragua, Russian Federation, Syrian Arab Republic, Zimbabwe

Abstaining:

Algeria, Angola, Armenia, Azerbaijan, Benin, Bolivia (Plurinational State of), China, Cuba, Ecuador, Eritrea, Iraq, Kazakhstan, Kenya, Kyrgyzstan, Mali, Namibia, Nigeria, Sudan, Tajikistan, Uganda, United Republic of Tanzania, Uzbekistan, Venezuela (Bolivarian Republic of)

Operative paragraph 2

In favour:

Afghanistan, Albania, Andorra, Antigua and Barbuda, Argentina, Australia, Austria, Bahamas, Bahrain, Barbados, Belgium, Belize, Bhutan, Bosnia and Herzegovina, Botswana, Brazil, Brunei Darussalam, Bulgaria, Burkina Faso, Cabo Verde, Canada, Chad, Chile, Colombia, Comoros, Congo, Costa Rica, Côte d'Ivoire, Croatia, Cyprus, Czech Republic, Denmark, Djibouti, Dominican Republic, Egypt, El Salvador, Equatorial Guinea, Estonia, Fiji, Finland, France, Gabon, Gambia, Georgia, Germany, Ghana, Greece, Guatemala, Guinea, Guinea-Bissau, Guyana, Haiti, Honduras, Hungary, Iceland, Indonesia, Ireland, Israel,

Italy, Jamaica, Japan, Jordan, Kiribati, Kuwait, Latvia, Lesotho, Liberia, Libya, Liechtenstein, Lithuania, Luxembourg, Madagascar, Malawi, Malaysia, Maldives, Malta, Marshall Islands, Mauritania, Mexico, Micronesia (Federated States of), Monaco, Mongolia, Montenegro, Morocco, Mozambique, Nepal, Netherlands, New Zealand, Norway, Panama, Papua New Guinea, Paraguay, Peru, Philippines, Poland, Portugal, Qatar, Republic of Korea, Republic of Moldova, Romania, Saint Kitts and Nevis, Saint Lucia, Saint Vincent and the Grenadines, Samoa, San Marino, Saudi Arabia, Senegal, Sierra Leone, Singapore, Slovakia, Slovenia, Solomon Islands, Somalia, Spain, Sri Lanka, Swaziland, Sweden, Switzerland, Thailand, the former Yugoslav Republic of Macedonia, Timor-Leste, Togo, Trinidad and Tobago, Tunisia, Turkey, Ukraine, United Arab Emirates, United Kingdom, United States, Uruguay, Vanuatu, Yemen, Zambia

Against:

Belarus, Bolivia (Plurinational State of), Burundi, China, Cuba, Democratic People's Republic of Korea, Iran (Islamic Republic of), Nicaragua, Russian Federation, Syrian Arab Republic, Venezuela (Bolivarian Republic of), Zimbabwe

Abstaining:

Algeria, Angola, Armenia, Azerbaijan, Bangladesh, Benin, Cambodia, Ecuador, Ethiopia, India, Iraq, Kazakhstan, Kenya, Kyrgyzstan, Mali, Mauritius, Namibia, Nigeria, Pakistan, Rwanda, South Africa, Sudan, Tajikistan, Uganda, United Republic of Tanzania

Operative paragraph 15

In favour:

Afghanistan, Albania, Andorra, Antigua and Barbuda, Argentina, Australia, Austria, Bahamas, Bahrain, Bangladesh, Barbados, Belgium, Belize, Bhutan, Bosnia and Herzegovina, Botswana, Brazil, Brunei Darussalam, Bulgaria, Burkina Faso, Cabo Verde, Canada, Chad, Chile, Colombia, Comoros, Congo, Costa Rica, Côte d'Ivoire, Croatia, Cyprus, Czech Republic, Denmark, Djibouti, Dominican Republic, Egypt, El Salvador, Equatorial Guinea, Estonia, Ethiopia, Fiji, Finland, France, Gabon, Gambia, Georgia, Germany, Ghana, Greece, Guatemala, Guinea, Guinea-Bissau, Guyana, Haiti, Honduras, Hungary, Iceland, India, Indonesia, Ireland, Israel, Italy, Jamaica, Japan, Jordan, Kiribati, Kuwait, Latvia, Lesotho, Liberia, Libya, Liechtenstein, Lithuania, Luxembourg, Madagascar, Malawi, Malaysia, Maldives, Malta, Marshall Islands, Mauritania, Mexico, Micronesia (Federated States of), Monaco, Mongolia, Montenegro, Morocco, Mozambique, Myanmar, Nepal, Netherlands, New Zealand, Norway, Oman, Panama, Papua New Guinea, Paraguay, Peru, Philippines, Poland, Portugal, Qatar, Republic of Korea,

Republic of Moldova, Romania, Saint Kitts and Nevis, Saint Lucia, Saint Vincent and the Grenadines, Samoa, San Marino, Saudi Arabia, Senegal, Sierra Leone, Singapore, Slovakia, Slovenia, Solomon Islands, Somalia, Spain, Sri Lanka, Swaziland, Sweden, Switzerland, Thailand, the former Yugoslav Republic of Macedonia, Timor-Leste, Togo, Trinidad and Tobago, Tunisia, Turkey, Ukraine, United Arab Emirates, United Kingdom, United States, Uruguay, Vanuatu, Yemen, Zambia

Against:

Belarus, Burundi, China, Democratic People's Republic of Korea, Iran (Islamic Republic of), Nicaragua, Russian Federation, Syrian Arab Republic, Venezuela (Bolivarian Republic of), Zimbabwe

Abstaining:

Algeria, Angola, Armenia, Azerbaijan, Benin, Bolivia (Plurinational State of), Cambodia, Cuba, Ecuador, Eritrea, Iraq, Kazakhstan, Kenya, Kyrgyzstan, Mali, Mauritius, Namibia, Nigeria, Pakistan, Rwanda, South Africa, Sudan, Tajikistan, Uganda, United Republic of Tanzania, Viet Nam

Action by the First Committee

Date: 2 November 2017   Meeting: 28th meeting

Vote: 150-6-12   Draft resolution: A/C.1/72/L.26/Rev.1

       134-7-19, p.p. 4

       122-11-24, o.p. 2

       123-9-27, o.p. 15

Agenda item 99 (x)

72/44   The Arms Trade Treaty

Text

The General Assembly,

Recalling its resolutions 61/89 of 6 December 2006, 63/240 of 24 December 2008, 64/48 of 2 December 2009, 67/234 A of 24 December 2012, 67/234 B of 2 April 2013, 68/31 of 5 December 2013, 69/49 of 2 December 2014, 70/58 of 7 December 2015 and 71/50 of 5 December 2016 and its decision 66/518 of 2 December 2011,

Recognizing that disarmament, arms control and non-proliferation are essential for the maintenance of international peace and security,

Recognizing also the security, social, economic and humanitarian consequences of the illicit and unregulated trade in conventional arms,

Recognizing further the legitimate political, security, economic and commercial interests of States in the international trade in conventional arms,

Underlining the need to prevent and eradicate the illicit trade in conventional arms and to prevent their diversion to the illicit market, or for unauthorized end use and end users, including the commission of terrorist acts,

Noting the contribution made by the Programme of Action to Prevent, Combat and Eradicate the Illicit Trade in Small Arms and Light Weapons in All Its Aspects,[1] as well as the Protocol against the Illicit Manufacturing of and Trafficking in Firearms, Their Parts and Components and Ammunition, supplementing the United Nations Convention against Transnational Organized Crime,[2] and the International Instrument to Enable States to Identify and Trace, in a Timely and Reliable Manner, Illicit Small Arms and Light Weapons,[3]

Highlighting the links and synergies between the Arms Trade Treaty[4] and the 2030 Agenda for Sustainable Development,[5] including Sustainable Development Goal 16 and target 16.4, which aims at significantly reducing illicit arms flows by 2030,

Recognizing the important role that civil society organizations, including non-governmental organizations, and industry play, by raising awareness, in

---

[1] *Report of the United Nations Conference on the Illicit Trade in Small Arms and Light Weapons in All Its Aspects, New York, 9–20 July 2001* (A/CONF.192/15), chap. IV, para. 24.
[2] United Nations, *Treaty Series*, vol. 2326, No. 39574.
[3] See decision 60/519 and A/60/88 and A/60/88/Corr.2, annex.
[4] See resolution 67/234 B.
[5] Resolution 70/1.

efforts to prevent and eradicate the unregulated and illicit trade in conventional arms and prevent their diversion and in supporting the implementation of the Arms Trade Treaty,

Welcoming the adoption by the General Assembly and the entry into force of the Treaty on 2 April 2013 and 24 December 2014, respectively, and noting that the Treaty remains open for accession by any State that has not signed it,

Welcoming also the latest ratifications of the Treaty, bearing in mind that universalization of the Treaty is essential to achieving its object and purpose,

Noting the efforts by the States parties to the Treaty to continue exploring ways and means to enhance national implementation of the Treaty through the working group on implementation and the voluntary trust fund for the implementation of the Arms Trade Treaty,

1.   *Welcomes* the decisions taken at the Third Conference of States Parties to the Arms Trade Treaty, held in Geneva from 11 to 15 September 2017, and notes that the Fourth Conference of States Parties is to be held in Japan from 20 to 24 August 2018, subject to the final confirmation of the Government of Japan;

2.   *Also welcomes* the establishment of the standing working groups on implementation, on transparency and reporting, and on universalization by the Third Conference of States Parties as important steps in advancing the object and purpose of the Arms Trade Treaty;[4]

3.   *Recognizes* that the consolidation of the institutional structure of the Treaty provides a framework for supporting further work under the Treaty, in particular its effective implementation, and in this regard calls upon States that have not yet done so to address their financial obligations under the Treaty in a prompt and timely manner;

4.   *Calls upon* all States that have not yet done so to ratify, accept, approve or accede to the Treaty, according to their respective constitutional processes, in order to achieve its universalization;

5.   *Calls upon* those States parties in a position to do so to provide assistance, including legal or legislative assistance, institutional capacity-building and technical, material or financial assistance, to requesting States in order to promote the universalization of the Treaty;

6.   *Stresses* the vital importance of the full and effective implementation of and compliance with all provisions of the Treaty by States parties, and urges them to meet their obligations under the Treaty;

7.   *Recognizes* the complementarity among all relevant international instruments on conventional arms and the Treaty, and to this end urges all States to implement effective national measures to prevent, combat and

eradicate the illicit and unregulated trade in conventional arms in fulfilment of their respective international obligations and commitments;

8. *Encourages* all States parties to make available their initial report, as well as their annual report for the preceding calendar year, as required under article 13 of the Treaty, thereby enhancing confidence, transparency, trust and accountability, and notes the endorsement by the Second Conference of States Parties of templates that may facilitate the reporting task;

9. *Welcomes* the successful operationalization of the voluntary trust fund for the implementation of the Arms Trade Treaty, encourages eligible States to make best use of the voluntary trust fund, and encourages all States parties in a position to do so to contribute to the voluntary trust fund;

10. *Encourages* States parties and signatory States in a position to do so to provide financial assistance, through a voluntary sponsorship fund, that could contribute to meeting the costs of participation in meetings under the Treaty for those States that would otherwise be unable to attend;

11. *Encourages* States parties to strengthen their cooperation with civil society, including non-governmental organizations, industry and relevant international organizations and to work with other States parties at the national and regional levels, with the aim of ensuring the effective implementation of the Treaty;

12. *Decides* to include in the provisional agenda of its seventy-third session, under the item entitled "General and complete disarmament", the sub-item entitled "The Arms Trade Treaty", and to review the implementation of the present resolution at that session.

Action by the General Assembly

Date: 4 December 2017   Meeting: 62nd plenary meeting
Vote: 155-0-29   Report: A/72/409

Sponsors

Albania, Angola, Argentina, Australia, Austria, Belgium, Bosnia and Herzegovina, Bulgaria, Canada, Costa Rica, Croatia, Czech Republic, Dominican Republic, El Salvador, Estonia, Finland, France, Germany, Ghana, Greece, Guatemala, Hungary, Iceland, Ireland, Italy, Jamaica, **Japan**, Latvia, Liechtenstein, Lithuania, Luxembourg, Malawi, Malta, Mongolia, Montenegro, Netherlands, Nigeria, Norway, Panama, Peru, Philippines, Poland, Portugal, Republic of Korea, Republic of Moldova, Romania, Samoa, Serbia, Slovakia, Slovenia, Spain, Sweden, Switzerland, the former Yugoslav Republic of Macedonia, Thailand, Togo, Ukraine, Uruguay, Zambia

Co-sponsors

> Antigua and Barbuda, Bahamas, Belize, Benin, Burkina Faso, Chile, Colombia, Cyprus, Denmark, Georgia, Guinea, Guyana, Haiti, Honduras, Kazakhstan, Liberia, Madagascar, Maldives, Mexico, Monaco, Namibia, New Zealand, Paraguay, Saint Kitts and Nevis, Saint Lucia, San Marino, Senegal, Sierra Leone, South Africa, Swaziland, Trinidad and Tobago, United Kingdom

Recorded vote

In favour:

> Afghanistan, Albania, Algeria, Andorra, Angola, Antigua and Barbuda, Argentina, Australia, Austria, Bahamas, Bahrain, Bangladesh, Barbados, Belgium, Belize, Benin, Bhutan, Bosnia and Herzegovina, Botswana, Brazil, Brunei Darussalam, Bulgaria, Burkina Faso, Burundi, Cabo Verde, Cambodia, Cameroon, Canada, Chad, Chile, China, Colombia, Comoros, Congo, Costa Rica, Côte d'Ivoire, Croatia, Cyprus, Czech Republic, Democratic Republic of the Congo, Denmark, Djibouti, Dominican Republic, El Salvador, Equatorial Guinea, Eritrea, Estonia, Ethiopia, Finland, France, Gabon, Gambia, Georgia, Germany, Ghana, Greece, Grenada, Guatemala, Guinea, Guinea-Bissau, Guyana, Haiti, Honduras, Hungary, Iceland, Iraq, Ireland, Israel, Italy, Jamaica, Japan, Jordan, Kazakhstan, Kenya, Kiribati, Kyrgyzstan, Latvia, Lebanon, Lesotho, Liberia, Libya, Liechtenstein, Lithuania, Luxembourg, Madagascar, Malawi, Malaysia, Maldives, Mali, Malta, Marshall Islands, Mauritania, Mauritius, Mexico, Monaco, Mongolia, Montenegro, Morocco, Mozambique, Myanmar, Namibia, Nepal, Netherlands, New Zealand, Nigeria, Norway, Pakistan, Palau, Panama, Papua New Guinea, Paraguay, Peru, Philippines, Poland, Portugal, Republic of Korea, Republic of Moldova, Romania, Rwanda, Saint Kitts and Nevis, Saint Lucia, Saint Vincent and the Grenadines, Samoa, San Marino, Senegal, Serbia, Sierra Leone, Singapore, Slovakia, Slovenia, Solomon Islands, Somalia, South Africa, Spain, Suriname, Sweden, Switzerland, Tajikistan, Thailand, the former Yugoslav Republic of Macedonia, Timor-Leste, Togo, Tonga, Trinidad and Tobago, Tunisia, Turkey, Turkmenistan, Tuvalu, Ukraine, United Arab Emirates, United Kingdom, United Republic of Tanzania, Uruguay, Vanuatu, Zambia

Against:

> None

Abstaining:

> Armenia, Azerbaijan, Belarus, Bolivia (Plurinational State of), Cuba, Democratic People's Republic of Korea, Ecuador, Egypt, Fiji, India, Indonesia, Iran (Islamic Republic of), Kuwait, Lao People's Democratic Republic, Nicaragua, Oman, Qatar, Russian Federation, Saudi Arabia,

Sri Lanka, Sudan, Swaziland, Syrian Arab Republic, Uganda, United States, Uzbekistan, Venezuela (Bolivarian Republic of), Yemen, Zimbabwe

Action by the First Committee

Date: 31 October 2017   Meeting: 26th meeting
Vote: 144-0-29   Draft resolution: A/C.1/72/L.27

Agenda item 99 (i)

72/45   Nuclear-weapon-free southern hemisphere and adjacent areas

Text

The General Assembly,

Recalling its resolutions 51/45 B of 10 December 1996, 52/38 N of 9 December 1997, 53/77 Q of 4 December 1998, 54/54 L of 1 December 1999, 55/33 I of 20 November 2000, 56/24 G of 29 November 2001, 57/73 of 22 November 2002, 58/49 of 8 December 2003, 59/85 of 3 December 2004, 60/58 of 8 December 2005, 61/69 of 6 December 2006, 62/35 of 5 December 2007, 63/65 of 2 December 2008, 64/44 of 2 December 2009, 65/58 of 8 December 2010, 67/55 of 3 December 2012, 69/35 of 2 December 2014, 70/45 of 7 December 2015 and 71/51 of 5 December 2016,

Recalling also the provisions on nuclear-weapon-free zones of the Final Document of the Tenth Special Session of the General Assembly, the first special session devoted to disarmament,[1]

Recalling further the adoption by the Disarmament Commission at its 1999 substantive session of a text entitled "Establishment of nuclear-weapon-free zones on the basis of arrangements freely arrived at among the States of the region concerned",[2]

Determined to pursue the total elimination of nuclear weapons,

Determined also to continue to contribute to the prevention of the proliferation of nuclear weapons in all its aspects and to the process of general and complete disarmament under strict and effective international control, in particular in the field of nuclear weapons and other weapons of mass destruction, with a view to strengthening international peace and security, in accordance with the purposes and principles of the Charter of the United Nations,

Welcoming the adoption on 7 July 2017 of the Treaty on the Prohibition of Nuclear Weapons[3] and its reaffirmation of the conviction that the establishment of the internationally recognized nuclear-weapon-free zones on the basis of arrangements freely arrived at among the States of the region concerned enhances global and regional peace and security, strengthens the nuclear non-proliferation regime and contributes towards realizing the objective of nuclear disarmament,

---

[1] Resolution S-10/2.
[2] *Official Records of the General Assembly, Fifty-fourth Session, Supplement No. 42* (A/54/42), annex I.
[3] A/CONF.229/2017/8.

Recalling the Final Document of the 2010 Review Conference of the Parties to the Treaty on the Non-Proliferation of Nuclear Weapons,[4] which reaffirmed the conviction that the establishment of nuclear-weapon-free zones contributes towards realizing the objectives of nuclear disarmament,

Stressing the importance of the treaties of Tlatelolco,[5] Rarotonga,[6] Bangkok[7] and Pelindaba[8] establishing nuclear-weapon-free zones, as well as the Antarctic Treaty,[9] inter alia, for achieving a world entirely free of nuclear weapons,

Welcoming the convening by Indonesia of the third Conference of States Parties and Signatories to Treaties that Establish Nuclear-Weapon-Free Zones and Mongolia, on 24 April 2015,

Noting that 115 States are currently parties and signatories to nuclear-weapon-free zone treaties,

Underlining the value of enhancing cooperation among the nuclear-weapon-free zone treaty members by means of mechanisms such as joint meetings of States parties, signatories and observers to those treaties,

Reaffirming the applicable principles and rules of international law relating to the freedom of the high seas and the rights of passage through maritime space, including those of the United Nations Convention on the Law of the Sea,[10]

1. *Reaffirms its conviction* of the important role of nuclear-weapon-free zones in strengthening the nuclear non-proliferation regime and in extending the areas of the world that are nuclear-weapon-free, and calls for greater progress towards the total elimination of all nuclear weapons;

2. *Welcomes* the continued contribution that the Antarctic Treaty[9] and the treaties of Tlatelolco,[5] Rarotonga,[6] Bangkok[7] and Pelindaba[8] are making towards freeing the southern hemisphere and adjacent areas covered by those treaties from nuclear weapons;

3. *Notes with satisfaction* that all nuclear-weapon-free zones in the southern hemisphere and adjacent areas are now in force;

4. *Calls upon* all States concerned to continue to work together in order to facilitate adherence to the protocols to nuclear-weapon-free zone treaties by all relevant States that have not yet done so, in this regard

---

4 *2010 Review Conference of the Parties to the Treaty on the Non-Proliferation of Nuclear Weapons, Final Document*, vols. I–III (NPT/CONF.2010/50 (Vol. I), NPT/CONF.2010/50 (Vol. II) and NPT/CONF.2010/50 (Vol. III)).

5 United Nations, *Treaty Series*, vol. 634, No. 9068.

6 The *United Nations Disarmament Yearbook*, vol. 10: 1985 (United Nations publication, Sales No. E.86.IX.7), appendix VII.

7 United Nations, *Treaty Series*, vol. 1981, No. 33873.

8 A/50/426, annex.

9 United Nations, *Treaty Series*, vol. 402, No. 5778.

10 Ibid., vol. 1833, No. 31363.

welcomes the ratification by China, France, the Russian Federation and the United Kingdom of Great Britain and Northern Ireland of the Protocol to the Treaty on a Nuclear-Weapon-Free Zone in Central Asia and the steps taken by the United States of America towards the ratification of the protocols to the Treaty on a Nuclear-Weapon-Free Zone in Central Asia, to the Treaty of Pelindaba and to the Treaty of Rarotonga, and encourages progress with a view to concluding consultations between the nuclear-weapon States and the parties to the Bangkok Treaty on the Protocol to that Treaty;

5.   *Calls upon* the nuclear-weapon States to withdraw any reservations or interpretive declarations contrary to the object and purpose of the treaties establishing nuclear-weapon-free zones;

6.   *Welcomes* the steps taken to conclude further nuclear-weapon-free zone treaties on the basis of arrangements freely arrived at among the States of the region concerned, and calls upon all States to consider all relevant proposals, including those reflected in its resolutions on the establishment of a nuclear-weapon-free zone in the Middle East;

7.   *Congratulates* the States parties and signatories to the treaties of Tlatelolco, Rarotonga, Bangkok and Pelindaba, as well as of Central Asia and Mongolia, for their efforts to pursue the common goals envisaged in those treaties and to promote the nuclear-weapon-free status of the southern hemisphere and adjacent areas, and calls upon them to explore and implement further ways and means of cooperation among themselves and their treaty agencies;

8.   *Encourages* efforts to reinforce coordination among nuclear-weapon-free zones;

9.   *Encourages* the competent authorities of the nuclear-weapon-free zone treaties to provide assistance to the States parties and signatories to those treaties so as to facilitate the accomplishment of the goals of the treaties;

10.   *Decides* to include in the provisional agenda of its seventy-fourth session, under the item entitled "General and complete disarmament", the sub-item entitled "Nuclear-weapon-free southern hemisphere and adjacent areas".

Action by the General Assembly

Date: 4 December 2017   Meeting: 62nd plenary meeting
Vote: 149-5-29   Report: A/72/409
       128-35-12, p.p. 6

Sponsors

Angola, Austria, **Brazil**, Costa Rica, Cuba, Ecuador, Indonesia, Ireland, Kazakhstan, Mexico, Mongolia, Namibia, New Zealand, Nicaragua, Panama, Papua New Guinea, Peru, Philippines, Samoa, South Africa, Suriname, Thailand, Trinidad and Tobago, Uruguay, Vanuatu, Venezuela (Bolivarian Republic of)

Co-sponsors

Argentina, Bangladesh, Brunei Darussalam, Chile, Guatemala, Guyana, Honduras, Jamaica, Liechtenstein, Malaysia, Nigeria, Paraguay, Singapore

Recorded vote

As a whole*

In favour:

Afghanistan, Algeria, Andorra, Angola, Antigua and Barbuda, Argentina, Armenia, Austria, Azerbaijan, Bahamas, Bahrain, Bangladesh, Barbados, Belarus, Belgium, Belize, Benin, Bhutan, Bolivia (Plurinational State of), Botswana, Brazil, Brunei Darussalam, Burkina Faso, Burundi, Cabo Verde, Cambodia, Canada, Central African Republic, Chad, Chile, China, Colombia, Comoros, Congo, Costa Rica, Côte d'Ivoire, Cuba, Cyprus, Democratic People's Republic of Korea, Democratic Republic of the Congo, Djibouti, Dominican Republic, Ecuador, Egypt, El Salvador, Equatorial Guinea, Eritrea, Ethiopia, Fiji, Finland, Gabon, Gambia, Ghana, Grenada, Guatemala, Guinea, Guinea-Bissau, Guyana, Honduras, India, Indonesia, Iran (Islamic Republic of), Iraq, Ireland, Jamaica, Japan, Jordan, Kazakhstan, Kenya, Kiribati, Kuwait, Kyrgyzstan, Lao People's Democratic Republic, Lebanon, Lesotho, Liberia, Libya, Liechtenstein, Madagascar, Malawi, Malaysia, Maldives, Mali, Malta, Mauritania, Mauritius, Mexico, Mongolia, Morocco, Mozambique, Myanmar, Namibia, Nauru, Nepal, Netherlands, New Zealand, Nicaragua, Nigeria, Oman, Pakistan, Palau, Panama, Papua New Guinea, Paraguay, Peru, Philippines, Qatar, Republic of Moldova, Rwanda, Saint Kitts and Nevis, Saint Lucia, Saint Vincent and the Grenadines, Samoa, San Marino, Saudi Arabia, Senegal, Serbia, Sierra Leone, Singapore, Solomon Islands, Somalia, South Africa, Sri Lanka, Sudan, Suriname, Swaziland, Sweden, Switzerland, Syrian Arab Republic, Tajikistan, Thailand, Timor-Leste, Togo, Tonga, Trinidad and Tobago, Tunisia, Turkmenistan, Tuvalu, Uganda, United Arab Emirates, United Republic of Tanzania, Uruguay, Uzbekistan, Vanuatu, Venezuela (Bolivarian Republic of), Viet Nam, Yemen, Zambia, Zimbabwe

Against:

France, Greece, Russian Federation, United Kingdom, United States

Abstaining:

Albania, Australia, Bosnia and Herzegovina, Bulgaria, Croatia, Czech Republic, Denmark, Estonia, Georgia, Germany, Hungary, Iceland, Israel, Italy, Latvia, Lithuania, Luxembourg, Montenegro, Norway,

---

* Subsequently, the delegation of Greece informed the Secretariat that it had intended to abstain. The voting tally above does not reflect this information.

Poland, Portugal, Republic of Korea, Romania, Slovakia, Slovenia, Spain, the former Yugoslav Republic of Macedonia, Turkey, Ukraine

Sixth preambular paragraph

In favour:

Afghanistan, Algeria, Angola, Antigua and Barbuda, Argentina, Austria, Azerbaijan, Bahamas, Bahrain, Bangladesh, Barbados, Belize, Benin, Bhutan, Bolivia (Plurinational State of), Botswana, Brazil, Brunei Darussalam, Burkina Faso, Burundi, Cabo Verde, Cambodia, Chad, Chile, Colombia, Comoros, Congo, Costa Rica, Côte d'Ivoire, Cuba, Cyprus, Democratic Republic of the Congo, Djibouti, Dominican Republic, Ecuador, Egypt, El Salvador, Equatorial Guinea, Eritrea, Ethiopia, Fiji, Gabon, Gambia, Ghana, Grenada, Guatemala, Guinea, Guinea-Bissau, Guyana, Honduras, Indonesia, Iran (Islamic Republic of), Iraq, Ireland, Jamaica, Jordan, Kazakhstan, Kenya, Kiribati, Kuwait, Lao People's Democratic Republic, Lebanon, Lesotho, Liberia, Libya, Liechtenstein, Madagascar, Malawi, Malaysia, Maldives, Mali, Malta, Mauritania, Mauritius, Mexico, Mongolia, Morocco, Mozambique, Myanmar, Namibia, Nepal, New Zealand, Nicaragua, Nigeria, Oman, Panama, Papua New Guinea, Paraguay, Peru, Philippines, Qatar, Republic of Moldova, Rwanda, Saint Kitts and Nevis, Saint Lucia, Saint Vincent and the Grenadines, Samoa, San Marino, Saudi Arabia, Senegal, Sierra Leone, Singapore, Solomon Islands, Somalia, South Africa, Sri Lanka, Sudan, Suriname, Swaziland, Sweden, Switzerland, Thailand, Timor-Leste, Togo, Trinidad and Tobago, Tunisia, Turkmenistan, Tuvalu, Uganda, United Arab Emirates, United Republic of Tanzania, Uruguay, Vanuatu, Venezuela (Bolivarian Republic of), Viet Nam, Yemen, Zambia, Zimbabwe

Against:

Albania, Australia, Belgium, Bosnia and Herzegovina, Bulgaria, Canada, China, Croatia, Czech Republic, Denmark, Estonia, France, Germany, Hungary, Iceland, Israel, Italy, Latvia, Lithuania, Luxembourg, Montenegro, Netherlands, Norway, Poland, Portugal, Republic of Korea, Romania, Russian Federation, Slovakia, Slovenia, Spain, Turkey, Ukraine, United Kingdom, United States

Abstaining:

Andorra, Armenia, Belarus, Democratic People's Republic of Korea, Finland, Georgia, Greece, India, Japan, Pakistan, Serbia, the former Yugoslav Republic of Macedonia

Action by the First Committee

Date: 27 October 2017   Meeting: 24th meeting
Vote: 142-4-29   Draft resolution: A/C.1/72/L.28
      121-35-11, p.p. 6

Agenda item 99 (d)

72/46   Relationship between disarmament and development

Text

The General Assembly,

Recalling that the Charter of the United Nations envisages the establishment and maintenance of international peace and security with the least diversion for armaments of the world's human and economic resources,

Recalling also the provisions of the Final Document of the Tenth Special Session of the General Assembly concerning the relationship between disarmament and development,[1] as well as the adoption on 11 September 1987 of the Final Document of the International Conference on the Relationship between Disarmament and Development,[2]

Recalling further its resolutions 49/75 J of 15 December 1994, 50/70 G of 12 December 1995, 51/45 D of 10 December 1996, 52/38 D of 9 December 1997, 53/77 K of 4 December 1998, 54/54 T of 1 December 1999, 55/33 L of 20 November 2000, 56/24 E of 29 November 2001, 57/65 of 22 November 2002, 59/78 of 3 December 2004, 60/61 of 8 December 2005, 61/64 of 6 December 2006, 62/48 of 5 December 2007, 63/52 of 2 December 2008, 64/32 of 2 December 2009, 65/52 of 8 December 2010, 66/30 of 2 December 2011, 67/40 of 3 December 2012, 68/37 of 5 December 2013, 69/56 of 2 December 2014, 70/32 of 7 December 2015 and 71/62 of 5 December 2016 and its decision 58/520 of 8 December 2003,

Bearing in mind the Final Document of the Seventeenth Conference of Heads of State or Government of Non-Aligned Countries, held on Margarita Island, Bolivarian Republic of Venezuela, from 13 to 18 September 2016,

Mindful of the changes in international relations that have taken place since the adoption in 1987 of the Final Document of the International Conference on the Relationship between Disarmament and Development, including the development agenda that has emerged over the past decade,

Bearing in mind the new challenges for the international community in the fields of development, poverty eradication and the elimination of the diseases that afflict humanity,

Stressing the importance of the symbiotic relationship between disarmament and development and the important role of security in this

---

[1] See resolution S-10/2.
[2] See *Report of the International Conference on the Relationship between Disarmament and Development, New York, 24 August–11 September 1987* (A/CONF.130/39).

connection, and concerned at increasing global military expenditure, which could otherwise be spent on development needs,

Recalling the report of the Group of Governmental Experts on the relationship between disarmament and development[3] and its reappraisal of this significant issue in the current international context,

Bearing in mind the importance of following up on the implementation of the action programme adopted at the 1987 International Conference on the Relationship between Disarmament and Development,[2]

Taking note of the report of the Secretary-General submitted pursuant to resolution 71/62,[4]

1.   *Stresses* the central role of the United Nations in the relationship between disarmament and development, and requests the Secretary-General to strengthen further the role of the Organization in this field, in particular the high-level Steering Group on Disarmament and Development, in order to ensure continued and effective coordination and close cooperation between the relevant United Nations departments, agencies and subagencies;

2.   *Requests* the Secretary-General to continue to take action, through appropriate organs and within available resources, for the implementation of the action programme adopted on 11 September 1987 at the International Conference on the Relationship between Disarmament and Development;[2]

3.   *Urges* the international community to devote part of the resources made available by the implementation of disarmament and arms limitation agreements to economic and social development, with a view to reducing the ever-widening gap between developed and developing countries;

4.   *Encourages* the international community to achieve the Sustainable Development Goals and to make reference to the contribution that disarmament could provide in meeting them when it reviews its progress towards this purpose, as well as to make greater efforts to integrate disarmament, humanitarian and development activities;

5.   *Encourages* the relevant regional and subregional organizations and institutions, non-governmental organizations and research institutes to incorporate issues related to the relationship between disarmament and development into their agendas and, in this regard, to take into account the report of the Group of Governmental Experts on the relationship between disarmament and development;[3]

6.   *Reiterates its invitation* to Member States to provide the Secretary-General with information regarding measures and efforts to devote part of the resources made available by the implementation of disarmament and arms

---

[3] See A/59/119.
[4] A/72/308.

limitation agreements to economic and social development, with a view to reducing the ever-widening gap between developed and developing countries;

7.   *Requests* the Secretary-General to report to the General Assembly at its seventy-third session on the implementation of the present resolution, including the information provided by Member States pursuant to paragraph 6 above;

8.   *Decides* to include in the provisional agenda of its seventy-third session, under the item entitled "General and complete disarmament", the sub-item entitled "Relationship between disarmament and development".

Action by the General Assembly

Date: 4 December 2017   Meeting: 62nd plenary meeting
Vote: Adopted without a vote   Report: A/72/409

Sponsors

Indonesia (on behalf of the States Members of the United Nations that are members of the Movement of Non-Aligned Countries)

Action by the First Committee

Date: 31 October 2017   Meeting: 26th meeting
Vote: Adopted without a vote   Draft resolution: A/C.1/72/L.30

Agenda item 99 (j)

72/47   Observance of environmental norms in the drafting and implementation of agreements on disarmament and arms control

Text

The General Assembly,

Recalling its resolutions 50/70 M of 12 December 1995, 51/45 E of 10 December 1996, 52/38 E of 9 December 1997, 53/77 J of 4 December 1998, 54/54 S of 1 December 1999, 55/33 K of 20 November 2000, 56/24 F of 29 November 2001, 57/64 of 22 November 2002, 58/45 of 8 December 2003, 59/68 of 3 December 2004, 60/60 of 8 December 2005, 61/63 of 6 December 2006, 62/28 of 5 December 2007, 63/51 of 2 December 2008, 64/33 of 2 December 2009, 65/53 of 8 December 2010, 66/31 of 2 December 2011, 67/37 of 3 December 2012, 68/36 of 5 December 2013, 69/55 of 2 December 2014, 70/30 of 7 December 2015 and 71/60 of 5 December 2016,

Emphasizing the importance of the observance of environmental norms in the preparation and implementation of disarmament and arms limitation agreements,

Recognizing that it is necessary to take duly into account the agreements adopted at the United Nations Conference on Environment and Development, as well as prior relevant agreements, in the drafting and implementation of agreements on disarmament and arms limitation,

Taking note of the report of the Secretary-General submitted pursuant to resolution 71/60,[1]

Noting that the Seventeenth Conference of Heads of State or Government of Non-Aligned Countries, held on Margarita Island, Bolivarian Republic of Venezuela, from 13 to 18 September 2016, welcomed the adoption by the General Assembly, without a vote, of resolution 70/30 on the observance of environmental norms in the drafting and implementation of agreements on disarmament and arms control,

Mindful of the detrimental environmental effects of the use of nuclear weapons,

1.   *Reaffirms* that international disarmament forums should take fully into account the relevant environmental norms in negotiating treaties and agreements on disarmament and arms limitation and that all States, through their actions, should contribute fully to ensuring compliance with the aforementioned norms in the implementation of treaties and conventions to which they are parties;

---

[1]   A/72/309.

2.   *Calls upon* States to adopt unilateral, bilateral, regional and multilateral measures so as to contribute to ensuring the application of scientific and technological progress within the framework of international security, disarmament and other related spheres, without detriment to the environment or to its effective contribution to attaining sustainable development;

3.   *Welcomes* the information provided by Member States on the implementation of the measures that they have adopted to promote the objectives envisaged in the present resolution;[1]

4.   *Invites* all Member States to communicate to the Secretary-General information on the measures that they have adopted to promote the objectives envisaged in the present resolution, and requests the Secretary-General to submit a report containing that information to the General Assembly at its seventy-third session;

5.   *Decides* to include in the provisional agenda of its seventy-third session, under the item entitled "General and complete disarmament", the sub-item entitled "Observance of environmental norms in the drafting and implementation of agreements on disarmament and arms control".

Action by the General Assembly

Date: 4 December 2017   Meeting: 62nd plenary meeting
Vote: Adopted without a vote   Report: A/72/409

Sponsors

Indonesia (on behalf of the States Members of the United Nations that are members of the Movement of Non-Aligned Countries)

Action by the First Committee

Date: 31 October 2017   Meeting: 26th meeting
Vote: Adopted without a vote   Draft resolution: A/C.1/72/L.31

Agenda item 99 (r)

72/48   Promotion of multilateralism in the area of disarmament and non-proliferation

Text

The General Assembly,

Determined to foster strict respect for the purposes and principles enshrined in the Charter of the United Nations,

Recalling its resolution 56/24 T of 29 November 2001 on multilateral cooperation in the area of disarmament and non-proliferation and global efforts against terrorism and other relevant resolutions, as well as its resolutions 57/63 of 22 November 2002, 58/44 of 8 December 2003, 59/69 of 3 December 2004, 60/59 of 8 December 2005, 61/62 of 6 December 2006, 62/27 of 5 December 2007, 63/50 of 2 December 2008, 64/34 of 2 December 2009, 65/54 of 8 December 2010, 66/32 of 2 December 2011, 67/38 of 3 December 2012, 68/38 of 5 December 2013, 69/54 of 2 December 2014, 70/31 of 7 December 2015 and 71/61 of 5 December 2016 on the promotion of multilateralism in the area of disarmament and non-proliferation,

Recalling also the purpose of the United Nations to maintain international peace and security and, to that end, to take effective collective measures for the prevention and removal of threats to the peace and for the suppression of acts of aggression or other breaches of the peace, and to bring about by peaceful means, and in conformity with the principles of justice and international law, adjustment or settlement of international disputes or situations which might lead to a breach of the peace, as enshrined in the Charter,

Recalling further the United Nations Millennium Declaration,[1] in which it is stated, inter alia, that the responsibility for managing worldwide economic and social development, as well as threats to international peace and security, must be shared among the nations of the world and should be exercised multilaterally and that, as the most universal and most representative organization in the world, the United Nations must play the central role,

Convinced that, in the globalization era and with the information revolution, arms regulation, non-proliferation and disarmament problems are more than ever the concern of all countries in the world, which are affected in one way or another by these problems and therefore should have the possibility to participate in the negotiations that arise to tackle them,

Bearing in mind the existence of a broad structure of disarmament and arms regulation agreements resulting from non-discriminatory and transparent multilateral negotiations with the participation of a large number of countries, regardless of their size and power,

---

[1] Resolution 55/2.

Aware of the need to advance further in the field of arms regulation, non-proliferation and disarmament on the basis of universal, multilateral, non-discriminatory and transparent negotiations with the goal of reaching general and complete disarmament under strict international control,

Recognizing the complementarity of bilateral, plurilateral and multilateral negotiations on disarmament,

Recognizing also that the proliferation and development of weapons of mass destruction, including nuclear weapons, are among the most immediate threats to international peace and security which need to be dealt with, with the highest priority,

Considering that the multilateral disarmament agreements provide the mechanism for States parties to consult one another and to cooperate in solving any problems which may arise in relation to the objective of, or in the application of, the provisions of the agreements and that such consultations and cooperation may also be undertaken through appropriate international procedures within the framework of the United Nations and in accordance with the Charter,

Stressing that international cooperation, the peaceful settlement of disputes, dialogue and confidence-building measures would make an essential contribution to the creation of multilateral and bilateral friendly relations among peoples and nations,

Being concerned at the continuous erosion of multilateralism in the field of arms regulation, non-proliferation and disarmament, and recognizing that a resort to unilateral actions by Member States in resolving their security concerns would jeopardize international peace and security and undermine confidence in the international security system as well as the foundations of the United Nations itself,

Noting that the Seventeenth Conference of Heads of State or Government of Non-Aligned Countries, held on Margarita Island, Bolivarian Republic of Venezuela, from 13 to 18 September 2016, welcomed the adoption of resolution 70/31 on the promotion of multilateralism in the area of disarmament and non-proliferation and underlined the fact that multilateralism and multilaterally agreed solutions, in accordance with the Charter, provide the only sustainable method of addressing disarmament and international security issues,

Reaffirming the absolute validity of multilateral diplomacy in the field of disarmament and non-proliferation, and determined to promote multilateralism as an essential way to develop arms regulation and disarmament negotiations,

1.   *Reaffirms* multilateralism as the core principle in negotiations in the area of disarmament and non-proliferation with a view to maintaining and strengthening universal norms and enlarging their scope;

2.   *Also reaffirms* multilateralism as the core principle in resolving disarmament and non-proliferation concerns;

3.   *Urges* the participation of all interested States in multilateral negotiations on arms regulation, non-proliferation and disarmament in a non-discriminatory and transparent manner;

4.   *Underlines* the importance of preserving the existing agreements on arms regulation and disarmament, which constitute an expression of the results of international cooperation and multilateral negotiations in response to the challenges facing mankind;

5.   *Calls once again upon* all Member States to renew and fulfil their individual and collective commitments to multilateral cooperation as an important means of pursuing and achieving their common objectives in the area of disarmament and non-proliferation;

6.   *Requests* the States parties to the relevant instruments on weapons of mass destruction to consult and cooperate among themselves in resolving their concerns with regard to cases of non-compliance as well as on implementation, in accordance with the procedures defined in those instruments, and to refrain from resorting or threatening to resort to unilateral actions or directing unverified non-compliance accusations against one another to resolve their concerns;

7.   *Takes note* of the report of the Secretary-General containing the replies of Member States on the promotion of multilateralism in the area of disarmament and non-proliferation, submitted pursuant to resolution 71/61;[2]

8.   *Requests* the Secretary-General to seek the views of Member States on the issue of the promotion of multilateralism in the area of disarmament and non-proliferation and to submit a report thereon to the General Assembly at its seventy-third session;

9.   *Decides* to include in the provisional agenda of its seventy-third session, under the item entitled "General and complete disarmament", the sub-item entitled "Promotion of multilateralism in the area of disarmament and non-proliferation".

Action by the General Assembly

Date: 4 December 2017   Meeting: 62nd plenary meeting
Vote: 130-4-51   Report: A/72/409

Sponsors

Indonesia (on behalf of the States Members of the United Nations that are members of the Movement of Non-Aligned Countries)

---

[2] A/72/302.

Recorded vote

In favour:
Afghanistan, Algeria, Angola, Antigua and Barbuda, Argentina, Azerbaijan, Bahamas, Bahrain, Bangladesh, Barbados, Belarus, Belize, Benin, Bhutan, Bolivia (Plurinational State of), Botswana, Brazil, Brunei Darussalam, Burkina Faso, Burundi, Cabo Verde, Cambodia, Central African Republic, Chad, Chile, China, Colombia, Comoros, Congo, Costa Rica, Côte d'Ivoire, Cuba, Democratic People's Republic of Korea, Democratic Republic of the Congo, Djibouti, Dominican Republic, Ecuador, Egypt, El Salvador, Equatorial Guinea, Eritrea, Ethiopia, Fiji, Gabon, Gambia, Ghana, Grenada, Guatemala, Guinea, Guinea-Bissau, Guyana, Honduras, India, Indonesia, Iran (Islamic Republic of), Iraq, Jamaica, Jordan, Kazakhstan, Kenya, Kiribati, Kuwait, Kyrgyzstan, Lao People's Democratic Republic, Lebanon, Lesotho, Liberia, Libya, Madagascar, Malawi, Malaysia, Maldives, Mali, Marshall Islands, Mauritania, Mauritius, Mexico, Mongolia, Morocco, Mozambique, Myanmar, Namibia, Nepal, Nicaragua, Nigeria, Oman, Pakistan, Palau, Panama, Papua New Guinea, Paraguay, Peru, Philippines, Qatar, Russian Federation, Rwanda, Saint Kitts and Nevis, Saint Lucia, Saint Vincent and the Grenadines, Saudi Arabia, Senegal, Serbia, Sierra Leone, Singapore, Solomon Islands, Somalia, South Africa, Sri Lanka, Sudan, Suriname, Swaziland, Syrian Arab Republic, Tajikistan, Thailand, Timor-Leste, Togo, Trinidad and Tobago, Tunisia, Turkmenistan, Uganda, United Arab Emirates, United Republic of Tanzania, Uruguay, Uzbekistan, Vanuatu, Venezuela (Bolivarian Republic of), Viet Nam, Yemen, Zambia, Zimbabwe

Against:
Israel, Micronesia (Federated States of), United Kingdom, United States

Abstaining:
Albania, Andorra, Armenia, Australia, Austria, Belgium, Bosnia and Herzegovina, Bulgaria, Canada, Croatia, Cyprus, Czech Republic, Denmark, Estonia, Finland, France, Georgia, Germany, Greece, Hungary, Iceland, Ireland, Italy, Japan, Latvia, Liechtenstein, Lithuania, Luxembourg, Malta, Monaco, Montenegro, Netherlands, New Zealand, Norway, Poland, Portugal, Republic of Korea, Republic of Moldova, Romania, Samoa, San Marino, Slovakia, Slovenia, Spain, Sweden, Switzerland, the former Yugoslav Republic of Macedonia, Tonga, Turkey, Tuvalu, Ukraine

Action by the First Committee

Date: 31 October 2017	Meeting:	26th meeting
Vote: 120-4-49	Draft resolution:	A/C.1/72/L.32

Agenda item 99 (h)

72/49 Convening of the fourth special session of the General Assembly devoted to disarmament

Text

The General Assembly,

Recalling its resolutions 49/75 I of 15 December 1994, 50/70 F of 12 December 1995, 51/45 C of 10 December 1996, 52/38 F of 9 December 1997, 53/77 AA of 4 December 1998, 54/54 U of 1 December 1999, 55/33 M of 20 November 2000, 56/24 D of 29 November 2001, 57/61 of 22 November 2002, 59/71 of 3 December 2004, 61/60 of 6 December 2006, 62/29 of 5 December 2007 and 65/66 of 8 December 2010, as well as its decisions 58/521 of 8 December 2003, 60/518 of 8 December 2005, 60/559 of 6 June 2006, 63/519 of 2 December 2008, 64/515 of 2 December 2009 and 70/551 of 23 December 2015,

Recalling also that, there being a consensus to do so in each case, three special sessions of the General Assembly devoted to disarmament were held in 1978, 1982 and 1988, respectively,

Bearing in mind the Final Document of the Tenth Special Session of the General Assembly, adopted by consensus at the first special session devoted to disarmament,[1]

Bearing in mind also the ultimate objective of general and complete disarmament under effective international control,

Reiterating its conviction that a special session of the General Assembly devoted to disarmament can set the future course of action in the fields of disarmament, arms control, non-proliferation and related international security matters,

Emphasizing the importance of multilateralism in the process of disarmament, arms control, non-proliferation and related international security matters,

Welcoming the successful conclusion of the work of the Open-ended Working Group on the fourth special session of the General Assembly devoted to disarmament to consider the objectives and agenda of the fourth special session, and to adopt its report and substantive recommendations by consensus,[2]

Having considered the report of the Open-ended Working Group and the recommendations contained therein,

---

[1] Resolution S-10/2.
[2] A/AC.268/2017/2.

1. *Welcomes* the adoption by consensus of the recommendations on the objectives and agenda of the fourth special session of the General Assembly devoted to disarmament by the Open-ended Working Group on the fourth special session of the General Assembly devoted to disarmament, which was established by the Assembly by its resolution 65/66 and its decision 70/551 and which met in New York in 2016 and 2017;

2. *Endorses* the report of the Open-ended Working Group and the substantive recommendations contained therein;[2]

3. *Expresses its appreciation* to the participants of the Open-ended Working Group for their constructive contribution to its work;

4. *Encourages* Member States to continue consultations on the next steps for convening of the fourth special session of the General Assembly devoted to disarmament;

5. *Decides* to include in the provisional agenda of its seventy-third session, under the item entitled "General and complete disarmament", the sub-item entitled "Convening of the fourth special session of the General Assembly devoted to disarmament".

Action by the General Assembly

Date: 4 December 2017   Meeting: 62nd plenary meeting
Vote: 181-0-3   Report: A/72/409

Sponsors

Indonesia (on behalf of the States Members of the United Nations that are members of the Movement of Non-Aligned Countries)

Recorded vote

In favour:

Afghanistan, Albania, Algeria, Andorra, Angola, Antigua and Barbuda, Argentina, Armenia, Australia, Austria, Azerbaijan, Bahamas, Bahrain, Bangladesh, Barbados, Belarus, Belgium, Belize, Benin, Bhutan, Bolivia (Plurinational State of), Bosnia and Herzegovina, Botswana, Brazil, Brunei Darussalam, Bulgaria, Burkina Faso, Burundi, Cabo Verde, Cambodia, Canada, Central African Republic, Chad, Chile, China, Colombia, Comoros, Congo, Costa Rica, Côte d'Ivoire, Croatia, Cuba, Cyprus, Czech Republic, Democratic People's Republic of Korea, Democratic Republic of the Congo, Denmark, Djibouti, Dominican Republic, Ecuador, Egypt, El Salvador, Equatorial Guinea, Eritrea, Estonia, Ethiopia, Fiji, Finland, Gabon, Gambia, Georgia, Germany, Ghana, Greece, Grenada, Guatemala, Guinea, Guinea-Bissau, Guyana, Haiti, Honduras, Hungary, Iceland, India, Indonesia, Iran (Islamic Republic of), Iraq, Ireland, Italy, Jamaica, Japan, Jordan, Kazakhstan, Kenya, Kiribati, Kuwait, Kyrgyzstan, Lao People's Democratic Republic,

Latvia, Lebanon, Lesotho, Liberia, Libya, Liechtenstein, Lithuania, Luxembourg, Madagascar, Malawi, Malaysia, Maldives, Mali, Malta, Marshall Islands, Mauritania, Mauritius, Mexico, Monaco, Mongolia, Montenegro, Morocco, Mozambique, Myanmar, Namibia, Nepal, Netherlands, New Zealand, Nicaragua, Nigeria, Norway, Oman, Pakistan, Palau, Panama, Papua New Guinea, Paraguay, Peru, Philippines, Poland, Portugal, Qatar, Republic of Korea, Republic of Moldova, Romania, Russian Federation, Rwanda, Saint Kitts and Nevis, Saint Lucia, Saint Vincent and the Grenadines, Samoa, San Marino, Saudi Arabia, Senegal, Serbia, Sierra Leone, Singapore, Slovakia, Slovenia, Solomon Islands, Somalia, South Africa, Spain, Sri Lanka, Sudan, Suriname, Swaziland, Sweden, Switzerland, Syrian Arab Republic, Tajikistan, Thailand, the former Yugoslav Republic of Macedonia, Timor-Leste, Togo, Trinidad and Tobago, Tunisia, Turkey, Turkmenistan, Tuvalu, Uganda, Ukraine, United Arab Emirates, United Kingdom, United Republic of Tanzania, Uruguay, Uzbekistan, Vanuatu, Venezuela (Bolivarian Republic of), Viet Nam, Yemen, Zambia, Zimbabwe

Against:
None

Abstaining:
France, Israel, United States

Action by the First Committee

Date:	1 November 2017	Meeting:	27th meeting
Vote:	170-0-3	Draft resolution:	A/C.1/72/L.33

Agenda item 99 (z)

72/50   United action with renewed determination towards the total elimination of nuclear weapons

Text

The General Assembly,

Reaffirming its commitment towards a peaceful and secure world free of nuclear weapons,

Recalling its resolution 71/49 of 5 December 2016,

Reaffirming the crucial importance of the Treaty on the Non-Proliferation of Nuclear Weapons[1] as the cornerstone of the international nuclear non-proliferation regime and an essential foundation for the pursuit of nuclear disarmament, nuclear non-proliferation and the peaceful uses of nuclear energy,

Reaffirming also its determination to further strengthen the universality of the regime of the Treaty on the Non-Proliferation of Nuclear Weapons, and recalling that nuclear disarmament, non-proliferation and peaceful uses of nuclear energy are mutually reinforcing and are essential for strengthening the Treaty regime,

Recalling the Final Documents of the 1995 Review and Extension Conference of the Parties to the Treaty on the Non-Proliferation of Nuclear Weapons[2] and the 2000[3] and 2010[4] Review Conferences of the Parties to the Treaty on the Non-Proliferation of Nuclear Weapons,

Stressing the importance of the Review Conference of the Parties to the Treaty on the Non-Proliferation of Nuclear Weapons to be held in 2020, on the occasion of the fiftieth anniversary of the entry into force of the Treaty, and of its review cycle towards the 2020 Review Conference,

Emphasizing the crucial importance of rebuilding trust and enhancing cooperation among all States in order to make substantive progress in nuclear disarmament and non-proliferation, bearing in mind there are various approaches towards the realization of a world free of nuclear weapons,

---

[1] United Nations, *Treaty Series*, vol. 729, No. 10485.

[2] *1995 Review and Extension Conference of the Parties to the Treaty on the Non-Proliferation of Nuclear Weapons, Final Document, Part I* (NPT/CONF.1995/32 (Part I) and NPT/CONF.1995/32 (Part I)/Corr.2).

[3] *2000 Review Conference of the Parties to the Treaty on the Non-Proliferation of Nuclear Weapons, Final Document*, vols. I–III (NPT/CONF.2000/28 (Parts I and II), NPT/CONF.2000/28 (Part III) and NPT/CONF.2000/28 (Part IV)).

[4] *2010 Review Conference of the Parties to the Treaty on the Non-Proliferation of Nuclear Weapons, Final Document*, vols. I–III (NPT/CONF.2010/50 (Vol. I), NPT/CONF.2010/50 (Vol. II) and NPT/CONF.2010/50 (Vol. III)).

Reaffirming that the enhancement of international peace and security and the promotion of nuclear disarmament are mutually reinforcing,

Expressing grave concern over the recent developments in regional security situations and the growing dangers posed by the proliferation of weapons of mass destruction, including nuclear weapons, and by related proliferation networks,

Recalling, in this context, that the repeated and frequent unlawful nuclear tests and the launches using ballistic missile technology conducted by the Democratic People's Republic of Korea, including its nuclear test of 3 September 2017, which it announced as a hydrogen bomb for an intercontinental ballistic missile, and the two launches of ballistic missiles which flew over Japan on 29 August and 15 September 2017, pose unprecedented, grave and imminent threats to the peace and security of the region and the world, present grave challenges to the regime centred on the Treaty on the Non-Proliferation of Nuclear Weapons, and constitute clear and repeated violations of the relevant Security Council resolutions, and reiterating the resolute opposition of the international community to the possession of nuclear weapons by the Democratic People's Republic of Korea,

Recognizing that the relevant Security Council resolutions, including resolution 2375 (2017) of 11 September 2017, express the Council's firm opposition to the unlawful nuclear and missile programmes of the Democratic People's Republic of Korea in violation of the relevant Council resolutions and the Council's determination to take further significant measures in the event of a further nuclear test or ballistic missile launch by the Democratic People's Republic of Korea,

Reaffirming that further consolidation of the international regime for nuclear non-proliferation, is, inter alia, essential to international peace and security,

Noting that the ultimate objective of the efforts of States in the disarmament process is general and complete disarmament under strict and effective international control,

Stressing the importance of the decisions and the resolution on the Middle East of the 1995 Review and Extension Conference of the Parties to the Treaty on the Non-Proliferation of Nuclear Weapons and the Final Documents of the 2000 and 2010 Review Conferences of the Parties to the Treaty on the Non-Proliferation of Nuclear Weapons, and reaffirming its support for the establishment of a Middle East zone free of nuclear weapons and all other weapons of mass destruction and their delivery systems, on the basis of arrangements freely arrived at by the States of the region and in accordance with the 1995 resolution on the Middle East, and for the resumption of dialogue towards this end involving the States concerned,

Welcoming the efforts undertaken towards the development of nuclear disarmament verification capabilities that can contribute to the pursuit of a world free of nuclear weapons, including the International Partnership for Nuclear Disarmament Verification, and stressing in this regard the importance of cooperation between nuclear-weapon States and non-nuclear-weapon States,

Stressing the need to continue to explore possibilities for overcoming the ongoing deadlock of two decades in the Conference on Disarmament,

Welcoming the continuing successful implementation of the Treaty between the Russian Federation and the United States of America on Measures for the Further Reduction and Limitation of Strategic Offensive Arms,

Commending the accomplishments of the Preparatory Commission for the Comprehensive Nuclear-Test-Ban Treaty Organization since the opening for signature of the Treaty,[5] in particular the significant progress made in the establishment of the International Monitoring System and the International Data Centre,

Expressing deep concern at the catastrophic humanitarian consequences of nuclear weapons use, and reaffirming the need for all States to comply at all times with applicable international law, including international humanitarian law, while convinced that every effort should be made to avoid the use of nuclear weapons,

Recognizing that the catastrophic humanitarian consequences that would result from the use of nuclear weapons should be fully understood by all, and noting in this regard that efforts should be made to increase such understanding,

Welcoming the recent visits of political leaders to Hiroshima and Nagasaki,

Recalling that nuclear and radiological terrorism remains a pressing and evolving challenge to the international community, and reaffirming the central role of the International Atomic Energy Agency in nuclear security,

1.   *Renews* the determination of all States to take united action towards the total elimination of nuclear weapons through the easing of international tension and the strengthening of trust between States as envisioned in the preamble to the Treaty on the Non-Proliferation of Nuclear Weapons[1] in order to facilitate disarmament and through strengthening the nuclear non-proliferation regime;

2.   *Reaffirms*, in this regard, the unequivocal undertaking of the nuclear-weapon States to fully implement the Treaty on the Non-Proliferation of Nuclear Weapons, towards a safer world for all and a peaceful and secure world free of nuclear weapons;

---

[5] See resolution 50/245 and A/50/1027.

3.   *Calls upon* all States parties to the Treaty on the Non-Proliferation of Nuclear Weapons to comply with their obligations under all the articles of the Treaty;

4.   *Encourages* all States to exert their utmost efforts towards the success of the 2020 Review Conference of the Parties to the Treaty on the Non-Proliferation of Nuclear Weapons, welcoming the successful convening of the first session of the Preparatory Committee for the Review Conference, which was held in Vienna in May 2017;

5.   *Calls upon* all States not parties to the Treaty on the Non-Proliferation of Nuclear Weapons to accede as non-nuclear-weapon States to the Treaty promptly and without any conditions to achieve its universality and, pending their accession to the Treaty, to adhere to its terms and to take practical steps in support of the Treaty;

6.   *Calls upon* all States to take further practical steps and effective measures towards the total elimination of nuclear weapons, based on the principle of undiminished and increased security for all;

7.   *Encourages* all States to further engage in meaningful dialogue that facilitates practical, concrete and effective measures on nuclear disarmament and non-proliferation;

8.   *Emphasizes* that deep concerns about the humanitarian consequences of the use of nuclear weapons continue to be a key factor that underpins efforts by all States towards a world free of nuclear weapons;

9.   *Encourages* the Russian Federation and the United States of America to take steps to create conditions that would allow for the commencement of negotiations at an early date to achieve greater reductions in their stockpiles of nuclear weapons, with a view to concluding such negotiations as soon as possible;

10.   *Calls upon* all States to ease international tension, strengthen trust between States, and create conditions that would allow for further reduction of nuclear weapons, and calls upon all nuclear-weapon States to undertake further efforts to reduce and ultimately eliminate all types of nuclear weapons, deployed and non-deployed, including through unilateral, bilateral, regional, and multilateral measures;

11.   *Also calls upon* all States to apply the principles of irreversibility, verifiability and transparency in relation to the process of nuclear disarmament and non-proliferation;

12.   *Encourages* the nuclear-weapon States to continue to convene regular meetings, with a view to creating the necessary environment for and thereby implementing further nuclear disarmament, and to build upon and expand their efforts to enhance transparency and to increase mutual confidence, including, inter alia, by providing more frequent and further

detailed reporting on nuclear weapons and delivery systems dismantled and reduced as part of nuclear disarmament efforts throughout the review process of the Treaty on the Non-Proliferation of Nuclear Weapons towards the 2020 Review Conference of the Parties to the Treaty;

13. *Calls upon* all States to ease international tension and strengthen trust between States, and create the necessary environment that would allow for further consideration of, and calls upon States concerned to continue to review, their military and security concepts, doctrines and policies with a view to reducing further the role and significance of nuclear weapons therein, taking into account the security environment;

14. *Recognizes* the legitimate interest of non-nuclear-weapon States that are party to the Treaty on the Non-Proliferation of Nuclear Weapons and in compliance with their nuclear non-proliferation obligations in receiving unequivocal and legally binding security assurances from nuclear-weapon States which could strengthen the nuclear non-proliferation regime;

15. *Recalls* Security Council resolution 984 (1995) of 11 April 1995, noting the unilateral statements by each of the nuclear-weapon States, and calls upon all nuclear-weapon States to fully respect their commitments with regard to security assurances;

16. *Encourages* the establishment of further nuclear-weapon-free zones, where appropriate, on the basis of arrangements freely arrived at by the States of the region concerned and in accordance with the 1999 guidelines of the Disarmament Commission,[6] and recognizes that, by signing and ratifying relevant protocols that contain negative security assurances, nuclear-weapon States would undertake individual legally binding commitments with respect to the status of such zones and not to use or threaten to use nuclear weapons against States that are party to such treaties;

17. *Urges* all States possessing nuclear weapons to continue to undertake all efforts necessary to comprehensively address the risks of unintended nuclear detonations;

18. *Encourages* further efforts towards the establishment of a Middle East zone free of nuclear weapons and all other weapons of mass destruction and their delivery systems, on the basis of arrangements freely arrived at by the States of the region and in accordance with the 1995 resolution on the Middle East,[7] and the resumption of dialogue towards that end involving the States concerned;

---

[6] See *Official Records of the General Assembly, Fifty-fourth Session, Supplement No. 42* (A/54/42).

[7] See *1995 Review and Extension Conference of the Parties to the Treaty on the Non-Proliferation of Nuclear Weapons, Final Document*, Part I (NPT/CONF.1995/32 (Part I) and NPT/CONF.1995/32 (Part I)/Corr.2), annex.

19. *Stresses* the vital importance and urgency of universal adherence to the moratoria on nuclear-weapon test explosions or any other nuclear explosions in the light of the tests conducted by the Democratic People's Republic of Korea, recognizing that the Democratic People's Republic of Korea is an annex 2 State and that the entry into force of the Comprehensive Nuclear-Test-Ban Treaty[5] will not be possible while such testing by the Democratic People's Republic of Korea continues, and urges the Democratic People's Republic of Korea to sign and ratify that Treaty without further delay and without waiting for any other State to do so;

20. *Also stresses* the vital importance and urgency for all States who have not done so to declare and maintain moratoria on the production of fissile material for use in nuclear weapons or other nuclear explosive devices, pending commencement of negotiations on a treaty banning the production of fissile material for nuclear weapons or other nuclear explosive devices and its early conclusion, as called for in document CD/1299 of 24 March 1995 and the mandate contained therein, and welcomes in this context the recent efforts of the high-level expert preparatory group established by the General Assembly in its resolution 71/259 of 23 December 2016 in order to attain recommendations on substantial elements of a future fissile material cut-off treaty, including by examining the report of the Group of Governmental Experts contained in document A/70/81;

21. *Acknowledges* the widespread call for the early entry into force of the Comprehensive Nuclear-Test-Ban Treaty, while recalling that all States, in particular the eight remaining States in annex 2 thereof, have been urged to take individual initiatives to sign and ratify that Treaty without waiting for any other State to do so, and the immediate commencement of negotiations on a treaty banning the production of fissile material for nuclear weapons or other nuclear explosive devices;

22. *Encourages* all States to implement the recommendations contained in the report of the Secretary-General on the United Nations study on disarmament and non-proliferation education,[8] in support of achieving a world free of nuclear weapons;

23. *Encourages* every effort to raise awareness of the realities of the use of nuclear weapons, including through, among others, visits by leaders, youth and others to and interactions with communities and people, including atomic bomb survivors, the hibakusha, that pass on their experiences to the future generations;

24. *Condemns in the strongest terms* all nuclear tests and launches using ballistic missile technology by the Democratic People's Republic of Korea, which cannot have the status of a nuclear-weapon State in accordance with the Treaty on the Non-Proliferation of Nuclear Weapons, strongly urges

---

[8] A/57/124.

the Democratic People's Republic of Korea to refrain from conducting further nuclear tests and to abandon all ongoing nuclear activities immediately in a complete, verifiable and irreversible manner, and calls upon the Democratic People's Republic of Korea to fully comply with all relevant Security Council resolutions, with special emphasis on Council resolutions 2356 (2017) of 2 June 2017, 2371 (2017) of 5 August 2017 and, most recently, resolution 2375 (2017) of 11 September 2017 adopted since the seventy-first session of the General Assembly, to implement the joint statement of the Six-Party Talks of 19 September 2005 and to return at an early date to full compliance with the Treaty, including that of the International Atomic Energy Agency safeguards;

25. *Calls upon* all States to make utmost efforts to address the unprecedented, grave and imminent threat posed by the nuclear and missile programmes of the Democratic People's Republic of Korea, including through the full implementation of all relevant Security Council resolutions, including Council resolution 2375 (2017);

26. *Also calls upon* all States to redouble their efforts to prevent and curb the proliferation of nuclear weapons and their means of delivery and to fully respect and comply with any obligations undertaken to forswear nuclear weapons;

27. *Further calls upon* all States to establish and enforce effective domestic controls to prevent proliferation of nuclear weapons and encourages cooperation among States and technical assistance to enhance international partnership and capacity-building in non-proliferation efforts;

28. *Stresses* the fundamental role of the International Atomic Energy Agency safeguards and the importance of the universalization of the comprehensive safeguards agreements, and, while noting that it is the sovereign decision of any State to conclude an additional protocol, strongly encourages all States that have not done so to conclude and bring into force as soon as possible an additional protocol based on the Model Additional Protocol to the Agreement(s) between States and the International Atomic Energy Agency for the Application of Safeguards, approved by the Board of Governors of the Agency on 15 May 1997;

29. *Calls upon* all States to fully implement relevant Security Council resolutions, including Council resolutions 1540 (2004) of 28 April 2004 and 2325 (2016) of 15 December 2016, based on the outcome of the comprehensive review of the status of implementation of Council resolution 1540 (2004);

30. *Encourages* all States to attach more importance to, and enhance the security of, nuclear and other radiological materials, and to further strengthen the global nuclear security architecture;

31. *Decides* to include in the provisional agenda of its seventy-third session, under the item entitled "General and complete disarmament", the

sub-item entitled "United action with renewed determination towards the total elimination of nuclear weapons".

Action by the General Assembly

Date: 4 December 2017   Meeting: 62nd plenary meeting
Vote: 156-4-24   Report: A/72/409
       158-1-17, p.p. 19
       166-1-8, p.p. 20
       142-7-27, o.p. 2
       169-4-5, o.p. 5
       157-2-16, o.p. 8
       164-3-11, o.p. 20
       154-4-19, o.p. 21
       164-1-11, o.p. 28

Sponsors

Afghanistan, Albania, Angola, Australia, Benin, Bosnia and Herzegovina, Bulgaria, Cabo Verde, Chad, Croatia, Czech Republic, Dominican Republic, El Salvador, Estonia, Finland, Georgia, Germany, Greece, Hungary, Iceland, Italy, **Japan**, Kenya, Latvia, Lithuania, Luxembourg, Malawi, Mauritania, Montenegro, Nicaragua, Papua New Guinea, Paraguay, Poland, Portugal, Republic of Moldova, Romania, Samoa, Sierra Leone, Slovakia, Spain, Turkey, United Arab Emirates, United Kingdom, United States, Uruguay, Vanuatu

Co-sponsors

Andorra, Belize, Burkina Faso, Central African Republic, Colombia, Côte d'Ivoire, Denmark, Equatorial Guinea, Haiti, Honduras, Lebanon, Madagascar, Marshall Islands, Micronesia (Federated States of), Morocco, Mozambique, Nepal, Norway, Panama, Serbia, Singapore, Slovenia, Sri Lanka, Swaziland, the former Yugoslav Republic of Macedonia, Togo, Tonga, Tunisia, Tuvalu, Uzbekistan, Zambia

Recorded vote

As a whole

In favour:

Afghanistan, Albania, Andorra, Antigua and Barbuda, Argentina, Armenia, Australia, Azerbaijan, Bahamas, Bahrain, Bangladesh, Barbados, Belarus, Belgium, Belize, Benin, Bhutan, Bolivia (Plurinational State of), Bosnia and Herzegovina, Botswana, Brunei Darussalam, Bulgaria, Burkina Faso, Burundi, Cabo Verde, Cambodia, Canada, Central African Republic, Chad, Chile, Colombia, Comoros, Congo, Côte d'Ivoire, Croatia, Cyprus, Czech Republic, Denmark,

Djibouti, Dominican Republic, El Salvador, Equatorial Guinea, Eritrea, Estonia, Ethiopia, Fiji, Finland, France, Gabon, Gambia, Georgia, Germany, Ghana, Greece, Guatemala, Guinea, Guinea-Bissau, Guyana, Haiti, Honduras, Hungary, Iceland, Iraq, Italy, Jamaica, Japan, Jordan, Kazakhstan, Kenya, Kuwait, Kyrgyzstan, Lao People's Democratic Republic, Latvia, Lebanon, Lesotho, Liberia, Libya, Lithuania, Luxembourg, Madagascar, Malawi, Malaysia, Maldives, Mali, Malta, Marshall Islands, Mauritania, Mauritius, Mexico, Micronesia (Federated States of), Monaco, Mongolia, Montenegro, Morocco, Mozambique, Nauru, Nepal, Netherlands, Nicaragua, Norway, Oman, Palau, Panama, Papua New Guinea, Paraguay, Peru, Philippines, Poland, Portugal, Qatar, Republic of Moldova, Romania, Rwanda, Saint Kitts and Nevis, Saint Lucia, Saint Vincent and the Grenadines, Samoa, Saudi Arabia, Senegal, Serbia, Sierra Leone, Singapore, Slovakia, Slovenia, Solomon Islands, Somalia, Spain, Sri Lanka, Sudan, Suriname, Swaziland, Sweden, Switzerland, Tajikistan, Thailand, the former Yugoslav Republic of Macedonia, Timor-Leste, Togo, Tonga, Trinidad and Tobago, Tunisia, Turkey, Turkmenistan, Tuvalu, Uganda, Ukraine, United Arab Emirates, United Kingdom, United Republic of Tanzania, United States, Uruguay, Uzbekistan, Vanuatu, Viet Nam, Yemen, Zambia

Against:

China, Democratic People's Republic of Korea, Russian Federation, Syrian Arab Republic

Abstaining:

Algeria, Angola, Austria, Brazil, Costa Rica, Cuba, Ecuador, Egypt, India, Indonesia, Iran (Islamic Republic of), Ireland, Israel, Liechtenstein, Myanmar, Namibia, New Zealand, Nigeria, Pakistan, Republic of Korea, San Marino, South Africa, Venezuela (Bolivarian Republic of), Zimbabwe

Nineteenth preambular paragraph*

In favour:

Afghanistan, Albania, Algeria, Andorra, Antigua and Barbuda, Argentina, Armenia, Australia, Austria, Azerbaijan, Bahamas, Bahrain, Bangladesh, Barbados, Belarus, Belgium, Belize, Benin, Bhutan, Bolivia (Plurinational State of), Bosnia and Herzegovina, Botswana, Brazil, Brunei Darussalam, Bulgaria, Burkina Faso, Burundi, Cabo Verde, Cambodia, Canada, Chad, Chile, Colombia, Comoros, Congo, Costa Rica, Côte d'Ivoire, Croatia, Cuba, Cyprus, Czech Republic, Denmark, Djibouti, Dominican Republic, Ecuador, Egypt, El Salvador, Equatorial Guinea, Eritrea, Estonia, Ethiopia, Fiji, Finland, Gabon, Gambia, Georgia, Germany, Ghana, Greece, Guatemala, Guinea-Bissau, Guyana,

---

* Subsequently, the delegation of South Africa informed the Secretariat that it had intended to vote against. The voting tally above does not reflect this information.

Haiti, Honduras, Hungary, Iceland, India, Indonesia, Iran (Islamic Republic of), Iraq, Italy, Jamaica, Japan, Jordan, Kazakhstan, Kenya, Kiribati, Kuwait, Kyrgyzstan, Lao People's Democratic Republic, Latvia, Lebanon, Lesotho, Liberia, Libya, Lithuania, Luxembourg, Madagascar, Malawi, Malaysia, Maldives, Mali, Marshall Islands, Mauritania, Mexico, Micronesia (Federated States of), Montenegro, Morocco, Mozambique, Myanmar, Nepal, Netherlands, Nicaragua, Nigeria, Norway, Oman, Panama, Papua New Guinea, Paraguay, Peru, Philippines, Poland, Portugal, Qatar, Republic of Moldova, Romania, Saint Kitts and Nevis, Saint Lucia, Saint Vincent and the Grenadines, Samoa, San Marino, Saudi Arabia, Senegal, Serbia, Sierra Leone, Singapore, Slovakia, Slovenia, Somalia, South Africa, Spain, Sri Lanka, Sudan, Suriname, Swaziland, Tajikistan, Thailand, the former Yugoslav Republic of Macedonia, Timor-Leste, Togo, Tonga, Trinidad and Tobago, Tunisia, Turkey, Turkmenistan, Tuvalu, Ukraine, United Arab Emirates, United Kingdom, United Republic of Tanzania, United States, Uruguay, Uzbekistan, Vanuatu, Venezuela (Bolivarian Republic of), Viet Nam, Yemen, Zambia

Against:
Russian Federation

Abstaining:
Angola, China, Democratic People's Republic of Korea, France, Ireland, Israel, Liechtenstein, Malta, Monaco, Mongolia, Namibia, New Zealand, Rwanda, Sweden, Switzerland, Uganda, Zimbabwe

Twentieth preambular paragraph

In favour:
Afghanistan, Albania, Algeria, Andorra, Antigua and Barbuda, Argentina, Armenia, Australia, Austria, Azerbaijan, Bahamas, Bahrain, Bangladesh, Barbados, Belarus, Belgium, Belize, Benin, Bhutan, Bolivia (Plurinational State of), Bosnia and Herzegovina, Botswana, Brazil, Brunei Darussalam, Bulgaria, Burkina Faso, Burundi, Cabo Verde, Cambodia, Canada, Chad, Chile, Colombia, Comoros, Congo, Costa Rica, Côte d'Ivoire, Croatia, Cuba, Cyprus, Czech Republic, Denmark, Djibouti, Dominican Republic, Ecuador, Egypt, El Salvador, Equatorial Guinea, Eritrea, Estonia, Ethiopia, Fiji, Finland, Gabon, Gambia, Georgia, Germany, Ghana, Greece, Guatemala, Guinea-Bissau, Guyana, Haiti, Honduras, Hungary, Iceland, India, Indonesia, Iran (Islamic Republic of), Iraq, Ireland, Italy, Jamaica, Japan, Jordan, Kazakhstan, Kenya, Kiribati, Kuwait, Kyrgyzstan, Lao People's Democratic Republic, Latvia, Lebanon, Lesotho, Liberia, Libya, Liechtenstein, Lithuania, Luxembourg, Madagascar, Malawi, Malaysia, Maldives, Mali, Malta, Marshall Islands, Mauritania, Mexico, Micronesia (Federated States

of), Mongolia, Montenegro, Morocco, Mozambique, Myanmar, Nepal, Netherlands, New Zealand, Nicaragua, Nigeria, Norway, Oman, Panama, Papua New Guinea, Paraguay, Peru, Philippines, Poland, Portugal, Qatar, Republic of Moldova, Romania, Saint Kitts and Nevis, Saint Lucia, Saint Vincent and the Grenadines, Samoa, San Marino, Saudi Arabia, Senegal, Serbia, Sierra Leone, Singapore, Slovakia, Slovenia, Solomon Islands, Somalia, South Africa, Spain, Sudan, Suriname, Swaziland, Sweden, Switzerland, Tajikistan, Thailand, the former Yugoslav Republic of Macedonia, Timor-Leste, Togo, Tonga, Trinidad and Tobago, Tunisia, Turkey, Turkmenistan, Tuvalu, Ukraine, United Arab Emirates, United Kingdom, United Republic of Tanzania, United States, Uruguay, Uzbekistan, Vanuatu, Venezuela (Bolivarian Republic of), Viet Nam, Yemen, Zambia, Zimbabwe

Against:

Russian Federation

Abstaining:

Angola, China, France, Israel, Monaco, Namibia, Rwanda, Uganda

Operative paragraph 2

In favour:

Afghanistan, Albania, Andorra, Antigua and Barbuda, Argentina, Armenia, Australia, Azerbaijan, Bahamas, Bahrain, Bangladesh, Barbados, Belarus, Belgium, Belize, Benin, Bhutan, Bosnia and Herzegovina, Botswana, Brunei Darussalam, Bulgaria, Burkina Faso, Burundi, Cabo Verde, Cambodia, Canada, Chad, China, Colombia, Comoros, Congo, Côte d'Ivoire, Croatia, Czech Republic, Denmark, Djibouti, Dominican Republic, El Salvador, Equatorial Guinea, Eritrea, Estonia, Ethiopia, Fiji, Finland, France, Gabon, Gambia, Georgia, Germany, Ghana, Greece, Guatemala, Guinea-Bissau, Guyana, Haiti, Honduras, Hungary, Iceland, Iraq, Italy, Jamaica, Japan, Jordan, Kazakhstan, Kenya, Kiribati, Kuwait, Kyrgyzstan, Latvia, Lebanon, Lesotho, Liberia, Libya, Lithuania, Luxembourg, Madagascar, Malawi, Maldives, Mali, Malta, Marshall Islands, Mauritania, Micronesia (Federated States of), Monaco, Montenegro, Morocco, Mozambique, Nepal, Netherlands, Nicaragua, Nigeria, Norway, Oman, Panama, Papua New Guinea, Paraguay, Peru, Philippines, Poland, Portugal, Qatar, Republic of Korea, Republic of Moldova, Romania, Saint Kitts and Nevis, Saint Lucia, Saint Vincent and the Grenadines, Samoa, Saudi Arabia, Senegal, Serbia, Sierra Leone, Singapore, Slovakia, Slovenia, Solomon Islands, Somalia, Spain, Sri Lanka, Sudan, Swaziland, Tajikistan, Thailand, the former Yugoslav Republic of Macedonia, Timor-Leste, Togo, Trinidad and Tobago, Tunisia, Turkey, Turkmenistan, Tuvalu, Ukraine, United Arab Emirates, United Kingdom, United

Republic of Tanzania, United States, Uruguay, Uzbekistan, Vanuatu, Viet Nam, Yemen, Zambia

Against:

Austria, Ecuador, Liechtenstein, Myanmar, New Zealand, South Africa, Switzerland

Abstaining:

Algeria, Angola, Bolivia (Plurinational State of), Brazil, Chile, Costa Rica, Cuba, Cyprus, Democratic People's Republic of Korea, Egypt, India, Indonesia, Iran (Islamic Republic of), Ireland, Israel, Malaysia, Mexico, Mongolia, Namibia, Pakistan, Russian Federation, Rwanda, San Marino, Sweden, Uganda, Venezuela (Bolivarian Republic of), Zimbabwe

Operative paragraph 5

In favour:

Afghanistan, Albania, Algeria, Andorra, Antigua and Barbuda, Argentina, Armenia, Australia, Austria, Azerbaijan, Bahamas, Bahrain, Bangladesh, Barbados, Belarus, Belgium, Belize, Benin, Bolivia (Plurinational State of), Bosnia and Herzegovina, Botswana, Brazil, Brunei Darussalam, Bulgaria, Burkina Faso, Burundi, Cabo Verde, Cambodia, Canada, Chad, Chile, China, Colombia, Comoros, Congo, Costa Rica, Côte d'Ivoire, Croatia, Cuba, Cyprus, Czech Republic, Denmark, Djibouti, Dominican Republic, Ecuador, Egypt, El Salvador, Equatorial Guinea, Eritrea, Estonia, Ethiopia, Fiji, Finland, France, Gabon, Gambia, Georgia, Germany, Ghana, Greece, Guatemala, Guinea-Bissau, Guyana, Haiti, Honduras, Hungary, Iceland, Indonesia, Iran (Islamic Republic of), Iraq, Ireland, Italy, Jamaica, Japan, Jordan, Kazakhstan, Kenya, Kiribati, Kuwait, Kyrgyzstan, Lao People's Democratic Republic, Latvia, Lebanon, Lesotho, Liberia, Libya, Liechtenstein, Lithuania, Luxembourg, Madagascar, Malawi, Malaysia, Maldives, Mali, Malta, Marshall Islands, Mauritania, Mexico, Micronesia (Federated States of), Monaco, Mongolia, Montenegro, Morocco, Mozambique, Myanmar, Nepal, Netherlands, New Zealand, Nicaragua, Nigeria, Norway, Oman, Panama, Papua New Guinea, Paraguay, Peru, Philippines, Poland, Portugal, Qatar, Republic of Korea, Republic of Moldova, Romania, Russian Federation, Saint Kitts and Nevis, Saint Lucia, Saint Vincent and the Grenadines, Samoa, San Marino, Saudi Arabia, Senegal, Serbia, Sierra Leone, Singapore, Slovakia, Slovenia, Solomon Islands, Somalia, South Africa, Spain, Sri Lanka, Sudan, Suriname, Swaziland, Sweden, Switzerland, Tajikistan, Thailand, the former Yugoslav Republic of Macedonia, Timor-Leste, Togo, Trinidad and Tobago, Tunisia, Turkey, Turkmenistan, Tuvalu, Ukraine, United Arab Emirates, United Kingdom, United Republic of Tanzania, United States, Uruguay, Uzbekistan,

Vanuatu, Venezuela (Bolivarian Republic of), Viet Nam, Yemen, Zambia, Zimbabwe

Against:

Democratic People's Republic of Korea, India, Israel, Pakistan

Abstaining:

Angola, Bhutan, Namibia, Rwanda, Uganda

Operative paragraph 8

In favour:

Afghanistan, Albania, Algeria, Andorra, Antigua and Barbuda, Argentina, Armenia, Australia, Austria, Azerbaijan, Bahamas, Bahrain, Bangladesh, Barbados, Belarus, Belgium, Belize, Benin, Bhutan, Bolivia (Plurinational State of), Bosnia and Herzegovina, Botswana, Brazil, Brunei Darussalam, Bulgaria, Burkina Faso, Burundi, Cabo Verde, Cambodia, Canada, Chad, Chile, Colombia, Comoros, Congo, Costa Rica, Côte d'Ivoire, Croatia, Cuba, Cyprus, Czech Republic, Denmark, Djibouti, Dominican Republic, Ecuador, Egypt, El Salvador, Equatorial Guinea, Eritrea, Estonia, Ethiopia, Fiji, Finland, Gabon, Gambia, Georgia, Germany, Ghana, Greece, Guatemala, Guinea-Bissau, Guyana, Haiti, Honduras, Hungary, Iceland, India, Indonesia, Iran (Islamic Republic of), Iraq, Italy, Jamaica, Japan, Jordan, Kazakhstan, Kenya, Kiribati, Kuwait, Kyrgyzstan, Lao People's Democratic Republic, Latvia, Lebanon, Lesotho, Liberia, Libya, Lithuania, Luxembourg, Madagascar, Malawi, Maldives, Mali, Marshall Islands, Mauritania, Mexico, Micronesia (Federated States of), Montenegro, Morocco, Mozambique, Myanmar, Nepal, Netherlands, Nicaragua, Nigeria, Norway, Oman, Panama, Papua New Guinea, Paraguay, Peru, Philippines, Poland, Portugal, Qatar, Republic of Moldova, Romania, Rwanda, Saint Kitts and Nevis, Saint Lucia, Saint Vincent and the Grenadines, Samoa, San Marino, Saudi Arabia, Senegal, Serbia, Sierra Leone, Singapore, Slovakia, Slovenia, Solomon Islands, Somalia, Spain, Sri Lanka, Sudan, Suriname, Swaziland, Tajikistan, Thailand, the former Yugoslav Republic of Macedonia, Timor-Leste, Togo, Trinidad and Tobago, Tunisia, Turkey, Turkmenistan, Tuvalu, Ukraine, United Arab Emirates, United Kingdom, United Republic of Tanzania, United States, Uruguay, Uzbekistan, Vanuatu, Venezuela (Bolivarian Republic of), Viet Nam, Yemen, Zambia

Against:

Russian Federation, South Africa

Abstaining:

Angola, China, France, Ireland, Israel, Liechtenstein, Malaysia, Malta, Monaco, Mongolia, Namibia, New Zealand, Sweden, Switzerland, Uganda, Zimbabwe

Operative paragraph 20**

In favour:

Afghanistan, Albania, Algeria, Andorra, Antigua and Barbuda, Argentina, Armenia, Australia, Austria, Azerbaijan, Bahamas, Bahrain, Bangladesh, Barbados, Belarus, Belgium, Belize, Benin, Bhutan, Bolivia (Plurinational State of), Bosnia and Herzegovina, Botswana, Brazil, Brunei Darussalam, Bulgaria, Burkina Faso, Burundi, Cabo Verde, Cambodia, Canada, Chad, Chile, Colombia, Comoros, Congo, Costa Rica, Côte d'Ivoire, Croatia, Cuba, Cyprus, Czech Republic, Denmark, Djibouti, Dominican Republic, Ecuador, El Salvador, Equatorial Guinea, Eritrea, Estonia, Ethiopia, Fiji, Finland, France, Gabon, Gambia, Georgia, Germany, Ghana, Greece, Guatemala, Guinea-Bissau, Guyana, Haiti, Honduras, Hungary, Iceland, Indonesia, Iraq, Ireland, Italy, Jamaica, Japan, Jordan, Kazakhstan, Kenya, Kiribati, Kuwait, Kyrgyzstan, Lao People's Democratic Republic, Latvia, Lebanon, Lesotho, Liberia, Libya, Liechtenstein, Lithuania, Luxembourg, Madagascar, Malawi, Malaysia, Maldives, Mali, Malta, Marshall Islands, Mauritania, Mexico, Micronesia (Federated States of), Monaco, Mongolia, Montenegro, Mozambique, Nepal, Netherlands, New Zealand, Nicaragua, Nigeria, Norway, Oman, Panama, Papua New Guinea, Paraguay, Peru, Philippines, Poland, Portugal, Qatar, Republic of Korea, Republic of Moldova, Romania, Russian Federation, Rwanda, Saint Kitts and Nevis, Saint Lucia, Saint Vincent and the Grenadines, Samoa, San Marino, Saudi Arabia, Senegal, Serbia, Sierra Leone, Singapore, Slovakia, Slovenia, Solomon Islands, Somalia, South Africa, Spain, Sri Lanka, Sudan, Suriname, Swaziland, Sweden, Switzerland, Tajikistan, the former Yugoslav Republic of Macedonia, Timor-Leste, Togo, Trinidad and Tobago, Tunisia, Turkey, Turkmenistan, Tuvalu, Ukraine, United Arab Emirates, United Kingdom, United Republic of Tanzania, United States, Uruguay, Uzbekistan, Vanuatu, Venezuela (Bolivarian Republic of), Viet Nam, Yemen, Zambia

Against:

China, Democratic People's Republic of Korea, Pakistan

Abstaining:

Angola, Egypt, India, Iran (Islamic Republic of), Israel, Morocco, Myanmar, Namibia, Thailand, Uganda, Zimbabwe

---

** Subsequently, the delegation of Morocco informed the Secretariat that it had intended to vote in favour. The voting tally above does not reflect this information.

Operative paragraph 21

In favour:

Afghanistan, Albania, Algeria, Andorra, Antigua and Barbuda, Argentina, Armenia, Australia, Azerbaijan, Bahamas, Bahrain, Bangladesh, Barbados, Belarus, Belgium, Belize, Benin, Bhutan, Bolivia (Plurinational State of), Bosnia and Herzegovina, Botswana, Brunei Darussalam, Bulgaria, Burkina Faso, Burundi, Cabo Verde, Cambodia, Canada, Chad, Chile, China, Colombia, Comoros, Congo, Côte d'Ivoire, Croatia, Czech Republic, Denmark, Djibouti, Dominican Republic, El Salvador, Equatorial Guinea, Eritrea, Estonia, Ethiopia, Fiji, Finland, France, Gabon, Gambia, Georgia, Germany, Ghana, Greece, Guatemala, Guinea-Bissau, Guyana, Haiti, Honduras, Hungary, Iceland, Iraq, Italy, Jamaica, Japan, Jordan, Kazakhstan, Kenya, Kiribati, Kuwait, Kyrgyzstan, Lao People's Democratic Republic, Latvia, Lebanon, Lesotho, Liberia, Libya, Lithuania, Luxembourg, Madagascar, Malawi, Maldives, Mali, Malta, Marshall Islands, Mauritania, Mexico, Micronesia (Federated States of), Monaco, Mongolia, Montenegro, Morocco, Mozambique, Nepal, Netherlands, New Zealand, Nicaragua, Nigeria, Norway, Oman, Panama, Papua New Guinea, Paraguay, Peru, Philippines, Poland, Portugal, Qatar, Republic of Korea, Republic of Moldova, Romania, Russian Federation, Rwanda, Saint Kitts and Nevis, Saint Lucia, Saint Vincent and the Grenadines, Samoa, San Marino, Saudi Arabia, Senegal, Serbia, Sierra Leone, Singapore, Slovakia, Slovenia, Solomon Islands, Somalia, South Africa, Spain, Sri Lanka, Sudan, Suriname, Swaziland, Sweden, Tajikistan, the former Yugoslav Republic of Macedonia, Timor-Leste, Togo, Trinidad and Tobago, Tunisia, Turkey, Turkmenistan, Tuvalu, Ukraine, United Arab Emirates, United Kingdom, United Republic of Tanzania, United States, Uruguay, Uzbekistan, Vanuatu, Viet Nam, Yemen, Zambia

Against:

Austria, Liechtenstein, Myanmar, Pakistan

Abstaining:

Angola, Brazil, Costa Rica, Cuba, Cyprus, Democratic People's Republic of Korea, Ecuador, Egypt, India, Indonesia, Iran (Islamic Republic of), Ireland, Israel, Malaysia, Namibia, Switzerland, Thailand, Venezuela (Bolivarian Republic of), Zimbabwe

Operative paragraph 28

In favour:

Afghanistan, Albania, Algeria, Andorra, Antigua and Barbuda, Argentina, Armenia, Australia, Austria, Azerbaijan, Bahamas, Bahrain, Bangladesh, Barbados, Belarus, Belgium, Belize, Benin, Bhutan, Bolivia (Plurinational State of), Bosnia and Herzegovina, Botswana, Brunei

Darussalam, Bulgaria, Burkina Faso, Burundi, Cabo Verde, Cambodia, Canada, Chad, Chile, China, Colombia, Comoros, Congo, Costa Rica, Côte d'Ivoire, Croatia, Cuba, Cyprus, Czech Republic, Denmark, Djibouti, Dominican Republic, Ecuador, El Salvador, Equatorial Guinea, Eritrea, Estonia, Ethiopia, Fiji, Finland, France, Gabon, Gambia, Georgia, Germany, Ghana, Greece, Guatemala, Guinea-Bissau, Guyana, Haiti, Honduras, Hungary, Iceland, Indonesia, Iraq, Ireland, Italy, Jamaica, Japan, Jordan, Kazakhstan, Kenya, Kiribati, Kuwait, Kyrgyzstan, Lao People's Democratic Republic, Latvia, Lebanon, Lesotho, Liberia, Libya, Liechtenstein, Lithuania, Luxembourg, Madagascar, Malawi, Malaysia, Maldives, Mali, Malta, Marshall Islands, Mauritania, Mexico, Micronesia (Federated States of), Monaco, Mongolia, Montenegro, Morocco, Mozambique, Nepal, Netherlands, New Zealand, Nicaragua, Nigeria, Norway, Oman, Panama, Papua New Guinea, Paraguay, Peru, Philippines, Poland, Portugal, Qatar, Republic of Korea, Republic of Moldova, Romania, Russian Federation, Rwanda, Saint Kitts and Nevis, Saint Lucia, Saint Vincent and the Grenadines, Samoa, San Marino, Saudi Arabia, Senegal, Serbia, Sierra Leone, Singapore, Slovakia, Slovenia, Solomon Islands, Somalia, South Africa, Spain, Sri Lanka, Sudan, Swaziland, Sweden, Switzerland, Tajikistan, Thailand, the former Yugoslav Republic of Macedonia, Timor-Leste, Togo, Trinidad and Tobago, Tunisia, Turkey, Turkmenistan, Tuvalu, Ukraine, United Arab Emirates, United Kingdom, United Republic of Tanzania, United States, Uruguay, Uzbekistan, Vanuatu, Viet Nam, Yemen, Zambia

Against:
Democratic People's Republic of Korea

Abstaining:
Angola, Brazil, Egypt, India, Israel, Myanmar, Namibia, Pakistan, Uganda, Venezuela (Bolivarian Republic of), Zimbabwe

Action by the First Committee

Date:	27 October 2017	Meeting:	24th meeting
Vote:	144-4-27	Draft resolution:	A/C.1/72/L.35
	147-1-19, p.p. 19		
	155-2-10, p.p. 20		
	128-7-27, o.p. 2		
	161-4-3, o.p. 5		
	149-2-16, o.p. 8		
	155-4-11, o.p. 20		
	143-4-22, o.p. 21		
	155-2-9, o.p. 28		

Agenda item 99

72/51   International Day against Nuclear Tests

Text

The General Assembly,

Recalling its resolution 64/35 of 2 December 2009, and that the promotion of peace and security is among the main purposes and principles of the United Nations embodied in the Charter,

Convinced that every effort should be made to end nuclear tests in order to avert devastating and harmful effects on the lives and health of people and the environment,

Convinced also that the end of nuclear tests is one of the key means of achieving the goal of a nuclear-weapon-free world,

Welcoming the recent positive momentum in the international community to work towards this goal,

Emphasizing in this context the essential role of Governments, intergovernmental organizations, civil society, academia and mass media,

Acknowledging the related importance of education as a tool for peace, security, disarmament and non-proliferation,

1.   *Reiterates* that 29 August was declared the International Day against Nuclear Tests, devoted to enhancing public awareness and education about the effects of nuclear weapon test explosions or any other nuclear explosions and the need for their cessation as one of the means of achieving the goal of a nuclear-weapon-free world;

2.   *Invites* Member States, the United Nations system, civil society, academia, the mass media and individuals to commemorate the International Day against Nuclear Tests in an appropriate manner, including through all means of educational and public awareness-raising activities;

3.   *Requests* the President of the General Assembly to organize annually a high-level plenary meeting of the Assembly to commemorate and promote the International Day against Nuclear Tests.

Action by the General Assembly

Date: 4 December 2017   Meeting: 62nd plenary meeting
Vote: Adopted without a vote   Report: A/72/409

Sponsors

Angola, Austria, Belarus, Brazil, Dominican Republic, Egypt, El Salvador, Eritrea, Italy, Japan, **Kazakhstan**, Kenya, Mongolia, Nicaragua, Panama,

Papua New Guinea, Philippines, Portugal, Sierra Leone, Sudan, Venezuela (Bolivarian Republic of), Zambia

Co-sponsors

Afghanistan, Azerbaijan, Bangladesh, Central African Republic, Costa Rica, Cyprus, Ecuador, Iran (Islamic Republic of), Kyrgyzstan, Lebanon, Maldives, Marshall Islands, Nigeria, Paraguay, Republic of Korea, Samoa, Spain, Tajikistan, Turkmenistan, Uzbekistan

Action by the First Committee

Date: 27 October 2017   Meeting: 24th meeting
Vote: Adopted without a vote   Draft resolution: A/C.1/72/L.36

Agenda item 99 (e)

72/52   Prohibition of the dumping of radioactive wastes

Text

The General Assembly,

Bearing in mind resolutions CM/Res.1153 (XLVIII) of 1988[1] and CM/Res.1225 (L) of 1989,[2] adopted by the Council of Ministers of the Organization of African Unity, concerning the dumping of nuclear and industrial wastes in Africa,

Welcoming resolution GC(XXXIV)/RES/530 establishing the Code of Practice on the International Transboundary Movement of Radioactive Waste, adopted on 21 September 1990 by the General Conference of the International Atomic Energy Agency at its thirty-fourth regular session,

Taking note of the commitment made by the participants in the Summit on Nuclear Safety and Security, held in Moscow on 19 and 20 April 1996, to ban the dumping at sea of radioactive wastes,[3]

Considering its resolution 2602 C (XXIV) of 16 December 1969, in which the General Assembly requested the Conference of the Committee on Disarmament,[4] inter alia, to consider effective methods of control against the use of radiological methods of warfare,

Aware of the potential hazards underlying any use of radioactive wastes that would constitute radiological warfare and its implications for regional and international security, in particular for the security of developing countries,

Recalling all its resolutions on the matter since its forty-third session in 1988, including its resolution 51/45 J of 10 December 1996,

Recalling also resolution GC(45)/RES/10, adopted by consensus on 21 September 2001 by the General Conference of the International Atomic Energy Agency at its forty-fifth regular session, in which States shipping radioactive materials are invited to provide, as appropriate, assurances to concerned States, upon their request, that the national regulations of the shipping State take into account the Agency's transport regulations and to provide them with relevant information relating to the shipment of such materials; with the information provided being in no case contradictory to the measures of physical security and safety,

---

[1] See A/43/398, annex I.

[2] See A/44/603, annex I.

[3] A/51/131, annex I, para. 20.

[4] The Conference of the Committee on Disarmament became the Committee on Disarmament as from the tenth special session of the General Assembly. The Committee on Disarmament was redesignated the Conference on Disarmament as from 7 February 1984.

Welcoming the adoption, in Vienna on 5 September 1997, of the Joint Convention on the Safety of Spent Fuel Management and on the Safety of Radioactive Waste Management,[5] as recommended by the participants in the Summit on Nuclear Safety and Security,

Welcoming also the convening by the International Atomic Energy Agency of the Ministerial Conference on Nuclear Safety, in Vienna from 20 to 24 June 2011, and its outcome, the Declaration of the International Atomic Energy Agency Ministerial Conference on Nuclear Safety, as well as the Action Plan on Nuclear Safety, endorsed by the General Conference of the Agency at its fifty-fifth regular session,

Noting the convening by the Secretary-General of the high-level meeting on nuclear safety and security, in New York on 22 September 2011,

Noting with satisfaction that the Joint Convention entered into force on 18 June 2001,

Noting that the first Review Meeting of the Contracting Parties to the Joint Convention on the Safety of Spent Fuel Management and on the Safety of Radioactive Waste Management was convened in Vienna from 3 to 14 November 2003,

Desirous of promoting the implementation of paragraph 76 of the Final Document of the Tenth Special Session of the General Assembly, the first special session devoted to disarmament,[6]

1.   *Takes note* of the part of the report of the Conference on Disarmament relating to radiological weapons;[7]

2.   *Also takes note* of the Declaration of the International Atomic Energy Agency Ministerial Conference on Nuclear Safety, the Action Plan on Nuclear Safety and the high-level meeting on nuclear safety and security convened by the Secretary-General;

3.   *Expresses grave concern* regarding any use of nuclear wastes that would constitute radiological warfare and have grave implications for the national security of all States;

4.   *Calls upon* all States to take appropriate measures with a view to preventing any dumping of nuclear or radioactive wastes that would infringe upon the sovereignty of States;

5.   *Requests* the Conference on Disarmament to take into account, in any negotiations for a convention on the prohibition of radiological weapons, radioactive wastes as part of the scope of such a convention;

---

[5] United Nations, *Treaty Series*, vol. 2153, No. 37605.
[6] Resolution S-10/2.
[7] *Official Records of the General Assembly, Seventy-second Session, Supplement No. 27* (A/72/27), sect. III.E.

6.   *Also requests* the Conference on Disarmament to continue to consider such a convention and to include in its report to the General Assembly at its seventy-third session the progress recorded in the negotiations on this subject;

7.   *Takes note* of resolution CM/Res.1356 (LIV) of 1991, adopted by the Council of Ministers of the Organization of African Unity,[8] on the Bamako Convention on the Ban on the Import of Hazardous Wastes into Africa and on the Control of Their Transboundary Movements within Africa;

8.   *Expresses the hope* that the effective implementation of the International Atomic Energy Agency Code of Practice on the International Transboundary Movement of Radioactive Waste will enhance the protection of all States from the dumping of radioactive wastes on their territories;

9.   *Appeals* to all Member States that have not yet taken the steps necessary to become party to the Joint Convention on the Safety of Spent Fuel Management and on the Safety of Radioactive Waste Management[5] to do so as soon as possible;

10.   *Decides* to include in the provisional agenda of its seventy-fourth session, under the item entitled "General and complete disarmament", the sub-item entitled "Prohibition of the dumping of radioactive wastes".

Action by the General Assembly

Date: 4 December 2017   Meeting: 62nd plenary meeting
Vote: Adopted without a vote   Report: A/72/409

Sponsors

Nigeria (on behalf of the States Members of the United Nations that are members of the Group of African States)

Co-sponsors

Maldives

Action by the First Committee

Date: 27 October 2017   Meeting: 24th meeting
Vote: Adopted without a vote   Draft resolution: A/C.1/72/L.38

---

[8] See A/46/390, annex I.

Agenda item 99 (m)

72/53 Implementation of the Convention on the Prohibition of the Use, Stockpiling, Production and Transfer of Anti-Personnel Mines and on Their Destruction

Text

The General Assembly,

Recalling its resolutions 54/54 B of 1 December 1999, 55/33 V of 20 November 2000, 56/24 M of 29 November 2001, 57/74 of 22 November 2002, 58/53 of 8 December 2003, 59/84 of 3 December 2004, 60/80 of 8 December 2005, 61/84 of 6 December 2006, 62/41 of 5 December 2007, 63/42 of 2 December 2008, 64/56 of 2 December 2009, 65/48 of 8 December 2010, 66/29 of 2 December 2011, 67/32 of 3 December 2012, 68/30 of 5 December 2013, 69/34 of 2 December 2014, 70/55 of 7 December 2015 and 71/34 of 5 December 2016,

Reaffirming its determination to put an end to the suffering and casualties caused by anti-personnel mines, which kill or injure thousands of people – women, girls, boys and men – every year, and which place people living in affected areas at risk and hinder the development of their communities,

Believing it necessary to do the utmost to contribute in an efficient and coordinated manner to facing the challenge of removing anti-personnel mines placed throughout the world and to assure their destruction,

Wishing to do the utmost to ensure assistance for the care and rehabilitation, including the social and economic reintegration, of mine victims,

Noting with satisfaction the work undertaken to implement the Convention on the Prohibition of the Use, Stockpiling, Production and Transfer of Anti-Personnel Mines and on Their Destruction[1] and the substantial progress made towards addressing the global anti-personnel landmine problem,

Recalling the first to fifteenth meetings of the States parties to the Convention, held in Maputo (1999), Geneva (2000), Managua (2001), Geneva (2002), Bangkok (2003), Zagreb (2005), Geneva (2006), the Dead Sea (2007), Geneva (2008 and 2010), Phnom Penh (2011), Geneva (2012, 2013 and 2015) and Santiago (2016), and the First, Second and Third Review Conferences of the States Parties to the Convention, held in Nairobi (2004), Cartagena, Colombia (2009), and Maputo (2014),

---

[1] United Nations, *Treaty Series*, vol. 2056, No. 35597.

Recalling also that, at the Third Review Conference of the States Parties to the Convention, the international community reviewed the implementation of the Convention and the States parties adopted a declaration and an action plan for the period 2014–2019 to support enhanced implementation and promotion of the Convention,

Underlining the importance of cooperation and assistance in the implementation of the Convention, including through the so-called individualized approach, which offers mine-affected countries a platform for presenting their challenges,

Noting with satisfaction that 162 States have ratified or acceded to the Convention and have formally accepted the obligations of the Convention,

Emphasizing the desirability of attracting the adherence of all States to the Convention, and determined to work strenuously towards the promotion of its universalization and norms,

Noting with regret that anti-personnel mines continue to be used in some conflicts around the world, causing human suffering and impeding post-conflict development,

1. *Invites* all States that have not signed the Convention on the Prohibition of the Use, Stockpiling, Production and Transfer of Anti-Personnel Mines and on Their Destruction[1] to accede to it without delay;

2. *Urges* the one remaining State that has signed but has not ratified the Convention to ratify it without delay;

3. *Stresses* the importance of the full and effective implementation of and compliance with the Convention, including through the continued implementation of the action plan for the period 2014–2019;

4. *Expresses strong concern* regarding the use of anti-personnel mines in various parts of the world, including use highlighted in recent allegations, reports and documented evidence;

5. *Urges* all States parties to provide the Secretary-General with complete and timely information as required under article 7 of the Convention in order to promote transparency and compliance with the Convention;

6. *Invites* all States that have not ratified the Convention or acceded to it to provide, on a voluntary basis, information to make global mine action efforts more effective;

7. *Renews its call upon* all States and other relevant parties to work together to promote, support and advance the care, rehabilitation and social and economic reintegration of mine victims, mine risk education programmes and the removal and destruction of anti-personnel mines placed or stockpiled throughout the world;

8. *Urges* all States to remain seized of the issue at the highest political level and, where in a position to do so, to promote adherence to the Convention through bilateral, subregional, regional and multilateral contacts, outreach, seminars and other means;

9. *Reiterates its invitation and encouragement* to all interested States, the United Nations, other relevant international organizations or institutions, regional organizations, the International Committee of the Red Cross and relevant non-governmental organizations to attend the Sixteenth Meeting of the States Parties to the Convention, to be held in Vienna from 18 to 21 December 2017, and to participate in the future programme of meetings of the States parties to the Convention;

10. *Requests* the Secretary-General, in accordance with article 11, paragraph 1, of the Convention, to undertake the preparations necessary to convene the Seventeenth Meeting of the States Parties to the Convention and, on behalf of the States parties and in accordance with article 11, paragraph 4, of the Convention, to invite States not parties to the Convention, as well as the United Nations, other relevant international organizations or institutions, regional organizations, the International Committee of the Red Cross and relevant non-governmental organizations, to attend the Seventeenth Meeting of the States Parties as observers;

11. *Calls upon* States parties and participating States to address issues arising from outstanding dues and from recently implemented United Nations financial and accounting practices;

12. *Decides* to include in the provisional agenda of its seventy-third session, under the item entitled "General and complete disarmament", the sub-item entitled "Implementation of the Convention on the Prohibition of the Use, Stockpiling, Production and Transfer of Anti-Personnel Mines and on Their Destruction".

Action by the General Assembly

Date: 4 December 2017   Meeting: 62nd plenary meeting
Vote: 167-0-17   Report: A/72/409

Sponsors

Afghanistan, **Austria**, Chile

Recorded vote*

In favour:

Afghanistan, Albania, Algeria, Andorra, Angola, Antigua and Barbuda, Argentina, Armenia, Australia, Austria, Azerbaijan, Bahamas, Bahrain,

---

* Subsequently, the delegation of Oman informed the Secretariat that it had intended to vote in favour. The voting tally above does not reflect this information.

Bangladesh, Barbados, Belarus, Belgium, Belize, Benin, Bhutan, Bolivia (Plurinational State of), Bosnia and Herzegovina, Botswana, Brazil, Brunei Darussalam, Bulgaria, Burkina Faso, Burundi, Cabo Verde, Cambodia, Cameroon, Canada, Central African Republic, Chad, Chile, China, Colombia, Comoros, Congo, Costa Rica, Côte d'Ivoire, Croatia, Cyprus, Czech Republic, Denmark, Djibouti, Dominican Republic, Ecuador, El Salvador, Equatorial Guinea, Eritrea, Estonia, Ethiopia, Fiji, Finland, France, Gabon, Gambia, Georgia, Germany, Ghana, Greece, Guatemala, Guinea, Guinea-Bissau, Guyana, Haiti, Honduras, Hungary, Iceland, Indonesia, Iraq, Ireland, Italy, Jamaica, Japan, Jordan, Kazakhstan, Kenya, Kiribati, Kuwait, Kyrgyzstan, Lao People's Democratic Republic, Latvia, Lesotho, Liberia, Libya, Liechtenstein, Lithuania, Luxembourg, Madagascar, Malawi, Malaysia, Maldives, Mali, Malta, Marshall Islands, Mauritania, Mauritius, Mexico, Micronesia (Federated States of), Monaco, Mongolia, Montenegro, Morocco, Mozambique, Namibia, Netherlands, New Zealand, Nicaragua, Nigeria, Norway, Palau, Panama, Papua New Guinea, Paraguay, Peru, Philippines, Poland, Portugal, Qatar, Republic of Moldova, Romania, Rwanda, Saint Kitts and Nevis, Saint Lucia, Saint Vincent and the Grenadines, Samoa, San Marino, Senegal, Serbia, Sierra Leone, Singapore, Slovakia, Slovenia, Solomon Islands, Somalia, South Africa, Spain, Sri Lanka, Sudan, Suriname, Swaziland, Sweden, Switzerland, Tajikistan, Thailand, the former Yugoslav Republic of Macedonia, Timor-Leste, Togo, Tonga, Trinidad and Tobago, Tunisia, Turkey, Turkmenistan, Tuvalu, Uganda, Ukraine, United Arab Emirates, United Kingdom, United Republic of Tanzania, Uruguay, Vanuatu, Venezuela (Bolivarian Republic of), Yemen, Zambia, Zimbabwe

Against:
None

Abstaining:
Cuba, Democratic People's Republic of Korea, Egypt, India, Iran (Islamic Republic of), Israel, Myanmar, Nepal, Oman, Pakistan, Republic of Korea, Russian Federation, Saudi Arabia, Syrian Arab Republic, United States, Uzbekistan, Viet Nam

Action by the First Committee

Date: 31 October 2017	Meeting:	26th meeting
Vote: 158-0-16	Draft resolution:	A/C.1/72/L.40

Agenda item 99 (hh)

72/54   Implementation of the Convention on Cluster Munitions

Text

The General Assembly,

Recalling its resolutions 63/71 of 2 December 2008 on the Convention on Cluster Munitions and 70/54 of 7 December 2015 and 71/45 of 5 December 2016 on the implementation of the Convention,

Reaffirming its determination to put an end for all time to the suffering and casualties caused by cluster munitions at the time of their use, when they fail to function as intended or when they are abandoned,

Deploring the recent rise in the use of cluster munitions and related civilian casualties, and calling upon those who continue to use cluster munitions to cease any such activity immediately,

Conscious that cluster munition remnants kill or maim civilians, including women and children, obstruct economic and social development, including through the loss of livelihood, impede post-conflict rehabilitation and reconstruction, delay or prevent the return of refugees and internally displaced persons, can have a negative impact on national and international peacebuilding and humanitarian assistance efforts, and have other severe consequences for many years after use,

Concerned about the dangers presented by the large national stockpiles of cluster munitions retained for operational use, and determined to ensure their rapid destruction,

Believing it necessary to contribute effectively in an efficient, coordinated manner to resolving the challenge of removing cluster munition remnants located throughout the world, and to ensure their destruction,

Mindful of the need to coordinate adequately efforts undertaken in various forums, including through the Convention on the Rights of Persons with Disabilities,[1] to address the rights and needs of victims of various types of weapons, and resolved to avoid discrimination among victims of various types of weapons,

Reaffirming that in cases not covered by the Convention on Cluster Munitions[2] or by other international agreements, civilians and combatants remain under the protection and authority of the principles of international law, derived from established custom, from the principles of humanity and from the dictates of public conscience,

---

[1] United Nations, *Treaty Series*, vol. 2515, No. 44910.
[2] Ibid., vol. 2688, No. 47713.

Welcoming the steps taken nationally, regionally and globally in recent years aimed at prohibiting, restricting or suspending the use, stockpiling, production and transfer of cluster munitions, and welcoming in this regard that, since 2014, all Central American States have joined the Convention, thus fulfilling their aspiration to become the first cluster munitions-free region in the world,

Stressing the role of public conscience in furthering the principles of humanity, as evidenced by the global call for an end to civilian suffering caused by cluster munitions, and recognizing the efforts to that end undertaken by the United Nations, the International Committee of the Red Cross, the Cluster Munition Coalition and numerous other non-governmental organizations around the world,

Noting that a total of 119 States have joined the Convention, 102 as States parties and 17 as signatories,

Taking note of the 2015 Dubrovnik Declaration[3] and the Dubrovnik Action Plan[4] adopted at the First Review Conference of States Parties to the Convention on Cluster Munitions, held in Dubrovnik, Croatia, from 7 to 11 September 2015,

Taking note also of the political declaration establishing 2030 as a target date to implement all individual and collective outstanding obligations under the Convention as adopted by consensus under the presidency of the Netherlands at the Sixth Meeting of States Parties to the Convention on Cluster Munitions, held in Geneva from 5 to 7 September 2016,

Welcoming the dialogue undertaken by the German presidency of the Seventh Meeting of States Parties with States not parties to the Convention, including the military-to-military dialogue, in support of universal adherence to the Convention, and recognizing the assistance that the country coalition concept can provide to affected countries in the implementation of their obligations under the Convention,

1. *Urges* all States outside the Convention on Cluster Munitions[2] to join as soon as possible, whether by ratifying or acceding to it, and all States parties that are in a position to do so to promote adherence to the Convention through bilateral, subregional and multilateral contacts, outreach and other means;

2. *Stresses* the importance of the full and effective implementation of and compliance with the Convention, including through the implementation of the Dubrovnik Action Plan;[4]

---

[3] CCM/CONF/2015/7 and CCM/CONF/2015/7/Corr.1, annex I.
[4] Ibid., annex III.

3. *Expresses strong concern* regarding the rising number of allegations, reports or documented evidence of the use of cluster munitions in different parts of the world and related civilian casualties;

4. *Urges* all States parties to provide the Secretary-General with complete and timely information as required under article 7 of the Convention in order to promote transparency and compliance with the Convention;

5. *Invites* all States that have not ratified the Convention or acceded to it to provide, on a voluntary basis, information that could make the clearance and destruction of cluster munition remnants and related activities more effective;

6. *Reiterates* the invitation to States not parties to participate in a continued dialogue on issues relevant to the Convention in order to enhance its humanitarian impact and to promote its universalization, as well as to engage in a military-to-military dialogue in order to address specific security issues related to cluster munitions;

7. *Reiterates its invitation and encouragement* to all States parties, interested States, the United Nations, other relevant international organizations or institutions, regional organizations, the International Committee of the Red Cross, the Cluster Munition Coalition and other relevant non-governmental organizations to participate in the future meetings of States parties to the Convention;

8. *Calls upon* States parties and participating States to address issues arising from outstanding dues and from recently implemented United Nations financial and accounting practices;

9. *Decides* to remain seized of the matter.

Action by the General Assembly

Date: 4 December 2017   Meeting: 62nd plenary meeting
Vote: 142-2-36   Report: A/72/409

Sponsors

Angola, Austria, Belgium, Bosnia and Herzegovina, Bulgaria, Croatia, Czech Republic, El Salvador, France, **Germany**, Hungary, Iceland, Iraq, Ireland, Italy, Lao People's Democratic Republic, Lebanon, Liechtenstein, Luxembourg, Malta, Montenegro, Netherlands, Nicaragua, Norway, Panama, Portugal, Slovakia, Slovenia, Spain, Sweden, Switzerland

Co-sponsors

Andorra, Australia, Benin, Chile, Costa Rica, Denmark, Ecuador, Guyana, Monaco, Mozambique, New Zealand, Republic of Moldova,

San Marino, the former Yugoslav Republic of Macedonia, Trinidad and Tobago, United Kingdom, Zambia

Recorded vote

In favour:

Afghanistan, Albania, Algeria, Andorra, Angola, Antigua and Barbuda, Australia, Austria, Azerbaijan, Bahamas, Bangladesh, Barbados, Belgium, Belize, Benin, Bhutan, Bolivia (Plurinational State of), Bosnia and Herzegovina, Botswana, Brunei Darussalam, Bulgaria, Burkina Faso, Burundi, Cabo Verde, Cameroon, Canada, Chad, Chile, Colombia, Comoros, Congo, Costa Rica, Côte d'Ivoire, Croatia, Cuba, Czech Republic, Denmark, Djibouti, Dominican Republic, Ecuador, El Salvador, Equatorial Guinea, Eritrea, Ethiopia, Fiji, France, Gabon, Gambia, Germany, Ghana, Guatemala, Guinea, Guinea-Bissau, Guyana, Haiti, Honduras, Hungary, Iceland, Indonesia, Iraq, Ireland, Italy, Jamaica, Japan, Jordan, Kazakhstan, Kenya, Kiribati, Kyrgyzstan, Lao People's Democratic Republic, Lebanon, Lesotho, Liberia, Libya, Liechtenstein, Lithuania, Luxembourg, Madagascar, Malawi, Malaysia, Maldives, Mali, Malta, Marshall Islands, Mauritania, Mauritius, Mexico, Micronesia (Federated States of), Monaco, Mongolia, Montenegro, Mozambique, Namibia, Nepal, Netherlands, New Zealand, Nicaragua, Nigeria, Norway, Palau, Panama, Papua New Guinea, Paraguay, Peru, Philippines, Portugal, Republic of Moldova, Rwanda, Saint Kitts and Nevis, Saint Lucia, Saint Vincent and the Grenadines, Samoa, San Marino, Senegal, Sierra Leone, Singapore, Slovakia, Slovenia, Solomon Islands, Somalia, South Africa, Spain, Sri Lanka, Sudan, Suriname, Swaziland, Sweden, Switzerland, Thailand, the former Yugoslav Republic of Macedonia, Timor-Leste, Togo, Trinidad and Tobago, Tunisia, Tuvalu, United Kingdom, United Republic of Tanzania, Uruguay, Vanuatu, Venezuela (Bolivarian Republic of), Yemen, Zambia

Against:

Russian Federation, Zimbabwe

Abstaining:

Argentina, Armenia, Bahrain, Belarus, Brazil, China, Cyprus, Egypt, Estonia, Finland, Georgia, Greece, India, Iran (Islamic Republic of), Israel, Kuwait, Latvia, Morocco, Myanmar, Oman, Pakistan, Poland, Qatar, Republic of Korea, Romania, Saudi Arabia, Serbia, Syrian Arab Republic, Tajikistan, Turkey, Uganda, Ukraine, United Arab Emirates, United States, Uzbekistan, Viet Nam

Action by the First Committee

Date: 31 October 2017	Meeting: 26th meeting
Vote: 134-2-36	Draft resolution: A/C.1/72/L.41

Agenda item 99 (u)

72/55   Problems arising from the accumulation of conventional ammunition stockpiles in surplus

Text

The General Assembly,

Mindful of the dangers posed by unplanned explosions at munitions sites and the diversion of materials from conventional ammunition stockpiles to the illicit market, including for the manufacture of improvised explosive devices,

Emphasizing that thousands of people have died and the livelihoods of entire communities have been disrupted as a result of accidental ammunition depot explosions and that diversion from ammunition stockpiles has contributed to the intensity and duration of armed conflict and sustained armed violence around the world,[1]

Noting that conventional weapons and their ammunition are items for which, in principle, action can be taken to improve the regulation of transfers and prevent their diversion to illicit trafficking,

Recognizing the urgency of addressing the security and safety risks emanating from ineffective stockpile management around the world,[2]

Welcoming the requirement of the Arms Trade Treaty[3] that States parties thereto establish and maintain a national control system to regulate the export of relevant ammunition and munitions,

Taking note of the report of the Group of Experts on the problem of ammunition and explosives,[4]

Welcoming the adoption of the 2030 Agenda for Sustainable Development[5] and its recognition of the relevance for development of a significant reduction in illicit arms flows and of strengthened institutions for building capacity at all levels, in particular in developing countries, to prevent violence and combat terrorism and crime,

Recalling the recommendation contained in paragraph 27 of the report of the Open-ended Working Group to Negotiate an International Instrument to Enable States to Identify and Trace, in a Timely and Reliable Manner, Illicit Small Arms and Light Weapons,[6] namely, to address the issue of small

---

[1] See S/2011/255.
[2] See S/2015/289.
[3] See resolution 67/234 B.
[4] See A/54/155.
[5] Resolution 70/1.
[6] A/60/88 and A/60/88/Corr.2.

arms and light weapons ammunition in a comprehensive manner as part of a separate process conducted within the framework of the United Nations,

Taking note of the discussions on munitions management practice in the framework of Protocol V[7] to the Convention on Prohibitions or Restrictions on the Use of Certain Conventional Weapons Which May Be Deemed to Be Excessively Injurious or to Have Indiscriminate Effects,[8]

Noting with satisfaction the work and measures pursued at the regional and subregional levels with regard to the issue of conventional ammunition,

Recalling its decision 59/515 of 3 December 2004 and its resolutions 60/74 of 8 December 2005 and 61/72 of 6 December 2006, its resolution 63/61 of 2 December 2008, by which it welcomed the report of the Group of Governmental Experts established pursuant to resolution 61/72 to consider further steps to enhance cooperation with regard to the issue of conventional ammunition stockpiles in surplus,[9] its resolution 64/51 of 2 December 2009, its resolution 66/42 of 2 December 2011, its resolution 68/52 of 5 December 2013 and its resolution 70/35 of 7 December 2015,

Taking note of the recommendations of the Group of Governmental Experts, and encouraging the use, as appropriate, of the voluntary International Ammunition Technical Guidelines to improve the safety and security of ammunition storage sites,

Taking note also of the recommendations of the Group on improving knowledge resource management on technical ammunition issues within the United Nations system, and noting the subsequent establishment, within the Secretariat, of the Saf*er*Guard knowledge resource management programme,[10] including its online implementation support tools,

Noting that the voluntary International Ammunition Technical Guidelines are used by national authorities and an expanding network of partners from international and regional organizations, non-governmental organizations and the private sector in an increasing number of States to support ammunition stockpile management efforts,

Emphasizing the need to consider integrating ammunition management measures in accordance with the International Ammunition Technical Guidelines, where relevant, in mandates of United Nations peacekeeping operations and special political missions,

Recognizing the importance of appropriate national ammunition management structures and procedures, including laws and regulations, training and doctrine, equipment and maintenance, personnel management

---

[7] United Nations, *Treaty Series*, vol. 2399, No. 22495.

[8] Ibid., vol. 1342, No. 22495.

[9] A/63/182.

[10] Ibid., paras. 72 and 73.

and finances and infrastructure in order to ensure sustainability in ammunition management, and emphasizing in this regard the central role of the provision of technical assistance and capacity-building to Member States, upon their request,

1.   *Encourages* all interested States to assess, on a voluntary basis, whether, in conformity with their legitimate security needs, parts of their stockpiles of conventional ammunition should be considered to be in surplus, and recognizes that the security of such stockpiles must be taken into consideration and that appropriate controls with regard to the security and safety of stockpiles of conventional ammunition are indispensable at the national level in order to eliminate the risk of explosion, pollution or diversion;

2.   *Appeals* to all interested States to determine the size and nature of their surplus stockpiles of conventional ammunition, whether they represent a security risk, their means of destruction, if appropriate, and whether external assistance is needed to eliminate this risk;

3.   *Encourages* States in a position to do so to assist interested States within a bilateral framework or through international or regional organizations, including through activities conducted under the umbrella of the SaferGuard knowledge resource management programme,[10] on a voluntary and transparent basis, in elaborating and implementing programmes to eliminate surplus stockpiles or to improve stockpile management;

4.   *Encourages* all Member States to examine the possibility of developing and implementing, within a national, regional or subregional framework, measures to address accordingly the illicit trafficking related to the accumulation of such stockpiles;

5.   *Continues to encourage* States to implement the recommendations contained in the report of the Group of Governmental Experts established pursuant to resolution 61/72 to consider further steps to enhance cooperation with regard to the issue of conventional ammunition stockpiles in surplus;[9]

6.   *Notes with appreciation* initiatives at the international, regional and national levels that shed light on improving the sustainable management of ammunition, including through the implementation of the International Ammunition Technical Guidelines, and recognizing the relevance of continued discussions and coordination in this regard;

7.   *Recalls* the release of the updated version of the International Ammunition Technical Guidelines in 2015 and the continued implementation of the SaferGuard programme for the management of conventional ammunition stockpiles, developed by the Office for Disarmament Affairs of the Secretariat, with the full involvement of the Mine Action Service of the Department of Peacekeeping Operations of the Secretariat, in accordance with

the recommendations contained in the report of the Group of Governmental Experts;

8. *Welcomes* the continued application of the International Ammunition Technical Guidelines in the field, including the online implementation support and training materials, also welcomes the availability of translations of the Guidelines in various languages, encourages States in a position to do so to offer support to the Safe*r*Guard programme in undertaking additional translations, and calls upon all United Nations agencies to make full use of the Guidelines when supporting national authorities;

9. *Encourages* the consideration of the integration of ammunition management measures, where relevant, in the mandates of peacekeeping operations, including through the training of personnel of national authorities and peacekeepers, utilizing the International Ammunition Technical Guidelines;

10. *Welcomes* the ongoing work carried out by the Safe*r*Guard programme to establish its quick-response mechanism, which allows ammunition experts to be deployed rapidly to assist States, upon request, in the urgent management of ammunition stockpiles, including in the aftermath of unintended explosions of ammunition, and encourages States in a position to do so to provide technical expertise or financial support to the mechanism;

11. *Encourages* States wishing to improve their national ammunition stockpile management capacity, wishing to prevent the growth of conventional ammunition surpluses and wishing to implement wider risk mitigation to contact the Safe*r*Guard programme, as well as potential national donors, regional organizations or other organizations, as appropriate;

12. *Encourages* States, as appropriate, to consider ammunition management as an intrinsic part of their actions for achieving relevant targets of the Sustainable Development Goals related to the reduction of illicit arms flows and the prevention of violence through strengthened institutions, and to consider, where relevant, developing national, regional and subregional indicators based on this understanding;

13. *Asks* the Secretariat to assist States in this regard, upon their request, within existing resources, by developing options for such indicators, which may serve as voluntary examples for those States interested in adopting additional national, regional and subregional indicators on ammunition management;

14. *Encourages* States, where relevant, to develop voluntary national action plans on the safe and secure management of conventional ammunition, and acknowledges the utility of information-sharing and the benefit of good practices among States, as appropriate;

15. *Also encourages* States to participate in open, informal consultations within the framework of the present resolution, focusing on matters of conventional ammunition management within the United Nations system and beyond, and with a view to identifying urgent issues pertaining to the accumulation of conventional ammunition stockpiles in surplus on which progress can be made and that may constitute a basis for convening a group of governmental experts;

16. *Requests* the Secretary-General to convene a group of governmental experts in 2020 on problems arising from the accumulation of conventional ammunition stockpiles in surplus, taking into account discussions in the open, informal consultations;

17. *Reiterates* its decision to address the issue of conventional ammunition stockpiles in surplus in a comprehensive manner;

18. *Decides* to include in the provisional agenda of its seventy-fourth session, under the item entitled "General and complete disarmament", the sub-item entitled "Problems arising from the accumulation of conventional ammunition stockpiles in surplus".

Action by the General Assembly

Date: 4 December 2017   Meeting: 62nd plenary meeting
Vote: Adopted without a vote   Report: A/72/409

Sponsors

Albania, Angola, Australia, Austria, Belgium, Bosnia and Herzegovina, Bulgaria, Croatia, Czech Republic, Estonia, Finland, France, **Germany**, Greece, Hungary, Ireland, Italy, Latvia, Liechtenstein, Lithuania, Luxembourg, Malta, Montenegro, Netherlands, Norway, Peru, Poland, Portugal, Republic of Moldova, Romania, Slovenia, Spain, Sweden, Switzerland

Co-sponsors

Andorra, Burkina Faso, Canada, Central African Republic, Chile, Cyprus, Denmark, Georgia, Ghana, Haiti, Japan, Monaco, San Marino, Slovakia, the former Yugoslav Republic of Macedonia, Turkey, Ukraine, United Kingdom, United States

Action by the First Committee

Date: 31 October 2017   Meeting: 26th meeting
Vote: Adopted without a vote   Draft resolution: A/C.1/72/L.43

Agenda item 99 (v)

72/56   Transparency and confidence-building measures in outer space activities

Text

The General Assembly,

Recalling its resolutions 60/66 of 8 December 2005, 61/75 of 6 December 2006, 62/43 of 5 December 2007, 63/68 of 2 December 2008, 64/49 of 2 December 2009, 65/68 of 8 December 2010, 68/50 of 5 December 2013, 69/38 of 2 December 2014, 70/53 of 7 December 2015, 71/42 of 5 December 2016 and 71/90 of 6 December 2016, as well as its decision 66/517 of 2 December 2011,

Recalling also the report of the Secretary-General of 15 October 1993 to the General Assembly at its forty-eighth session, the annex to which contains the study by governmental experts on the application of confidence-building measures in outer space,[1]

Reaffirming the right of all countries to explore and use outer space in accordance with international law,

Reaffirming also that preventing an arms race in outer space is in the interest of maintaining international peace and security and is an essential condition for the promotion and strengthening of international cooperation in the exploration and use of outer space for peaceful purposes,

Recalling, in this context, its resolutions 45/55 B of 4 December 1990 and 48/74 B of 16 December 1993, in which, inter alia, it recognized the need for increased transparency and confirmed the importance of confidence-building measures as a means of reinforcing the objective of preventing an arms race in outer space,

Noting the constructive debates that the Conference on Disarmament has held on this subject and the views expressed by Member States,

Noting also the introduction by China and the Russian Federation at the Conference on Disarmament of the draft treaty on prevention of the placement of weapons in outer space and of the threat or use of force against outer space objects,[2] and the submission of its updated version[3] in 2014,

Noting further that, since 2004, several States[4] have introduced a policy of not being the first State to place weapons in outer space,

---

[1] A/48/305 and A/48/305/Corr.1.

[2] See CD/1839.

[3] See CD/1985.

[4] Argentina, Armenia, Belarus, Bolivia (Plurinational State of), Brazil, Cuba, Ecuador, Indonesia, Kazakhstan, Kyrgyzstan, Nicaragua, Russian Federation, Sri Lanka, Tajikistan, Uruguay, Venezuela (Bolivarian Republic of) and Viet Nam.

Noting with satisfaction the proposal put forward by China, the Russian Federation and the United States of America to include in the agenda of the Disarmament Commission an additional item relating to the practical implementation of transparency and confidence-building measures in outer space activities, with the goal of preventing an arms race in outer space,

Noting the presentation by the European Union of a draft of a non-legally binding international code of conduct for outer space activities,

Recognizing the work that takes place within the Committee on the Peaceful Uses of Outer Space, its Scientific and Technical Subcommittee and its Legal Subcommittee, which makes a significant contribution to the promotion of the long-term sustainability of outer space activities,

Noting the contribution of Member States that have submitted to the Secretary-General concrete proposals on international outer space transparency and confidence-building measures pursuant to paragraph 1 of resolution 61/75, paragraph 2 of resolution 62/43, paragraph 2 of resolution 63/68 and paragraph 2 of resolution 64/49,

Welcoming the work done in 2012 and 2013 by the Group of Governmental Experts on Transparency and Confidence-building Measures in Outer Space Activities, which was convened by the Secretary-General, on the basis of equitable geographical distribution, to conduct a study on outer space transparency and confidence-building measures,

Noting the consideration of the report of the Group of Governmental Experts,[5] as well as views on the modalities of making practical use of the recommendations contained therein, as set out in the report of the Committee on its fifty-eighth session, held in 2015,[6] at which it found that the Committee had a fundamental role to play in enhancing transparency and confidence-building among States, as well as in ensuring that outer space is maintained for peaceful purposes,

Noting also that, in its report, the Group of Governmental Experts recognized the value of the work of the Committee on the Peaceful Uses of Outer Space in developing a set of voluntary, non-legally binding guidelines for the long-term sustainability of outer space activities, some of which could be considered as potential transparency and confidence-building measures, while others could enhance the safety of outer space activities and thereby provide the technical basis for the further implementation of additional transparency and confidence-building measures,

Taking note of the special report by the Inter-Agency Meeting on Outer Space Activities (UN-Space) on the implementation of the report of the Group of Governmental Experts on Transparency and Confidence-building Measures

---

[5] A/68/189.

[6] *Official Records of the General Assembly, Seventieth Session, Supplement No. 20* (A/70/20).

in Outer Space Activities, and the recommendations contained therein, as submitted to the Committee at its fifty-ninth session, in 2016,[7]

Welcoming resolution 186 of 7 November 2014 of the International Telecommunication Union on strengthening the role of the Union with regard to transparency and confidence-building measures in outer space activities, adopted by the 2014 Plenipotentiary Conference of the Union, held in Busan, Republic of Korea, from 20 October to 7 November 2014,

1.   *Stresses* the importance of the report of the Group of Governmental Experts on Transparency and Confidence-building Measures in Outer Space Activities,[5] considered by the General Assembly on 5 December 2013;

2.   *Encourages* Member States to continue to review and implement, to the greatest extent practicable, the proposed transparency and confidence-building measures contained in the report, through the relevant national mechanisms, on a voluntary basis and in a manner consistent with the national interests of Member States;

3.   *Also encourages* Member States, in accordance with the recommendations contained in the report, with a view to promoting the practical implementation of transparency and confidence-building measures, to hold regular discussions in the Committee on the Peaceful Uses of Outer Space, the Disarmament Commission and the Conference on Disarmament on the prospects for their implementation;

4.   *Requests* the relevant entities and organizations of the United Nations system, to which, in accordance with its resolution 68/50, the report was circulated, to assist in effectively implementing the conclusions and recommendations contained therein, as appropriate;

5.   *Encourages* the relevant entities and organizations of the United Nations system to coordinate, as appropriate, on matters related to the recommendations contained in the report;

6.   *Welcomes* the joint ad hoc meetings of the First and Fourth Committees, held on 22 October 2015 and 12 October 2017, on possible challenges to space security and sustainability, convened in accordance with the report and its resolutions 69/38 and 71/90, and the substantive exchanges of opinions on various aspects of security in outer space that took place during the meetings;

7.   *Calls upon* Member States and the relevant entities and organizations of the United Nations system to support the implementation of the full range of conclusions and recommendations contained in the report;

8.   *Takes note* of the report of the Secretary-General on transparency and confidence-building measures in outer space activities in the United

---

[7] A/AC.105/1116.

Nations system, which contains summaries of the submissions received from Member States giving their views on transparency and confidence-building measures in outer space activities;[8]

9.   *Decides* to include in the provisional agenda of its seventy-third session, under the item entitled "General and complete disarmament", the sub-item entitled "Transparency and confidence-building measures in outer space activities".

Action by the General Assembly

Date: 4 December 2017   Meeting: 62nd plenary meeting
Vote: Adopted without a vote   Report: A/72/409

Sponsors

China, **Russian Federation**, United States

Co-sponsors

Albania, Algeria, Angola, Argentina, Armenia, Australia, Austria, Belarus, Belgium, Benin, Bosnia and Herzegovina, Bulgaria, Canada, Colombia, Croatia, Cuba, Cyprus, Czech Republic, Denmark, Ecuador, Eritrea, Estonia, Finland, France, Germany, Ghana, Greece, Haiti, Hungary, Iceland, Ireland, Italy, Japan, Kazakhstan, Latvia, Liechtenstein, Lithuania, Luxembourg, Maldives, Mali, Malta, Mongolia, Montenegro, Myanmar, Netherlands, Norway, Poland, Portugal, Republic of Korea, Romania, Senegal, Singapore, Slovakia, Slovenia, South Africa, Spain, Suriname, Sweden, Switzerland, Syrian Arab Republic, the former Yugoslav Republic of Macedonia, Turkey, United Kingdom, Uzbekistan

Action by the First Committee

Date: 30 October 2017   Meeting: 25th meeting
Vote: Adopted without a vote   Draft resolution: A/C.1/72/L.46

---

[8] A/72/65 and A/72/65/Add.1.

Agenda item 99 (p)

72/57   The illicit trade in small arms and light weapons in all its aspects

Text

The General Assembly,

Recalling its resolution 71/48 of 5 December 2016, as well as all previous resolutions on the illicit trade in small arms and light weapons in all its aspects, including resolution 56/24 V of 24 December 2001,

Emphasizing the importance of the continued and full implementation of the Programme of Action to Prevent, Combat and Eradicate the Illicit Trade in Small Arms and Light Weapons in All Its Aspects, adopted by the United Nations Conference on the Illicit Trade in Small Arms and Light Weapons in All Its Aspects,[1] and recognizing its important contribution to international efforts on this matter,

Emphasizing also the importance of the continued and full implementation of the International Instrument to Enable States to Identify and Trace, in a Timely and Reliable Manner, Illicit Small Arms and Light Weapons (the International Tracing Instrument),[2]

Recalling the commitment of States to the Programme of Action as the main framework for measures within the activities of the international community to prevent, combat and eradicate the illicit trade in small arms and light weapons in all its aspects,

Underlining the need for States to enhance their efforts to build national capacity for the effective implementation of the Programme of Action and the International Tracing Instrument,

Mindful of the implementation of the outcomes adopted by the follow-up meetings on the Programme of Action,

Recalling the convening of the Second Open-ended Meeting of Governmental Experts on the Implementation of the Programme of Action to Prevent, Combat and Eradicate the Illicit Trade in Small Arms and Light Weapons in All Its Aspects, in New York from 1 to 5 June 2015, and the Sixth Biennial Meeting of States to Consider the Implementation of the Programme of Action to Prevent, Combat and Eradicate the Illicit Trade in Small Arms and Light Weapons in All Its Aspects, held in New York from 6 to 10 June

---

[1] *Report of the United Nations Conference on the Illicit Trade in Small Arms and Light Weapons in All Its Aspects, New York, 9–20 July 2001* (A/CONF.192/15), chap. IV, para. 24.

[2] See decision 60/519 and A/60/88 and A/60/88/Corr.2, annex.

2016, to consider the full and effective implementation of the Programme of Action, and the final document adopted at the Sixth Biennial Meeting,[3]

Welcoming the early designation of France as the Chair of the third United Nations Conference to Review Progress Made in the Implementation of the Programme of Action to Prevent, Combat and Eradicate the Illicit Trade in Small Arms and Light Weapons in All Its Aspects, to be held in 2018, as well as the early commencement of informal consultations by France to prepare for this Conference,

Welcoming also the consensus outcome document of Working Group II of the Disarmament Commission, entitled "Recommendations on practical confidence-building measures in the field of conventional weapons", contained in the report of the Disarmament Commission for 2017,[4]

Noting that tools developed by the Office for Disarmament Affairs of the Secretariat, including the Programme of Action Implementation Support System, and those developed by Member States could be used to assess progress made in the implementation of the Programme of Action,

Welcoming the coordinated efforts within the United Nations to implement the Programme of Action, including by developing the Programme of Action Implementation Support System, which forms an integrated clearing house for international cooperation and assistance for capacity-building in the area of small arms and light weapons,

Noting that voluntary national reports on the implementation of the Programme of Action can serve, inter alia, to provide a baseline for measuring progress in its implementation, build confidence and promote transparency, provide a basis for information exchange and action and serve to identify needs and opportunities for international assistance and cooperation, including the matching of needs with available resources and expertise,

Noting with satisfaction regional and subregional efforts being undertaken in support of the implementation of the Programme of Action, and commending the progress that has already been made in this regard, including the tackling of both supply and demand factors that are relevant to addressing the illicit trade in small arms and light weapons,

Reaffirming that international cooperation and assistance are an essential aspect of the full and effective implementation of the Programme of Action and the International Tracing Instrument,

Recognizing the efforts undertaken by non-governmental organizations in the provision of assistance to States for the implementation of the Programme of Action,

---

[3] A/CONF.192/BMS/2016/2, annex.
[4] *Official Records of the General Assembly, Seventy-second Session, Supplement No. 42* (A/72/42).

Recalling that Governments bear the primary responsibility for preventing, combating and eradicating the illicit trade in small arms and light weapons in all its aspects, in accordance with the sovereignty of States and their relevant international obligations,

Reiterating that illicit brokering in small arms and light weapons is a serious problem that the international community should address urgently,

Highlighting new challenges and potential opportunities with regard to effective marking, record-keeping and tracing resulting from developments in the manufacturing, technology and design of small arms and light weapons, and bearing in mind the different situations, capacities and priorities of States and regions,

Taking note of the report of the Secretary-General,[5] which includes an overview of the implementation of resolution 71/48,

Welcoming the inclusion of small arms and light weapons in the scope of the Arms Trade Treaty,[6]

Acknowledging efforts related to the transfer of conventional arms that may also contribute to the prevention and eradication of the illicit trade in small arms and light weapons,

1.   *Underlines* the fact that the issue of the illicit trade in small arms and light weapons in all its aspects requires concerted efforts at the national, regional and international levels to prevent, combat and eradicate the illicit manufacture, transfer and circulation of small arms and light weapons, and that their uncontrolled spread in many regions of the world has a wide range of humanitarian and socioeconomic consequences and poses a serious threat to peace, reconciliation, safety, security, stability and sustainable development at the individual, local, national, regional and international levels;

2.   *Recognizes* the urgent need to maintain and enhance national controls, in accordance with the Programme of Action to Prevent, Combat and Eradicate the Illicit Trade in Small Arms and Light Weapons in All Its Aspects,[1] to prevent, combat and eradicate the illicit trade in small arms and light weapons, including their diversion to illicit trade, illegal armed groups, terrorists and other unauthorized recipients, taking into account, inter alia, their adverse humanitarian and socioeconomic consequences for the affected States;

3.   *Calls upon* all States to implement the International Instrument to Enable States to Identify and Trace, in a Timely and Reliable Manner, Illicit Small Arms and Light Weapons (the International Tracing Instrument)[2] by, inter alia, including in their national reports the name and contact information of the national points of contact and information on national marking

---

[5] A/72/122.
[6] See resolution 67/234 B.

practices used to indicate country of manufacture and/or country of import, as applicable;

4. *Encourages* all relevant initiatives, including those of the United Nations, other international organizations, regional and subregional organizations, non-governmental organizations and civil society, for the successful implementation of the Programme of Action, and calls upon all Member States to contribute towards the continued implementation of the Programme of Action at the national, regional and global levels;

5. *Encourages* States to implement the recommendations contained in the report of the Group of Governmental Experts established pursuant to resolution 60/81 to consider further steps to enhance international cooperation in preventing, combating and eradicating illicit brokering in small arms and light weapons;[7]

6. *Reaffirms* its endorsement of the report adopted at the Sixth Biennial Meeting of States to Consider the Implementation of the Programme of Action to Prevent, Combat and Eradicate the Illicit Trade in Small Arms and Light Weapons in All Its Aspects,[3] and encourages all States to implement, as appropriate, the measures highlighted in the annex to the report under the sections entitled "Way forward";

7. *Recalls* the decision of the second United Nations Conference to Review Progress Made in the Implementation of the Programme of Action to Prevent, Combat and Eradicate the Illicit Trade in Small Arms and Light Weapons in All Its Aspects,[8] and decides to convene the third United Nations Conference to Review Progress Made in the Implementation of the Programme of Action to Prevent, Combat and Eradicate the Illicit Trade in Small Arms and Light Weapons in All Its Aspects in New York from 18 to 29 June 2018, preceded by the meeting of the preparatory committee in New York, from 19 to 23 March 2018;

8. *Underlines* the importance of the full and effective implementation of the Programme of Action and the International Tracing Instrument for attaining Goal 16 and target 16.4 of the Sustainable Development Goals;[9]

9. *Emphasizes* that international cooperation and assistance remain essential to the full and effective implementation of the Programme of Action and the International Tracing Instrument, while being mindful of the need to ensure the adequacy, effectiveness and sustainability of international cooperation and assistance;

10. *Also emphasizes* the fact that initiatives by the international community with respect to international cooperation and assistance remain

---

[7] See A/62/163 and A/62/163/Corr.1.

[8] See A/CONF.192/2012/RC/4, annex I, sect. III, paras. 1 and 2.

[9] See resolution 70/1.

essential and complementary to national implementation efforts, as well as to those at the regional and global levels;

11. *Recognizes* the necessity for interested States to develop effective coordination mechanisms, where they do not exist, in order to match the needs of States with existing resources to enhance the implementation of the Programme of Action and to make international cooperation and assistance more effective, and in this regard encourages States to make use, as appropriate, of the Programme of Action Implementation Support System;

12. *Encourages* States to consider, among other mechanisms, the coherent identification of needs, priorities, national plans and programmes that may require international cooperation and assistance from States and regional and international organizations in a position to do so;

13. *Also encourages* States, on a voluntary basis, to make increasing use of their national reports as another tool for communicating assistance needs and information on the resources and mechanisms available to address such needs, and encourages States in a position to render such assistance to make use of these national reports;

14. *Encourages* States, relevant international and regional organizations and civil society with the capacity to do so to cooperate with and provide assistance to other States, upon request, in the preparation of comprehensive reports on their implementation of the Programme of Action;

15. *Encourages* States to reinforce, as necessary, cross-border cooperation at the national, subregional and regional levels in addressing the common problem of the illicit trade in small arms and light weapons in all its aspects, with full respect for each State's sovereignty over its own borders;

16. *Also encourages* States to take full advantage of the benefits of cooperation with the United Nations regional centres for peace and disarmament, the World Customs Organization, the International Criminal Police Organization (INTERPOL) and the United Nations Office on Drugs and Crime, in accordance with their mandates and consistent with national priorities;

17. *Encourages* all efforts to build national capacity for the effective implementation of the Programme of Action, including those highlighted in the outcome documents of the second United Nations Conference to Review Progress Made in the Implementation of the Programme of Action to Prevent, Combat and Eradicate the Illicit Trade in Small Arms and Light Weapons in All Its Aspects[10] and in the final document of the Sixth Biennial Meeting of States to Consider the Implementation of the Programme of Action;

---

[10] See A/CONF.192/2012/RC/4, annexes I and II.

18. *Encourages* States to submit, on a voluntary basis, national reports on their implementation of the Programme of Action, notes that States will submit national reports on their implementation of the International Tracing Instrument, encourages those States in a position to do so to use the reporting template made available by the Office for Disarmament Affairs of the Secretariat, and reaffirms the utility of synchronizing such reports with biennial meetings of States and review conferences as a means of increasing the submission rate and improving the utility of reports, as well as contributing substantively to meeting discussions;

19. *Encourages* States in a position to do so to provide financial assistance, through a voluntary sponsorship fund, that could be distributed, upon request, to States otherwise unable to participate in meetings on the Programme of Action;

20. *Encourages* interested States and relevant international and regional organizations in a position to do so to convene regional meetings to consider and advance the implementation of the Programme of Action, as well as the International Tracing Instrument, including in preparation for the meetings on the Programme of Action;

21. *Encourages* civil society and relevant organizations to strengthen their cooperation and work with States at the respective national and regional levels to achieve the implementation of the Programme of Action;

22. *Requests* the Secretary-General to report to the General Assembly at its seventy-third session on the implementation of the present resolution;

23. *Decides* to include in the provisional agenda of its seventy-third session, under the item entitled "General and complete disarmament", the sub-item entitled "The illicit trade in small arms and light weapons in all its aspects".

Action by the General Assembly

Date: 4 December 2017   Meeting: 62nd plenary meeting
Vote: Adopted without a vote   Report: A/72/409

Sponsors

Albania, Angola, Argentina, Australia, Austria, Belgium, Bosnia and Herzegovina, Bulgaria, Colombia, Croatia, Czech Republic, Dominican Republic, El Salvador, Finland, France, Germany, Ghana, Greece, Hungary, Iceland, Ireland, Italy, **Japan**, Luxembourg, Malta, Montenegro, Netherlands, Panama, Peru, Poland, Portugal, Republic of Korea, Republic of Moldova, Romania, Serbia, Slovenia, South Africa, Spain, Sweden, Switzerland, Thailand, Ukraine, Uruguay

Co-sponsors

Andorra, Bahamas, Benin, Brazil, Burkina Faso, Chile, Costa Rica, Cyprus, Denmark, Georgia, Guatemala, Guinea-Bissau, Guyana, Jamaica, Latvia, Liberia, Liechtenstein, Lithuania, Maldives, Monaco, Mozambique, New Zealand, Nigeria, Norway, Papua New Guinea, Paraguay, Saint Kitts and Nevis, Saint Lucia, Samoa, San Marino, Senegal, Slovakia, the former Yugoslav Republic of Macedonia, Togo, Trinidad and Tobago, Tunisia, Turkey, United Kingdom, United States, Zambia

Action by the First Committee

Date: 31 October 2017   Meeting: 26th meeting
Vote: Adopted without a vote   Draft resolution: A/C.1/72/L.56/Rev.1

Agenda item 99 (k)

72/58 Follow-up to the advisory opinion of the International Court of Justice on the legality of the threat or use of nuclear weapons

Text

The General Assembly,

Recalling its resolutions 49/75 K of 15 December 1994, 51/45 M of 10 December 1996, 52/38 O of 9 December 1997, 53/77 W of 4 December 1998, 54/54 Q of 1 December 1999, 55/33 X of 20 November 2000, 56/24 S of 29 November 2001, 57/85 of 22 November 2002, 58/46 of 8 December 2003, 59/83 of 3 December 2004, 60/76 of 8 December 2005, 61/83 of 6 December 2006, 62/39 of 5 December 2007, 63/49 of 2 December 2008, 64/55 of 2 December 2009, 65/76 of 8 December 2010, 66/46 of 2 December 2011, 67/33 of 3 December 2012, 68/42 of 5 December 2013, 69/43 of 2 December 2014, 70/56 of 7 December 2015 and 71/58 of 5 December 2016,

Convinced that the continuing existence of nuclear weapons poses a threat to humanity and all life on Earth, and recognizing that the only defence against a nuclear catastrophe is the total elimination of nuclear weapons and the certainty that they will never be produced again,

Reaffirming the commitment of the international community to the realization of the goal of a nuclear-weapon-free world through the total elimination of nuclear weapons,

Mindful of the solemn obligations of States parties, in particular the obligations undertaken in article VI of the Treaty on the Non-Proliferation of Nuclear Weapons,[1] to pursue negotiations in good faith on effective measures relating to cessation of the nuclear arms race at an early date and to nuclear disarmament,

Recalling the principles and objectives for nuclear non-proliferation and disarmament adopted at the 1995 Review and Extension Conference of the Parties to the Treaty on the Non-Proliferation of Nuclear Weapons,[2] the unequivocal commitment of nuclear-weapon States to accomplish the total elimination of their nuclear arsenals leading to nuclear disarmament, agreed at the 2000 Review Conference of the Parties to the Treaty on the Non-Proliferation of Nuclear Weapons,[3] and the action points agreed at the

---

[1] United Nations, *Treaty Series*, vol. 729, No. 10485.

[2] *1995 Review and Extension Conference of the Parties to the Treaty on the Non-Proliferation of Nuclear Weapons, Final Document, Part I* (NPT/CONF.1995/32 (Part I) and NPT/CONF.1995/32 (Part I)/Corr.2), annex, decision 2.

[3] See *2000 Review Conference of the Parties to the Treaty on the Non-Proliferation of Nuclear Weapons, Final Document*, vol. I (NPT/CONF.2000/28 (Parts I and II)), part I, section entitled "Article VI and eighth to twelfth preambular paragraphs", para. 15.

2010 Review Conference of the Parties to the Treaty on the Non-Proliferation of Nuclear Weapons as part of the conclusions and recommendations for follow-on actions on nuclear disarmament,[4]

Sharing the deep concern at the catastrophic humanitarian consequences of any use of nuclear weapons, and in this context reaffirming the need for all States at all times to comply with applicable international law, including international humanitarian law,

Calling upon all nuclear-weapon States to undertake concrete disarmament efforts, and stressing that all States need to make special efforts to achieve and maintain a world without nuclear weapons,

Noting the five-point proposal for nuclear disarmament of the Secretary-General, in which he proposes, inter alia, the consideration of negotiations on a nuclear weapons convention or agreement on a framework of separate mutually reinforcing instruments, backed by a strong system of verification,

Recalling the adoption of the Comprehensive Nuclear-Test-Ban Treaty in its resolution 50/245 of 10 September 1996, and expressing its satisfaction at the increasing number of States that have signed and ratified the Treaty,

Recognizing with satisfaction that the Antarctic Treaty,[5] the treaties of Tlatelolco,[6] Rarotonga,[7] Bangkok[8] and Pelindaba[9] and the Treaty on a Nuclear-Weapon-Free Zone in Central Asia, as well as Mongolia's nuclear-weapon-free status, are gradually freeing the entire southern hemisphere and adjacent areas covered by those treaties from nuclear weapons,

Recognizing the need for a multilaterally negotiated and legally binding instrument to assure non-nuclear-weapon States against the threat or use of nuclear weapons pending the total elimination of nuclear weapons,

Reaffirming the central role of the Conference on Disarmament as the sole multilateral disarmament negotiating forum,

Emphasizing the need for the Conference on Disarmament to commence negotiations on a phased programme for the complete elimination of nuclear weapons with a specified framework of time,

Stressing the urgent need for the nuclear-weapon States to accelerate concrete progress on the 13 practical steps to implement article VI of the Treaty on the Non-Proliferation of Nuclear Weapons leading to nuclear

---

[4] See *2010 Review Conference of the Parties to the Treaty on the Non-Proliferation of Nuclear Weapons, Final Document*, vol. I (NPT/CONF.2010/50 (Vol. I)), part I.

[5] United Nations, *Treaty Series*, vol. 402, No. 5778.

[6] Ibid., vol. 634, No. 9068.

[7] The *United Nations Disarmament Yearbook*, vol. 10: 1985 (United Nations publication, Sales No. E.86.IX.7), appendix VII.

[8] United Nations, *Treaty Series*, vol. 1981, No. 33873.

[9] A/50/426, annex.

disarmament, contained in the Final Document of the 2000 Review Conference,

Taking note of the Model Nuclear Weapons Convention submitted to the Secretary-General by Costa Rica and Malaysia in 2007 and circulated by the Secretary-General,[10]

Welcoming the adoption on 7 July 2017 of the Treaty on the Prohibition of Nuclear Weapons,[11] which contributed to achieving the objective of a legally binding prohibition of the development, production, testing, deployment, stockpiling, threat or use of nuclear weapons and their destruction under effective international control,

Recalling the advisory opinion of the International Court of Justice on the legality of the threat or use of nuclear weapons, issued on 8 July 1996,[12]

1. *Underlines once again* the unanimous conclusion of the International Court of Justice that there exists an obligation to pursue in good faith and bring to a conclusion negotiations leading to nuclear disarmament in all its aspects under strict and effective international control;

2. *Calls once again upon* all States to immediately engage in multilateral negotiations leading to nuclear disarmament in all its aspects under strict and effective international control, including under the Treaty on the Prohibition of Nuclear Weapons;[11]

3. *Requests* all States to inform the Secretary-General of the efforts and measures they have taken with respect to the implementation of the present resolution and nuclear disarmament, and requests the Secretary-General to apprise the General Assembly of that information at its seventy-third session;

4. *Decides* to include in the provisional agenda of its seventy-third session, under the item entitled "General and complete disarmament", the sub-item entitled "Follow-up to the advisory opinion of the International Court of Justice on the legality of the threat or use of nuclear weapons".

Action by the General Assembly

Date:	4 December 2017	Meeting:	62nd plenary meeting
Vote:	131-31-18	Report:	A/72/409
	125-35-13, p.p. 16		
	123-35-15, o.p. 2		

Sponsors

Angola, Cuba, Ecuador, Indonesia, Lao People's Democratic Republic, **Malaysia**, Myanmar, Nicaragua, Peru, Uruguay, Viet Nam

---

[10] A/62/650, annex.
[11] A/CONF.229/2017/8.
[12] A/51/218, annex.

Co-sponsors

Algeria, Bahamas, Bangladesh, Belize, Benin, Bolivia (Plurinational State of), Brazil, Brunei Darussalam, Burkina Faso, Cambodia, Central African Republic, Chad, Chile, Costa Rica, Côte d'Ivoire, Dominican Republic, Egypt, El Salvador, Fiji, Grenada, Guatemala, Guinea-Bissau, Honduras, Iran (Islamic Republic of), Iraq, Jamaica, Kazakhstan, Kenya, Lebanon, Libya, Madagascar, Malawi, Maldives, Mexico, Morocco, Namibia, Nepal, Nigeria, Palau, Papua New Guinea, Philippines, Samoa, Senegal, Singapore, Sri Lanka, Swaziland, Thailand, Timor-Leste, Trinidad and Tobago, Tunisia, Tuvalu, Vanuatu, Venezuela (Bolivarian Republic of), Zimbabwe

Recorded vote

As a whole

In favour:

Afghanistan, Algeria, Angola, Antigua and Barbuda, Argentina, Austria, Azerbaijan, Bahamas, Bahrain, Bangladesh, Barbados, Belize, Benin, Bhutan, Bolivia (Plurinational State of), Botswana, Brazil, Brunei Darussalam, Burkina Faso, Burundi, Cabo Verde, Cambodia, Central African Republic, Chad, Chile, China, Colombia, Comoros, Congo, Costa Rica, Côte d'Ivoire, Cuba, Cyprus, Djibouti, Dominican Republic, Ecuador, Egypt, El Salvador, Equatorial Guinea, Eritrea, Ethiopia, Fiji, Gabon, Gambia, Ghana, Guatemala, Guinea-Bissau, Guyana, Honduras, Indonesia, Iran (Islamic Republic of), Iraq, Ireland, Jamaica, Jordan, Kazakhstan, Kenya, Kiribati, Kuwait, Kyrgyzstan, Lao People's Democratic Republic, Lebanon, Lesotho, Liberia, Libya, Liechtenstein, Madagascar, Malawi, Malaysia, Maldives, Mali, Malta, Mauritania, Mauritius, Mexico, Mongolia, Morocco, Mozambique, Myanmar, Namibia, Nepal, New Zealand, Nicaragua, Nigeria, Oman, Pakistan, Palau, Panama, Papua New Guinea, Paraguay, Peru, Philippines, Qatar, Saint Kitts and Nevis, Saint Lucia, Saint Vincent and the Grenadines, Samoa, San Marino, Saudi Arabia, Senegal, Sierra Leone, Singapore, Solomon Islands, Somalia, South Africa, Sri Lanka, Sudan, Suriname, Swaziland, Sweden, Switzerland, Syrian Arab Republic, Tajikistan, Thailand, Timor-Leste, Togo, Tonga, Trinidad and Tobago, Tunisia, Turkmenistan, Tuvalu, Uganda, United Arab Emirates, United Republic of Tanzania, Uruguay, Vanuatu, Venezuela (Bolivarian Republic of), Viet Nam, Yemen, Zambia, Zimbabwe

Against:

Albania, Australia, Belgium, Bulgaria, Croatia, Czech Republic, Denmark, Estonia, France, Germany, Greece, Hungary, Israel, Italy, Latvia, Lithuania, Luxembourg, Montenegro, Netherlands, Norway,

Poland, Portugal, Republic of Korea, Romania, Russian Federation, Slovakia, Slovenia, Spain, Turkey, United Kingdom, United States

Abstaining:

Andorra, Armenia, Belarus, Bosnia and Herzegovina, Canada, Finland, Georgia, Iceland, India, Japan, Marshall Islands, Micronesia (Federated States of), Republic of Moldova, Rwanda, Serbia, the former Yugoslav Republic of Macedonia, Ukraine, Uzbekistan

Sixteenth preambular paragraph

In favour:

Afghanistan, Algeria, Angola, Antigua and Barbuda, Argentina, Austria, Azerbaijan, Bahamas, Bahrain, Bangladesh, Barbados, Belize, Benin, Bhutan, Bolivia (Plurinational State of), Botswana, Brazil, Brunei Darussalam, Burkina Faso, Burundi, Cabo Verde, Cambodia, Chad, Chile, Colombia, Comoros, Congo, Costa Rica, Côte d'Ivoire, Cuba, Cyprus, Djibouti, Dominican Republic, Ecuador, Egypt, El Salvador, Equatorial Guinea, Eritrea, Ethiopia, Fiji, Gabon, Gambia, Ghana, Guatemala, Guinea-Bissau, Guyana, Honduras, Indonesia, Iran (Islamic Republic of), Iraq, Ireland, Jamaica, Jordan, Kazakhstan, Kenya, Kiribati, Kuwait, Lao People's Democratic Republic, Lebanon, Lesotho, Liberia, Libya, Liechtenstein, Madagascar, Malawi, Malaysia, Maldives, Mali, Malta, Mauritania, Mauritius, Mexico, Mongolia, Morocco, Mozambique, Myanmar, Namibia, Nepal, New Zealand, Nicaragua, Nigeria, Oman, Palau, Panama, Papua New Guinea, Paraguay, Peru, Philippines, Qatar, Republic of Moldova, Saint Kitts and Nevis, Saint Lucia, Saint Vincent and the Grenadines, Samoa, San Marino, Saudi Arabia, Senegal, Sierra Leone, Singapore, Solomon Islands, Somalia, South Africa, Sri Lanka, Sudan, Suriname, Swaziland, Sweden, Switzerland, Thailand, Timor-Leste, Togo, Trinidad and Tobago, Tunisia, Turkmenistan, Tuvalu, Uganda, United Arab Emirates, United Republic of Tanzania, Uruguay, Vanuatu, Venezuela (Bolivarian Republic of), Viet Nam, Yemen, Zambia, Zimbabwe

Against:

Albania, Australia, Belgium, Bosnia and Herzegovina, Bulgaria, Canada, China, Croatia, Czech Republic, Denmark, Estonia, France, Germany, Greece, Hungary, Iceland, Israel, Italy, Latvia, Lithuania, Luxembourg, Montenegro, Netherlands, Norway, Poland, Portugal, Republic of Korea, Romania, Russian Federation, Slovakia, Slovenia, Spain, Turkey, United Kingdom, United States

Abstaining:

Andorra, Armenia, Belarus, Democratic People's Republic of Korea, Finland, Georgia, India, Japan, Pakistan, Rwanda, Serbia, the former Yugoslav Republic of Macedonia, Ukraine

Operative paragraph 2

In favour:

Afghanistan, Algeria, Angola, Antigua and Barbuda, Argentina, Austria, Azerbaijan, Bahamas, Bahrain, Bangladesh, Barbados, Belize, Benin, Bhutan, Bolivia (Plurinational State of), Botswana, Brazil, Brunei Darussalam, Burkina Faso, Burundi, Cabo Verde, Cambodia, Chad, Chile, Colombia, Comoros, Congo, Costa Rica, Côte d'Ivoire, Cuba, Cyprus, Djibouti, Dominican Republic, Ecuador, Egypt, El Salvador, Equatorial Guinea, Eritrea, Ethiopia, Fiji, Gabon, Gambia, Ghana, Guatemala, Guinea-Bissau, Guyana, Honduras, Indonesia, Iran (Islamic Republic of), Iraq, Ireland, Jamaica, Jordan, Kazakhstan, Kenya, Kiribati, Kuwait, Lao People's Democratic Republic, Lebanon, Lesotho, Liberia, Libya, Liechtenstein, Madagascar, Malawi, Malaysia, Maldives, Mali, Malta, Mauritania, Mauritius, Mexico, Mongolia, Morocco, Mozambique, Myanmar, Namibia, Nepal, New Zealand, Nicaragua, Nigeria, Oman, Panama, Papua New Guinea, Paraguay, Peru, Philippines, Qatar, Saint Kitts and Nevis, Saint Lucia, Saint Vincent and the Grenadines, Samoa, San Marino, Saudi Arabia, Senegal, Sierra Leone, Singapore, Solomon Islands, Somalia, South Africa, Sri Lanka, Sudan, Suriname, Swaziland, Syrian Arab Republic, Tajikistan, Thailand, Timor-Leste, Togo, Trinidad and Tobago, Tunisia, Turkmenistan, Tuvalu, Uganda, United Arab Emirates, United Republic of Tanzania, Uruguay, Vanuatu, Venezuela (Bolivarian Republic of), Viet Nam, Yemen, Zambia, Zimbabwe

Against:

Albania, Australia, Belgium, Bosnia and Herzegovina, Bulgaria, Canada, China, Croatia, Czech Republic, Denmark, Estonia, France, Germany, Greece, Hungary, Iceland, Israel, Italy, Latvia, Lithuania, Luxembourg, Montenegro, Netherlands, Norway, Poland, Portugal, Republic of Korea, Romania, Russian Federation, Slovakia, Slovenia, Spain, Turkey, United Kingdom, United States

Abstaining:

Andorra, Armenia, Belarus, Democratic People's Republic of Korea, Finland, Georgia, India, Japan, Pakistan, Rwanda, Serbia, Sweden, Switzerland, the former Yugoslav Republic of Macedonia, Ukraine

Action by the First Committee

Date:	1 November 2017	Meeting:	27th meeting
Vote:	124-31-17	Draft resolution:	A/C.1/72/L.57
	117-35-13, p.p. 16		
	117-35-14, o.p. 2		

Agenda item 100 (a)

72/59 Convention on the Prohibition of the Use of Nuclear Weapons

Text

The General Assembly,

Convinced that the use of nuclear weapons poses the most serious threat to the survival of humankind,

Bearing in mind the advisory opinion of the International Court of Justice of 8 July 1996 on the legality of the threat or use of nuclear weapons,[1]

Convinced that a multilateral, universal and binding agreement prohibiting the use or threat of use of nuclear weapons would contribute to the elimination of the nuclear threat and to the climate for negotiations leading to the ultimate elimination of nuclear weapons, thereby strengthening international peace and security,

Conscious that some steps have been taken by the Russian Federation and the United States of America towards a reduction of their nuclear weapons and that further steps – in all relevant formats – on nuclear arms control and disarmament can contribute to the improvement of the international climate and the goal of the complete elimination of nuclear weapons,

Recalling that in paragraph 58 of the Final Document of the Tenth Special Session of the General Assembly[2] it is stated that all States should actively participate in efforts to bring about conditions in international relations among States in which a code of peaceful conduct of nations in international affairs could be agreed upon and which would preclude the use or threat of use of nuclear weapons,

Reaffirming that any use of nuclear weapons would be a violation of the Charter of the United Nations and a crime against humanity, as declared in its resolutions 1653 (XVI) of 24 November 1961, 33/71 B of 14 December 1978, 34/83 G of 11 December 1979, 35/152 D of 12 December 1980 and 36/92 I of 9 December 1981,

Recognizing that a legally binding prohibition of the use of nuclear weapons is not contrary to but in fact contributes to international efforts for the achievement and maintenance of a world free of nuclear weapons,

Stressing that an international convention on the prohibition of the use of nuclear weapons would be an important step in a phased programme towards the complete elimination of nuclear weapons, with a specified framework of time,

---

[1] A/51/218, annex.
[2] Resolution S-10/2.

Noting with regret that the Conference on Disarmament, during its 2016 session, was unable to undertake negotiations on this subject as called for in General Assembly resolution 70/62 of 7 December 2015,

1. *Reiterates its request* to the Conference on Disarmament to commence negotiations in order to reach agreement on an international convention prohibiting the use or threat of use of nuclear weapons under any circumstances;

2. *Requests* the Conference on Disarmament to report to the General Assembly on the results of those negotiations.

Action by the General Assembly

Date: 4 December 2017　　　Meeting: 62nd plenary meeting
Vote: 123-50-10　　　　　　Report: A/72/410

Sponsors

Bhutan, Cuba, **India**, Kenya, Lao People's Democratic Republic, Mauritius, Myanmar, Samoa, Viet Nam

Co-sponsors

Afghanistan, Angola, Bangladesh, Bolivia (Plurinational State of), Guinea-Bissau, Honduras, Indonesia, Iran (Islamic Republic of), Kazakhstan, Maldives, Nepal, Sri Lanka

Recorded vote

In favour:

Afghanistan, Algeria, Angola, Antigua and Barbuda, Argentina, Azerbaijan, Bahamas, Bahrain, Bangladesh, Barbados, Belize, Benin, Bhutan, Bolivia (Plurinational State of), Botswana, Brunei Darussalam, Burkina Faso, Burundi, Cabo Verde, Cambodia, Chad, Chile, China, Colombia, Comoros, Congo, Costa Rica, Côte d'Ivoire, Cuba, Democratic Republic of the Congo, Djibouti, Dominican Republic, Ecuador, Egypt, El Salvador, Equatorial Guinea, Eritrea, Ethiopia, Fiji, Gabon, Gambia, Ghana, Guatemala, Guinea, Guinea-Bissau, Guyana, Honduras, India, Indonesia, Iran (Islamic Republic of), Iraq, Jamaica, Jordan, Kazakhstan, Kenya, Kiribati, Kuwait, Kyrgyzstan, Lao People's Democratic Republic, Lebanon, Lesotho, Liberia, Libya, Madagascar, Malawi, Malaysia, Maldives, Mauritania, Mauritius, Mexico, Mongolia, Morocco, Mozambique, Myanmar, Namibia, Nauru, Nepal, Nicaragua, Nigeria, Oman, Pakistan, Palau, Panama, Papua New Guinea, Paraguay, Peru, Philippines, Qatar, Rwanda, Saint Kitts and Nevis, Saint Lucia, Saint Vincent and the Grenadines, Samoa, Saudi Arabia, Senegal, Sierra Leone, Singapore, Solomon Islands, Somalia, South Africa, Sri Lanka, Sudan, Swaziland, Syrian Arab Republic, Tajikistan, Thailand, Timor-

Leste, Togo, Tonga, Trinidad and Tobago, Tunisia, Turkmenistan, Tuvalu, Uganda, United Arab Emirates, United Republic of Tanzania, Uruguay, Vanuatu, Venezuela (Bolivarian Republic of), Viet Nam, Yemen, Zambia, Zimbabwe

Against:

Albania, Andorra, Australia, Austria, Belgium, Bosnia and Herzegovina, Bulgaria, Canada, Croatia, Cyprus, Czech Republic, Denmark, Estonia, Finland, France, Georgia, Germany, Greece, Hungary, Iceland, Ireland, Israel, Italy, Latvia, Liechtenstein, Lithuania, Luxembourg, Malta, Micronesia (Federated States of), Monaco, Montenegro, Netherlands, New Zealand, Norway, Poland, Portugal, Republic of Korea, Republic of Moldova, Romania, San Marino, Slovakia, Slovenia, Spain, Sweden, Switzerland, the former Yugoslav Republic of Macedonia, Turkey, Ukraine, United Kingdom, United States

Abstaining:

Armenia, Belarus, Brazil, Democratic People's Republic of Korea, Japan, Mali, Russian Federation, Serbia, Suriname, Uzbekistan

Action by the First Committee

Date:	27 October 2017	Meeting:	24th meeting
Vote:	115-50-11	Draft resolution:	A/C.1/72/L.47

Agenda item 100 (b)

72/60   United Nations Regional Centre for Peace and Disarmament in Africa

Text

The General Assembly,

Mindful of the provisions of Article 11, paragraph 1, of the Charter of the United Nations, in which it is stipulated that a function of the General Assembly is to consider the general principles of cooperation in the maintenance of international peace and security, including the principles governing disarmament and arms limitation,

Recalling its resolutions 40/151 G of 16 December 1985, 41/60 D of 3 December 1986, 42/39 J of 30 November 1987 and 43/76 D of 7 December 1988 on the United Nations Regional Centre for Peace and Disarmament in Africa and its resolutions 46/36 F of 6 December 1991 and 47/52 G of 9 December 1992 on regional disarmament, including confidence-building measures,

Recalling also its subsequent resolutions on the Regional Centre, the most recent of which is resolution 71/76 of 5 December 2016,

Recalling further its resolution 71/56 of 5 December 2016, in which the General Assembly recognized the role of women in disarmament, non-proliferation and arms control,

Reaffirming the role of the Regional Centre in promoting disarmament, peace and security at the regional level,

Welcoming the continuing and deepening cooperation between the Regional Centre, the African Union and African subregional organizations in the context of the adoption of Agenda 2063 by the Assembly of Heads of State and Government of the African Union, and in particular the objective of silencing the guns in Africa by 2020,

Welcoming also the work of the Regional Centre in support of the achievement of the Sustainable Development Goals,[1] in particular Goal 16 on peace, justice and strong institutions, and target 16.4, which addresses the reduction of illicit arms flows,

Recalling the decision taken by the Executive Council of the African Union at its eighth ordinary session, held in Khartoum from 16 to 21 January 2006,[2] in which the Council called upon member States to make voluntary contributions to the Regional Centre to maintain its operations,

---

[1] See resolution 70/1.
[2] A/60/693, annex II, decision EX.CL/Dec.263 (VIII).

Recalling also the call by the Secretary-General for continued financial and in-kind support from Member States, which would enable the Regional Centre to discharge its mandate in full and to respond more effectively to requests for assistance from African States,

1.   *Takes note* of the report of the Secretary-General;[3]

2.   *Commends* the United Nations Regional Centre for Peace and Disarmament in Africa for its sustained support to Member States in implementing disarmament, arms control and non-proliferation activities through seminars and conferences, capacity-building and training, policy and technical expertise, and information and advocacy at the regional and national levels;

3.   *Welcomes* the continental dimension of the activities of the Regional Centre in response to the evolving needs of African Member States and the region's new and emerging challenges in the areas of disarmament, peace and security, including maritime security;

4.   *Also welcomes* the undertaking by the Regional Centre to deepen its partnership with the African Union Commission in the context of the Joint United Nations-African Union Framework for Enhanced Partnership in Peace and Security, signed on 19 April 2017, as well as with African subregional organizations, and requests the Secretary-General to continue to facilitate close cooperation between the Regional Centre and the African Union, in particular in the areas of disarmament, peace and security;

5.   *Further welcomes* the contribution of the Regional Centre to continental disarmament, peace and security, in particular its contribution to the implementation of Agenda 2063 adopted by the Assembly of Heads of State and Government of the African Union, the objective of silencing the guns in Africa and its master road map of practical steps to silence the guns in Africa by the year 2020, as well as its assistance to the African Commission on Nuclear Energy in its implementation of the African Nuclear-Weapon-Free Zone Treaty (Treaty of Pelindaba);[4]

6.   *Welcomes* efforts by the Regional Centre to promote the role and representation of women in disarmament, non-proliferation and arms control activities;

7.   *Notes with appreciation* the tangible achievements of the Regional Centre and the impact of the assistance that it provided to African States, in particular in Central Africa and the Sahel, to control small arms and light weapons through capacity-building for national commissions on small arms and light weapons, defence and security forces, and United Nations peacekeeping mission personnel, as well as the support that the Centre

---

[3] A/72/97.

[4] A/50/426, annex.

provided to States in preventing the diversion of such weapons, in particular to non-State armed groups and terrorist groups,[5] and also notes with appreciation the assistance provided by the Centre in the implementation of the Central African Convention for the Control of Small Arms and Light Weapons, Their Ammunition and All Parts and Components That Can Be Used for Their Manufacture, Repair and Assembly (Kinshasa Convention),[6] which entered into force on 8 March 2017, and its substantive support to the United Nations Standing Advisory Committee on Security Questions in Central Africa, in the implementation of the Economic Community of West African States Convention on Small Arms and Light Weapons, Their Ammunition and Other Related Materials and on security sector reform initiatives, and to East Africa on programmes to control brokering of small arms and light weapons, including the additional assistance provided by the Centre to African Member States in the implementation of Security Council resolution 1540 (2004) of 28 April 2004 and the Convention on the Prohibition of the Development, Production and Stockpiling of Bacteriological (Biological) and Toxin Weapons and on Their Destruction;[7]

8.   *Commends* the Regional Centre for the support and assistance that it provided to African States, upon request, on the Arms Trade Treaty,[8] including through the organization of subregional and regional seminars and workshops;

9.   *Urges* all States, as well as international, governmental and non-governmental organizations and foundations, to make voluntary contributions to enable the Regional Centre to carry out its programmes and activities and meet the needs of African States;

10.   *Urges*, in particular, States members of the African Union to make voluntary contributions to the trust fund for the United Nations Regional Centre for Peace and Disarmament in Africa, in conformity with the decision taken by the Executive Council of the African Union in Khartoum in January 2006;[2]

11.   *Requests* the Secretary-General to continue to provide the Regional Centre with the support necessary for greater achievements and results;

12.   *Also requests* the Secretary-General to report to the General Assembly at its seventy-third session on the implementation of the present resolution;

13.   *Decides* to include in the provisional agenda of its seventy-third session, under the item entitled "Review and implementation of the Concluding Document of the Twelfth Special Session of the General

---

[5] Security Council resolution 2370 (2017).
[6] See A/65/517-S/2010/534, annex.
[7] United Nations, *Treaty Series*, vol. 1015, No. 14860.
[8] See resolution 67/234 B.

Assembly", the sub-item entitled "United Nations Regional Centre for Peace and Disarmament in Africa".

Action by the General Assembly

    Date: 4 December 2017   Meeting: 62nd plenary meeting
    Vote: Adopted without a vote   Report: A/72/410

Sponsors

    Australia, Austria, Germany, **Nigeria** (on behalf of the States Members of the United Nations that are members of the Group of African States)

Co-sponsors

    Georgia, Maldives

Action by the First Committee

    Date: 1 November 2017   Meeting: 27th meeting
    Vote: Adopted without a vote   Draft resolution: A/C.1/72/L.39

Agenda item 100 (c)

72/61   United Nations Regional Centre for Peace, Disarmament and Development in Latin America and the Caribbean

Text

The General Assembly,

Recalling its resolutions 41/60 J of 3 December 1986, 42/39 K of 30 November 1987 and 43/76 H of 7 December 1988 on the United Nations Regional Centre for Peace, Disarmament and Development in Latin America and the Caribbean, with headquarters in Lima,

Recalling also its resolution 71/77 of 5 December 2016 and all previous resolutions on the Regional Centre,

Recognizing that the Regional Centre has continued to provide substantive support for the implementation of regional and subregional initiatives and has intensified its contribution to the coordination of United Nations efforts towards peace and disarmament and for the promotion of economic and social development, and emphasizing the role of the Centre in providing support for the realization of the 2030 Agenda for Sustainable Development,[1]

Reaffirming the mandate of the Regional Centre to provide, on request, substantive support for the initiatives and other activities of the Member States of the region for the implementation of measures for peace and disarmament and for the promotion of economic and social development,

Taking note of the report of the Secretary-General,[2] and expressing its appreciation for the important assistance provided, upon request, by the Regional Centre to several countries in the region, including through capacity-building and technical assistance activities for the implementation of disarmament, non-proliferation and arms control instruments,

Welcoming the support provided by the Regional Centre to Member States in the implementation of disarmament and non-proliferation instruments,

Emphasizing the need for the Regional Centre to develop and strengthen its activities and programmes in a comprehensive and balanced manner, in accordance with its mandate and in line with the requests for assistance by Member States,

---

[1] Resolution 70/1.
[2] A/72/99.

Welcoming the ongoing support provided by the Regional Centre to Member States in the implementation of the Programme of Action to Prevent, Combat and Eradicate the Illicit Trade in Small Arms and Light Weapons in All Its Aspects,[3]

Welcoming also the assistance provided by the Regional Centre to some States, upon request, in the management and securing of national weapons stockpiles and in the identification and destruction of surplus, obsolete or seized weapons and ammunition, as declared by competent national authorities, in particular the establishment of a regional training centre in Port of Spain to manage weapons stockpiles,

Welcoming further the technical advisory assistance provided by the Regional Centre to the United Nations Mission in Colombia,

Welcoming the initiative of the Regional Centre to continue to conduct activities in line with efforts to promote the equitable representation of women in all decision-making processes with regard to matters related to disarmament, non-proliferation and arms control, as encouraged in its resolutions 65/69 of 8 December 2010 and subsequent resolutions, including resolution 71/56 of 5 December 2016,

Recalling the report of the Group of Governmental Experts on the relationship between disarmament and development,[4] referred to in General Assembly resolution 59/78 of 3 December 2004, which is of utmost interest with regard to the role that the Regional Centre plays in promoting the issue in the region in pursuit of its mandate to promote economic and social development related to peace and disarmament,

Noting that security, disarmament and development issues have always been recognized as significant topics in Latin America and the Caribbean, the first inhabited region in the world to be declared a nuclear-weapon-free zone,

Recognizing the cooperation between the Regional Centre and the Agency for the Prohibition of Nuclear Weapons in Latin America and the Caribbean on strengthening the nuclear-weapon-free zone established by the Treaty for the Prohibition of Nuclear Weapons in Latin America and the Caribbean (Treaty of Tlatelolco),[5] as well as its efforts in promoting peace and disarmament education,

Bearing in mind the important role of the Regional Centre in promoting confidence-building measures, arms control and limitation, disarmament and development at the regional level,

---

[3] *Report of the United Nations Conference on the Illicit Trade in Small Arms and Light Weapons in All Its Aspects, New York, 9–20 July 2001* (A/CONF.192/15), chap. IV, para. 24.

[4] See A/59/119.

[5] United Nations, *Treaty Series*, vol. 634, No. 9068.

Recognizing the importance of information, research, education and training for peace, disarmament and development in order to achieve understanding and cooperation among States,

Recalling the thirtieth anniversary, in 2016, of the United Nations regional centres for peace and disarmament,

1. *Reiterates its strong support* for the role of the United Nations Regional Centre for Peace, Disarmament and Development in Latin America and the Caribbean in the promotion of activities of the United Nations at the regional and subregional levels to strengthen peace, disarmament, stability, security and development among its Member States;

2. *Welcomes* the activities carried out in the past year by the Regional Centre, and requests the Centre to continue to take into account the proposals to be submitted by the countries of the region for the implementation of the mandate of the Centre in the areas of peace, disarmament and development and for the promotion of, inter alia, nuclear disarmament, the prevention, combating and eradication of the illicit trade in small arms and light weapons, ammunition and explosives, the non-proliferation of weapons of mass destruction, confidence-building measures, arms control and limitation, transparency, and the reduction and prevention of armed violence at the regional and subregional levels;

3. *Expresses its appreciation* for the political support provided by Member States, as well as for the financial contributions made by Member States and international governmental and non-governmental organizations, to strengthen the Regional Centre, its programme of activities and the implementation thereof, and encourages them to continue to make and to increase voluntary contributions;

4. *Invites* all States of the region to continue to take part in the activities of the Regional Centre, proposing items for inclusion in its programme of activities and maximizing the potential of the Centre to meet the current challenges facing the international community with a view to fulfilling the aims of the Charter of the United Nations in the areas of peace, disarmament and development;

5. *Recognizes* that the Regional Centre has an important role in the promotion and development of regional and subregional initiatives agreed upon by the countries of Latin America and the Caribbean in the field of weapons of mass destruction, in particular nuclear weapons, and conventional arms, including small arms and light weapons, in the relationship between disarmament and development, including the implementation of the Sustainable Development Goals, in the promotion of the participation of women in this field and in strengthening voluntary confidence-building measures among the countries of the region;

6.   *Encourages* the Regional Centre to further develop activities in all countries of the region in the important areas of peace, disarmament and development and to provide, upon request and in accordance with its mandate, support to Member States of the region in the national implementation of relevant instruments, inter alia, the Programme of Action to Prevent, Combat and Eradicate the Illicit Trade in Small Arms and Light Weapons in All Its Aspects[3] and the Arms Trade Treaty,[6] as well as in the implementation of the Caribbean 1540 programme on the non-proliferation of weapons of mass destruction;

7.   *Requests* the Secretary-General to report to the General Assembly at its seventy-third session on the implementation of the present resolution;

8.   *Decides* to include in the provisional agenda of its seventy-third session, under the item entitled "Review and implementation of the Concluding Document of the Twelfth Special Session of the General Assembly", the sub-item entitled "United Nations Regional Centre for Peace, Disarmament and Development in Latin America and the Caribbean".

Action by the General Assembly

Date: 4 December 2017   Meeting: 62nd plenary meeting
Vote: Adopted without a vote   Report: A/72/410

Sponsors

Peru (on behalf of the States Members of the United Nations that are members of the Group of Latin American and Caribbean States)

Action by the First Committee

Date: 1 November 2017   Meeting: 27th meeting
Vote: Adopted without a vote   Draft resolution: A/C.1/72/L.51

---

[6] See resolution 67/234 B.

Agenda item 100 (d)

72/62   United Nations Regional Centre for Peace and Disarmament in Asia and the Pacific

Text

The General Assembly,

Recalling its resolutions 42/39 D of 30 November 1987 and 44/117 F of 15 December 1989, by which it established the United Nations Regional Centre for Peace and Disarmament in Asia and renamed it the United Nations Regional Centre for Peace and Disarmament in Asia and the Pacific, with headquarters in Kathmandu and with the mandate of providing, on request, substantive support for the initiatives and other activities mutually agreed upon by the Member States of the Asia-Pacific region for the implementation of measures for peace and disarmament, through appropriate utilization of available resources,

Welcoming the physical operation of the Regional Centre from Kathmandu in accordance with General Assembly resolution 62/52 of 5 December 2007,

Recalling the mandate of the Regional Centre to provide, on request, substantive support for the initiatives and other activities mutually agreed upon by the Member States of the Asia-Pacific region for the implementation of measures for peace and disarmament,

Taking note of the report of the Secretary-General,[1] and expressing its appreciation to the Regional Centre for its important work in promoting confidence-building measures through the organization of meetings, conferences and workshops in the region, including: national and subregional workshops on the control of small arms and light weapons; the fifteenth United Nations-Republic of Korea Joint Conference on Disarmament and Non-Proliferation Issues, held on Jeju Island, Republic of Korea, on 17 and 18 November 2016; the twenty-sixth United Nations Conference on Disarmament Issues, held in Nagasaki, Japan, on 12 and 13 December 2016; a technical and legal assistance project to assist the Philippines in the implementation of the Programme of Action to Prevent, Combat and Eradicate the Illicit Trade in Small Arms and Light Weapons in All Its Aspects[2] and to help build capacity towards ratification of the Arms Trade Treaty;[3] and a joint project with the Organization for Security and Cooperation in Europe

---

[1] A/72/98 and A/72/98/Corr.1.

[2] *Report of the United Nations Conference on the Illicit Trade in Small Arms and Light Weapons in All Its Aspects, New York, 9–20 July 2001* (A/CONF.192/15), chap. IV, para. 24.

[3] See resolution 67/234 B.

in support of regional implementation of Security Council resolution 1540 (2004) of 28 April 2004 in Central Asia and Mongolia,

Expressing appreciation for the timely execution by Nepal of its host country commitments for the physical operation of the Regional Centre,

Welcoming the work by the Regional Centre in support of the achievement of the Sustainable Development Goals,[4] in particular Goal 16 on peace, justice and strong institutions, as well as target 16.4, which addresses the reduction of illicit arms flows,

Welcoming also the efforts by the Regional Centre to promote the role and representation of women in disarmament, non-proliferation and arms control activities,

1.   *Expresses its satisfaction* at the activities carried out over the past year by the United Nations Regional Centre for Peace and Disarmament in Asia and the Pacific, and invites all States of the region to continue to support the activities of the Regional Centre, including by continuing to take part in them, where possible, and by proposing items for inclusion in the programme of activities of the Centre, in order to contribute to the implementation of measures for peace and disarmament;

2.   *Expresses its gratitude* to the Government of Nepal for its cooperation and financial support, which has enabled the Regional Centre to operate from Kathmandu;

3.   *Expresses its appreciation* to the Secretary-General and the Office for Disarmament Affairs of the Secretariat for providing the necessary support with a view to ensuring the smooth operation of the Regional Centre and to enabling the Centre to function effectively;

4.   *Appeals* to Member States, in particular those within the Asia-Pacific region, as well as to international governmental and non-governmental organizations and foundations, to make voluntary contributions, the only resources of the Regional Centre, to strengthen its programme of activities and the implementation thereof;

5.   *Reaffirms its strong support* for the role of the Regional Centre in the promotion of activities of the United Nations at the regional level to strengthen peace, stability and security among its Member States;

6.   *Underlines* the importance of the Kathmandu process for the development of the practice of region-wide security and disarmament dialogues;

7.   *Requests* the Secretary-General to report to the General Assembly at its seventy-third session on the implementation of the present resolution;

---

[4]   See resolution 70/1.

8.   *Decides* to include in the provisional agenda of its seventy-third session, under the item entitled "Review and implementation of the Concluding Document of the Twelfth Special Session of the General Assembly", the sub-item entitled "United Nations Regional Centre for Peace and Disarmament in Asia and the Pacific".

Action by the General Assembly

Date: 4 December 2017   Meeting: 62nd plenary meeting
Vote: Adopted without a vote   Report: A/72/410

Sponsors

Afghanistan, Angola, Australia, Austria, China, Japan, Kazakhstan, Malaysia, Mongolia, Myanmar, **Nepal**, Nigeria, Republic of Korea, Samoa, Singapore, Thailand, Vanuatu, Viet Nam

Co-sponsors

Bangladesh, Bhutan, Eritrea, India, Indonesia, Kyrgyzstan, Maldives, Micronesia (Federated States of), New Zealand, Pakistan, Philippines, Sri Lanka

Action by the First Committee

Date: 1 November 2017   Meeting: 27th meeting
Vote: Adopted without a vote   Draft resolution: A/C.1/72/L.48

Agenda item 100 (e)

72/63   Regional confidence-building measures: activities of the United Nations Standing Advisory Committee on Security Questions in Central Africa

Text

The General Assembly,

Recalling its previous relevant resolutions, in particular resolution 71/79 of 5 December 2016,

Recalling also the guidelines for general and complete disarmament adopted at its tenth special session, the first special session devoted to disarmament,

Bearing in mind the establishment by the Secretary-General on 28 May 1992 of the United Nations Standing Advisory Committee on Security Questions in Central Africa, the purpose of which is to encourage arms limitation, disarmament, non-proliferation and development in the Central Africa subregion,

Recalling that the purpose of the Standing Advisory Committee is to conduct reconstruction and confidence-building activities in Central Africa among its member States, including through confidence-building and arms limitation measures,

Reaffirming the importance and relevance of the Standing Advisory Committee as an instrument of preventive diplomacy in the subregional architecture for the promotion of peace and security in Central Africa,

Bearing in mind the revitalization of the activities of the Standing Advisory Committee decided upon at the forty-fourth meeting of the Committee, held in Yaoundé from 29 May to 2 June 2017, with a view to enhancing its contribution to the achievement of the objectives of peace, security and development in Central Africa,

Noting the entry into force of the Central African Convention for the Control of Small Arms and Light Weapons, Their Ammunition and All Parts and Components That Can Be Used for Their Manufacture, Repair and Assembly (Kinshasa Convention) on 8 March 2017,[1] and also the Third Conference of States Parties to the Arms Trade Treaty, held in Geneva from 11 to 15 September 2017,

Convinced that the resources released by disarmament, including regional disarmament, can be devoted to economic and social development

---

[1]   See A/65/517-S/2010/534, annex.

and to the protection of the environment for the benefit of all peoples, in particular those of developing countries,

Welcoming the Libreville Declaration on the adoption and implementation of the regional strategy and plan of action for combating terrorism and the trafficking in small arms and light weapons in Central Africa, adopted by the States members of the Standing Advisory Committee on 26 November 2015 at their forty-first ministerial meeting, held in Libreville from 23 to 27 November 2015,[2]

Also welcoming the adoption, at the forty-fourth meeting of the Standing Advisory Committee, of the plan of action and schedule for the implementation of the regional strategy under the auspices of the Economic Community of Central African States,

Considering the importance and effectiveness of confidence-building measures taken on the initiative and with the participation of all States concerned and taking into account the specific characteristics of each region, since such measures can contribute to regional stability and to international peace and security,

Convinced that development can be achieved only in a climate of peace, security and mutual confidence both within and among States,

Recalling the Brazzaville Declaration on Cooperation for Peace and Security in Central Africa,[3] the Bata Declaration for the Promotion of Lasting Democracy, Peace and Development in Central Africa[4] and the Yaoundé Declaration on Peace, Security and Stability in Central Africa,[5]

Bearing in mind resolutions 1196 (1998) and 1197 (1998), adopted by the Security Council on 16 and 18 September 1998, respectively, following its consideration of the report of the Secretary-General on the causes of conflict and the promotion of durable peace and sustainable development in Africa,[6]

Welcoming the successful conclusion of the Summit of Heads of State and Government on Maritime Safety and Security in the Gulf of Guinea, held in Yaoundé on 24 and 25 June 2013, the inauguration in Yaoundé, on 11 September 2014, of the Interregional Coordination Centre for Maritime Security in the Gulf of Guinea, the effective commencement of its activities with the installation of its statutory officials in Yaoundé on 22 February 2017, the inauguration of new offices of the Regional Centre for Maritime Security in Central Africa in Pointe Noire, Congo, on 20 October 2014, and the launch of the Multinational Maritime Coordination Centre in Cotonou, Benin, in March 2015, and also the conclusion of the African Union Extraordinary

---

[2] See A/70/682-S/2016/39, annex 3.
[3] A/50/474, annex I.
[4] A/53/258-S/1998/763, annex II, appendix I.
[5] A/53/868-S/1999/303, annex II.
[6] A/52/871-S/1998/318.

Summit of Heads of State and Government on Maritime Security and Safety and Development in Africa, held in Lomé on 15 October 2016,

Recalling its resolution 69/314 of 30 July 2015, the first such resolution on tackling illicit trafficking in wildlife, and also its resolutions 70/301 of 9 September 2016 and 71/326 of 11 September 2017, and welcoming the outcome of the high-level meetings on poaching and illicit wildlife trafficking, hosted by Gabon and Germany and held on the margins of the high-level segments of the sixty-eighth and sixty-ninth sessions of the General Assembly,

Emphasizing the need to strengthen the capacity for conflict prevention and peacekeeping in Africa, and taking note in this regard of the concrete conflict prevention initiatives facilitated by the Department of Political Affairs of the Secretariat,

Welcoming the close cooperation established between the United Nations Regional Office for Central Africa and the Economic Community of Central African States, as well as the signing of a new framework of cooperation agreement between the two entities on 14 June 2016,

Bearing in mind the increased focus of the Standing Advisory Committee on human security questions, such as trafficking in persons, especially women and children, as an important consideration for subregional peace, stability and conflict prevention, and welcoming the adoption by the General Assembly at its seventy-second session of the political declaration on the implementation of the United Nations Global Plan of Action to Combat Trafficking in Persons[7] following the high-level meeting on the appraisal of the United Nations global plan of action to combat trafficking in persons,

Welcoming the holding of the presidential and legislative elections in the Central African Republic, which led to the re-establishment of the constitutional order with the election of a President and the formation of a new Government, and taking note in that context of the reinstatement of the Central African Republic as a member of the African Union on 7 April 2016,

Expressing continued concern about the fragile situation in the Central African Republic and in the neighbouring countries affected, and noting the importance of promoting the political process, including through rationalization of the multiple peace initiatives, in order to make tangible progress, in particular with regard to protection of civilians, disarmament, demobilization and reintegration of former combatants, and strengthening the authority of the State,

Expressing concern about the increasing impact of cross-border criminality, in particular the activities of the Lord's Resistance Army, the terrorist attacks by Boko Haram in the Lake Chad Basin region and incidents of piracy in the Gulf of Guinea, on peace, security and development in Central Africa,

---

[7] Resolution 72/1.

Welcoming the progress made by the States members of the Lake Chad Basin Commission and Benin in making the Multinational Joint Task Force operational in order to effectively combat the threat posed by the Boko Haram terrorist group to the Lake Chad Basin region, and taking note of the signing of a memorandum of understanding between the Lake Chad Basin Commission and the African Union to support the Task Force,

Also welcoming the visit made by the Security Council to the countries of the Lake Chad Basin region from 2 to 7 March 2017, and welcoming resolution 2349 (2017) of 31 March 2017 adopted by the Council at the end of the visit, in which the Council called for, inter alia, increased assistance to the countries of the region,

Considering the urgent need to prevent the possible movement of illicit weapons, mercenaries and combatants involved in conflicts in the Sahel and in neighbouring countries in the Central African subregion,

1.   *Reaffirms its support* for efforts aimed at promoting confidence-building measures at the regional and subregional levels in order to ease tensions and conflicts in Central Africa and to further sustainable peace, stability and development in the subregion;

2.   *Welcomes* the measures taken at the forty-fourth ministerial meeting of the United Nations Standing Advisory Committee on Security Questions in Central Africa with a view to revitalizing the work of the Standing Advisory Committee, in particular the adoption of a more dynamic agenda and the strengthening of synergies between the Committee and the Economic Community of Central African States and the new format for ministerial meetings, including closed meetings, and takes note of the institutionalization of the role of the Committee focal point to ensure follow-up of the recommendations concerning the competent national institutions;

3.   *Welcomes and encourages* the initiative of the States members of the Standing Advisory Committee to develop collaboration and synergies with the Economic Community of Central African States and organs of the Council for Peace and Security in Central Africa, in particular the Commission for Defence and Security, including with a view to promoting the implementation of the regional strategy for combating terrorism and the trafficking in small arms and light weapons in Central Africa adopted by the Committee;

4.   *Encourages* the Standing Advisory Committee decision to develop a communications strategy in order to increase its visibility, including among the populations of the subregion, in cooperation with civil society;

5.   *Reaffirms* the importance of disarmament and arms control programmes in Central Africa carried out by the States of the subregion with the support of the United Nations, the African Union and other international partners;

6.   *Encourages* Member States to provide assistance to those States members of the Standing Advisory Committee that have ratified the Arms Trade Treaty,[8] and encourages those that have not yet done so to ratify the Treaty;

7.   *Welcomes* the entry into force of the Central African Convention for the Control of Small Arms and Light Weapons, Their Ammunition and All Parts and Components That Can Be Used for Their Manufacture, Repair and Assembly (Kinshasa Convention),[1] and encourages States members of the Standing Advisory Committee and other interested States to provide financial support for the implementation of the Convention;

8.   *Calls upon* the Secretary-General to convene the first Conference of States Parties to the Central African Convention for the Control of Small Arms and Light Weapons, Their Ammunition and All Parts and Components That Can Be Used for Their Manufacture, Repair and Assembly, in accordance with article 34, paragraph 3, of the Kinshasa Convention, and requests States parties to inform him of the logistical details, including the venue of the meeting, the composition of the bureau and the source of funding for the meeting;

9.   *Encourages* the States members of the Standing Advisory Committee to assist States parties in the organization of the first Conference of States Parties and in coordination activities for the control of small arms and light weapons at the regional and national level, including funding thereof, as expeditiously as possible;

10.   *Encourages* States members of the Standing Advisory Committee to provide assistance to the secretariat of the Economic Community of Central African States, as the mechanism for the coordination and implementation of the Convention at the subregional level, with a view to carrying out related activities in accordance with articles 29 and 31 of the Convention;

11.   *Urges* the States members of the Standing Advisory Committee to implement the Libreville Declaration on the adoption and implementation of the regional strategy and plan of action for combating terrorism and the trafficking in small arms and light weapons in Central Africa, and requests the United Nations Regional Office for Central Africa, the United Nations Regional Centre for Peace and Disarmament in Africa, the Security Council Committee established pursuant to resolution 1373 (2001) concerning counter-terrorism and the international community to support those measures;

12.   *Urges* the States members of the Economic Community of Central African States to implement the integrated strategy and plan of action for combating terrorism and the trafficking in small arms and light weapons in Central Africa, and requests the United Nations Regional Office for Central Africa to support the efforts of States members of the Economic Community of Central African States in this regard;

---

[8]   See resolution 67/234 B.

13. *Encourages* the Economic Community of Central African States and the Economic Community of West African States, in coordination with the African Union Commission, to accelerate joint efforts to adopt a comprehensive strategy to more effectively and urgently combat the threat posed by Boko Haram, and in this regard urges the two subregional organizations to convene their joint summit at the earliest opportunity in order to adopt a common strategy and develop active cooperation and coordination;

14. *Encourages* the States members of the Standing Advisory Committee to carry out the programmes of activities adopted at their ministerial meetings;

15. *Appeals* to the international community to support the efforts undertaken by the States concerned to implement disarmament, demobilization and reintegration programmes;

16. *Welcomes* the efforts of the Republic of Cameroon and the Republic of the Congo in providing assistance, respectively, to the Interregional Coordination Centre for Maritime Security in the Gulf of Guinea and the Regional Centre for Maritime Security in Central Africa, and urges other member States to honour their financial commitments in order to ensure the predictable and sustainable operation of the two Centres;

17. *Encourages* Member States to continue to implement the outcomes of the Summit of Heads of State and Government on Maritime Safety and Security in the Gulf of Guinea by operationalizing the Interregional Coordination Centre for Maritime Security in the Gulf of Guinea and activities of the Regional Centre for Maritime Security in Central Africa, and also encourages the implementation of the African Charter on Maritime Security and Safety and Development in Africa adopted at the African Union Extraordinary Summit of Heads of State and Government on Maritime Security and Safety and Development in Africa;

18. *Calls upon* Member States and subregional bodies to take immediate concerted action to counter the phenomenon of poaching and trafficking in wildlife, including through the implementation of the provisions of its resolutions 69/314, 70/301 and 71/326;

19. *Expresses its full support* for the efforts of the Economic Community of Central African States, the African Union and the United Nations in the Central African Republic, and calls upon the international community to support these efforts;

20. *Requests* the Security Council to consider strengthening the mandate of the United Nations Multidimensional Integrated Stabilization Mission in the Central African Republic in order to reinforce and support the internal security forces and the defence forces of the Central African Republic in coordination with the European Union Training Mission in the Central African Republic in their efforts to stabilize the country, including in the east, in the context of combating the Lord's Resistance Army and other armed groups;

21. *Encourages* the States members of the Standing Advisory Committee to pursue their discussions on concrete conflict prevention initiatives, and requests in this regard the assistance of the Secretary-General;

22. *Requests* the United Nations Regional Office for Central Africa, in collaboration with the United Nations Regional Centre for Peace and Disarmament in Africa, to facilitate the efforts undertaken by the States members of the Standing Advisory Committee, in particular for their execution of the Implementation Plan for the Kinshasa Convention;[9]

23. *Requests* the Secretary-General and the Office of the United Nations High Commissioner for Refugees to continue to assist the countries of Central Africa in tackling the problems of refugees and displaced persons in their territories;

24. *Requests* the Secretary-General and the United Nations High Commissioner for Human Rights to continue to provide their full assistance for the proper functioning of the Subregional Centre for Human Rights and Democracy in Central Africa;

25. *Welcomes* the increased contributions made by several Member States to the Trust Fund of the United Nations Standing Advisory Committee on Security Questions in Central Africa, reminds the States members of the Standing Advisory Committee of the commitments they undertook on the adoption of the Declaration on the Trust Fund of the United Nations Standing Advisory Committee on Security Questions in Central Africa on 8 May 2009[10] and the Bangui Declaration on 10 June 2016,[11] and invites those States members of the Committee that have not already done so to contribute to the Trust Fund;

26. *Urges* other States Members of the United Nations and intergovernmental and non-governmental organizations to support the activities of the Standing Advisory Committee effectively through voluntary contributions to the Trust Fund;

27. *Urges* the States members of the Standing Advisory Committee, in accordance with Security Council resolution 1325 (2000) of 31 October 2000, to strengthen the gender component of the various meetings of the Committee relating to disarmament and international security, in line with the Sao Tome Declaration on the participation of women in the statutory meetings of the Committee, adopted on 1 December 2016,[12] whereby States members were invited to increase the "representation of women in delegations participating in the statutory meetings of the Committee";

---

[9] See A/65/717-S/2011/53, annex.
[10] A/64/85-S/2009/288, annex I.
[11] A/71/293, annex I.
[12] A/72/363, annex II.

28. *Expresses its satisfaction* to the Secretary-General for his support to the Standing Advisory Committee, expresses appreciation for the role played by the United Nations Regional Office for Central Africa, welcomes the strengthening of the Office, and strongly encourages the States members of the Standing Advisory Committee and international partners to support the work of the Office;

29. *Welcomes* the efforts of the Standing Advisory Committee towards addressing cross-border security threats in Central Africa, including activities of Boko Haram and the Lord's Resistance Army, and acts of piracy and armed robbery at sea in the Gulf of Guinea, as well as the fallout from the situation in the Central African Republic, and also welcomes the role of the United Nations Regional Office for Central Africa in coordinating those efforts, working closely with the Economic Community of Central African States, the African Union and all relevant regional and international partners;

30. *Expresses its satisfaction* to the Secretary-General for his support for the revitalization of the activities of the Standing Advisory Committee, and requests him to continue to provide the assistance needed to ensure the success of its regular biannual meetings;

31. *Calls upon* the Secretary-General to submit to the General Assembly at its seventy-third session a report on the implementation of the present resolution;

32. *Decides* to include in the provisional agenda of its seventy-third session, under the item entitled "Review and implementation of the Concluding Document of the Twelfth Special Session of the General Assembly", the sub-item entitled "Regional confidence-building measures: activities of the United Nations Standing Advisory Committee on Security Questions in Central Africa".

Action by the General Assembly

Date: 4 December 2017   Meeting: 62nd plenary meeting
Vote: Adopted without a vote   Report: A/72/410

Sponsors

Cameroon (on behalf of the States Members of the United Nations that are members of the Economic Community of Central African States)

Co-sponsors

Malawi, Maldives

Action by the First Committee

Date: 1 November 2017   Meeting: 27th meeting
Vote: Adopted without a vote   Draft resolution: A/C.1/72/L.20

Agenda item 100 (f)

72/64 United Nations regional centres for peace and disarmament

Text

The General Assembly,

Recalling its resolutions 60/83 of 8 December 2005, 61/90 of 6 December 2006, 62/50 of 5 December 2007, 63/76 of 2 December 2008, 64/58 of 2 December 2009, 65/78 of 8 December 2010, 66/53 of 2 December 2011, 67/63 of 3 December 2012, 68/57 of 5 December 2013, 69/70 of 2 December 2014, 70/61 of 7 December 2015 and 71/80 of 5 December 2016 regarding the maintenance and revitalization of the three United Nations regional centres for peace and disarmament,

Recalling also the reports of the Secretary-General on the United Nations Regional Centre for Peace and Disarmament in Africa,[1] the United Nations Regional Centre for Peace and Disarmament in Asia and the Pacific[2] and the United Nations Regional Centre for Peace, Disarmament and Development in Latin America and the Caribbean,[3]

Reaffirming its decision, taken in 1982 at its twelfth special session, to establish the United Nations Disarmament Information Programme, the purpose of which is to inform, educate and generate public understanding and support for the objectives of the United Nations in the field of arms control and disarmament,

Bearing in mind its resolutions 40/151 G of 16 December 1985, 41/60 J of 3 December 1986, 42/39 D of 30 November 1987 and 44/117 F of 15 December 1989 on the regional centres for peace and disarmament in Nepal, Peru and Togo,

Noting that the thirtieth anniversary of the establishment by the General Assembly of the United Nations Regional Centre for Peace and Disarmament in Africa, the United Nations Regional Centre for Peace and Disarmament in Asia and the Pacific, and the United Nations Regional Centre for Peace, Disarmament and Development in Latin America and the Caribbean was celebrated in 2016 and will also be marked in 2017,

Recognizing that the changes that have taken place in the world have created new opportunities and posed new challenges for the pursuit of disarmament, and bearing in mind in this regard that the regional centres for peace and disarmament can contribute substantially to understanding and

---

[1] A/72/97.
[2] A/72/98 and A/72/98/Corr.1.
[3] A/72/99.

cooperation among States in each particular region in the areas of peace, disarmament and development,

Noting that, in paragraph 201 of the Final Document of the Seventeenth Conference of Heads of State or Government of Non-Aligned Countries, held on Margarita Island, Bolivarian Republic of Venezuela, on 17 and 18 September 2016, the Heads of State or Government emphasized the importance of United Nations activities at the regional level to increase the stability and security of its Member States, which could be promoted in a substantive manner by the maintenance and revitalization of the three regional centres for peace and disarmament,

1.   *Reiterates* the importance of United Nations activities at the regional level to advance disarmament and to increase the stability and security of its Member States, which could be promoted in a substantive manner by the maintenance and further strengthening of the three regional centres for peace and disarmament;

2.   *Commends* the three regional centres for peace and disarmament for their sustained support to Member States over the past 30 years in implementing disarmament, arms control and non-proliferation activities through seminars and conferences, capacity-building and training, policy and technical expertise, and information and advocacy at the global, regional and national levels;

3.   *Reaffirms* that, in order to achieve positive results, it is useful for the three regional centres to carry out dissemination and educational programmes that promote regional peace and security and that are aimed at changing basic attitudes with respect to peace and security and disarmament so as to support the achievement of the purposes and principles of the United Nations;

4.   *Appeals* to Member States in each region that are able to do so, as well as to international governmental and non-governmental organizations and foundations, to make voluntary contributions to the regional centres in their respective regions in order to strengthen their activities and initiatives;

5.   *Emphasizes* the importance of the activities of the Regional Disarmament Branch of the Office for Disarmament Affairs of the Secretariat;

6.   *Requests* the Secretary-General to provide all support necessary, within existing resources, to the regional centres in carrying out their programmes of activities;

7.   *Decides* to include in the provisional agenda of its seventy-third session, under the item entitled "Review and implementation of the Concluding Document of the Twelfth Special Session of the General Assembly", the sub-item entitled "United Nations regional centres for peace and disarmament".

Action by the General Assembly

Date: 4 December 2017   Meeting: 62nd plenary meeting
Vote: Adopted without a vote   Report: A/72/410

Sponsors

Indonesia (on behalf of the States Members of the United Nations that are members of the Movement of Non-Aligned Countries)

Action by the First Committee

Date: 1 November 2017   Meeting: 27th meeting
Vote: Adopted without a vote   Draft resolution: A/C.1/72/L.34

Agenda item 101 (a)

72/65 Report of the Conference on Disarmament

Text

The General Assembly,

Having considered the report of the Conference on Disarmament,[1]

Convinced that the Conference on Disarmament, as the single multilateral disarmament negotiating forum of the international community, has the primary role in substantive negotiations on priority questions of disarmament,

Recognizing the message of the Secretary-General of the United Nations, as well as the addresses of Ministers for Foreign Affairs and other high-level officials in the Conference on Disarmament, as expressions of support and concern for the endeavours of the Conference and as calls for the Conference to immediately commence negotiations to advance disarmament goals through the adoption of a balanced and comprehensive programme of work,

Recognizing also the need to conduct multilateral negotiations with the aim of reaching agreement on concrete issues, and considering that the present international climate should give additional impetus to multilateral negotiations,

Noting with renewed concern that, despite the intensive efforts by States members and Presidents of the Conference on Disarmament at its 2017 session to reach consensus on a programme of work on the basis of relevant proposals and suggestions, the Conference did not succeed in commencing its substantive work, including negotiations, as called for by the General Assembly in its resolution 71/81 of 5 December 2016, or in agreeing on and implementing a programme of work,

Recalling, in this respect, that the Conference on Disarmament has a number of urgent and important issues for negotiation to achieve disarmament goals,

Welcoming the overwhelming call for greater flexibility with respect to commencing the substantive work of the Conference on Disarmament without further delay, on the basis of a balanced and comprehensive programme of work,

Appreciating the continued cooperation among the States members of the Conference on Disarmament as well as the six successive Presidents of the Conference at its 2017 session,

---

[1] *Official Records of the General Assembly, Seventy-second Session, Supplement No. 27* (A/72/27).

Noting with appreciation the significant contributions made at the 2017 session to promote substantive discussions on issues on the agenda, including the informal discussions held pursuant to the decision adopted on 17 February 2017,[2] and noting the discussions on the functioning of the Conference on Disarmament, as well as the discussions held on other issues that could also be relevant to the current international security environment,

Emphasizing the importance of the United Nations Institute for Disarmament Research, as a stand-alone, autonomous institution, and the contribution that its research makes,

Recognizing the importance of engagement between civil society and the Conference on Disarmament according to decisions taken by the Conference,

Stressing the urgent need for the Conference on Disarmament to commence its substantive work at the beginning of its 2018 session,

1.   *Reaffirms* the role of the Conference on Disarmament as the single multilateral disarmament negotiating forum of the international community;

2.   *Appreciates* the strong support expressed for the Conference on Disarmament at its 2017 session by Ministers for Foreign Affairs and other high-level officials, while also acknowledging their concern about its ongoing impasse, and takes into account their calls for greater flexibility with respect to commencing the substantive work of the Conference without further delay;

3.   *Calls upon* the Conference on Disarmament to further intensify consultations and to explore possibilities for overcoming its ongoing deadlock of two decades by adopting and implementing a balanced and comprehensive programme of work at the earliest possible date during its 2018 session, bearing in mind the decision on the programme of work adopted by the Conference on 29 May 2009,[3] as well as other relevant present, past and future proposals;

4.   *Takes note with appreciation* of the decision of the Conference on Disarmament to establish the working group on the way ahead with a mandate to take stock of the progress on all agenda items of the Conference, identify issues for substantive work under the agenda, identify common ground for a programme of work with a negotiating mandate and consider steps for the way ahead,[2] and appreciates the efforts of the Chair and the facilitators of the working group;

5.   *Welcomes* the decision of the Conference on Disarmament to request the current President and the incoming President of the Conference to conduct consultations during the intersessional period and, if possible, to make recommendations, taking into account all relevant proposals, past, present and future, including those submitted as documents of the Conference, views

---

[2] Ibid., para. 15.

[3] Ibid., *Sixty-fourth Session, Supplement No. 27* (A/64/27), para. 18.

presented and discussions held, and to endeavour to keep the membership of the Conference informed, as appropriate, of their consultations;

6. *Requests* all States members of the Conference on Disarmament to cooperate with the current President and successive Presidents in their efforts to guide the Conference to the early commencement of its substantive work, including negotiations, at its 2018 session;

7. *Recognizes* the importance of continuing consultations in 2018 on the question of the expansion of the membership of the Conference on Disarmament;

8. *Requests* the Secretary-General to continue to ensure and to strengthen, if needed, the provision to the Conference on Disarmament of all necessary administrative, substantive and conference support services;

9. *Requests* the Conference on Disarmament to submit to the General Assembly at its seventy-third session a report on its work;

10. *Decides* to include in the provisional agenda of its seventy-third session, under the item entitled "Review of the implementation of the recommendations and decisions adopted by the General Assembly at its tenth special session", the sub-item entitled "Report of the Conference on Disarmament".

Action by the General Assembly

Date: 4 December 2017	Meeting: 62nd plenary meeting
Vote: Adopted without a vote	Report: A/72/411

Sponsors

Spain

Action by the First Committee

Date: 1 November 2017	Meeting: 27th meeting
Vote: Adopted without a vote	Draft resolution: A/C.1/72/L.14

Agenda item 101 (b)

72/66   Report of the Disarmament Commission

Text

The General Assembly,

Having considered the report of the Disarmament Commission,[1]

Recalling its resolutions 47/54 A of 9 December 1992, 47/54 G of 8 April 1993, 48/77 A of 16 December 1993, 49/77 A of 15 December 1994, 50/72 D of 12 December 1995, 51/47 B of 10 December 1996, 52/40 B of 9 December 1997, 53/79 A of 4 December 1998, 54/56 A of 1 December 1999, 55/35 C of 20 November 2000, 56/26 A of 29 November 2001, 57/95 of 22 November 2002, 58/67 of 8 December 2003, 59/105 of 3 December 2004, 60/91 of 8 December 2005, 61/98 of 6 December 2006, 62/54 of 5 December 2007, 63/83 of 2 December 2008, 64/65 of 2 December 2009, 65/86 of 8 December 2010, 66/60 of 2 December 2011, 67/71 of 3 December 2012, 68/63 of 5 December 2013, 69/77 of 2 December 2014, 70/68 of 7 December 2015 and 71/82 of 5 December 2016,

Considering the role that the Disarmament Commission has been called upon to play and the contribution that it should make in examining and submitting recommendations on various problems in the field of disarmament and in promoting the implementation of the relevant decisions adopted by the General Assembly at its tenth special session,

Recalling in particular General Assembly resolution 45/62 B of 4 December 1990, in which it noted with satisfaction the adoption by consensus of a set of "Ways and means to enhance the functioning of the Disarmament Commission",[2] Assembly decision 52/492 of 8 September 1998 concerning the efficient functioning of the Commission and Assembly resolution 61/98, which contains additional measures for improving the effectiveness of the methods of work of the Commission,

Reaffirming the mandate of the Disarmament Commission as the specialized, deliberative subsidiary body of the General Assembly that allows for in-depth deliberations on specific disarmament issues, leading to the submission of concrete recommendations on those issues, and recalling that the Commission shall make every effort to ensure that, insofar as possible, decisions on substantive issues be adopted by consensus, as set forth in paragraph 118 of the Final Document of the Tenth Special Session of the General Assembly,[3]

---

[1] *Official Records of the General Assembly, Seventy-second Session, Supplement No. 42* (A/72/42).

[2] Resolution 44/119 C, annex.

[3] Resolution S-10/2.

Emphasizing once again the important place of the Disarmament Commission within the United Nations multilateral disarmament machinery,

1.   *Takes note* of the report of the Disarmament Commission;[1]

2.   *Commends* the Disarmament Commission for the successful conclusion of its consideration of the item entitled "Practical confidence-building measures in the field of conventional weapons", and endorses the consensus text adopted thereon;[1]

3.   *Notes with regret* that the Disarmament Commission was not able to reach a consensus on the item entitled "Recommendations for achieving the objective of nuclear disarmament and non-proliferation of nuclear weapons";

4.   *Reaffirms* the importance of further enhancing the dialogue and cooperation among the First Committee, the Disarmament Commission and the Conference on Disarmament;

5.   *Requests* the Disarmament Commission to continue its work in accordance with its mandate, as set forth in paragraph 118 of the Final Document of the Tenth Special Session of the General Assembly,[3] and with paragraph 3 of Assembly resolution 37/78 H of 9 December 1982 and to that end to make every effort to achieve specific recommendations on the items on its agenda, taking into account the adopted "Ways and means to enhance the functioning of the Disarmament Commission";[2]

6.   *Recommends* that the Disarmament Commission consider the following items at its substantive session of 2018:

(a)   [To be determined];

(b)   [To be determined];

7.   *Encourages* the Disarmament Commission to invite, as appropriate, the United Nations Institute for Disarmament Research to prepare background papers on the items on its agenda and, if need be, other disarmament experts to present their views, as provided for in paragraph 3 (e) of resolution 61/98, upon the invitation of the Chair and with the prior approval of the Commission;

8.   *Requests* the Disarmament Commission to meet for a period not exceeding three weeks during 2018, namely from 2 to 20 April, and to submit a substantive report to the General Assembly at its seventy-third session, and stresses that the report of the Commission should contain a summary by the Chair of the proceedings to reflect different views or positions if no agreement can be reached on the specific agenda item deliberated on, as provided for in paragraph 3.4 of the adopted "Ways and means to enhance the functioning of the Disarmament Commission";

9.   *Requests* the Secretary-General to ensure full provision to the Disarmament Commission and its subsidiary bodies of interpretation and translation facilities in the official languages and to assign, as a matter of

priority, all the resources and services necessary, including verbatim records, to that end, and also requests the Secretary-General to transmit to the Commission the annual report of the Conference on Disarmament on its 2017 session,[4] together with all the official records of the seventy-second session of the General Assembly relating to disarmament matters, and to render all assistance that the Commission may require for implementing the present resolution;

10. *Invites* Member States to submit their views and proposals on the matter early enough to enable practical consultations among them prior to the beginning of the substantive session of 2018 of the Disarmament Commission, with a view to facilitating its constructive outcome, and in this regard encourages the Chair-designate to commence consultations and preparations for the substantive session of 2018 in a timely manner upon his or her nomination;

11. *Decides* to include in the provisional agenda of its seventy-third session, under the item entitled "Review of the implementation of the recommendations and decisions adopted by the General Assembly at its tenth special session", the sub-item entitled "Report of the Disarmament Commission".

Action by the General Assembly

  Date: 4 December 2017   Meeting: 62nd plenary meeting
  Vote: Adopted without a vote   Report: A/72/411

Sponsors

  Argentina (on behalf of the members of the Bureau of the Disarmament Commission)

Action by the First Committee

  Date: 1 November 2017   Meeting: 27 meeting
  Vote: Adopted without a vote   Draft resolution: A/C.1/72/L.25

---

[4] *Official Records of the General Assembly, Seventy-second Session, Supplement No. 27* (A/72/27).

Agenda item 102

72/67   The risk of nuclear proliferation in the Middle East

Text

The General Assembly,

Bearing in mind its relevant resolutions, the latest of which is resolution 71/83 of 5 December 2016,

Taking note of the relevant resolutions adopted by the General Conference of the International Atomic Energy Agency, the latest of which is resolution GC(61)/RES/14, adopted on 21 September 2017,

Cognizant that the proliferation of nuclear weapons in the region of the Middle East would pose a serious threat to international peace and security,

Mindful of the immediate need for placing all nuclear facilities in the region of the Middle East under full-scope safeguards of the Agency,

Recalling the decision on principles and objectives for nuclear non-proliferation and disarmament adopted by the 1995 Review and Extension Conference of the Parties to the Treaty on the Non-Proliferation of Nuclear Weapons on 11 May 1995,[1] in which the Conference urged universal adherence to the Treaty on the Non-Proliferation of Nuclear Weapons[2] as an urgent priority and called upon all States not yet parties to the Treaty to accede to it at the earliest date, particularly those States that operate unsafeguarded nuclear facilities,

Recognizing with satisfaction that, in the Final Document of the 2000 Review Conference of the Parties to the Treaty on the Non-Proliferation of Nuclear Weapons,[3] the Conference undertook to make determined efforts towards the achievement of the goal of universality of the Treaty, called upon those remaining States not parties to the Treaty to accede to it, thereby accepting an international legally binding commitment not to acquire nuclear weapons or nuclear explosive devices and to accept Agency safeguards on all their nuclear activities, and underlined the necessity of universal adherence to the Treaty and of strict compliance by all parties with their obligations under the Treaty,

Recalling the resolution on the Middle East adopted by the 1995 Review and Extension Conference of the Parties to the Treaty on 11 May 1995,[1] in

---

[1] See *1995 Review and Extension Conference of the Parties to the Treaty on the Non-Proliferation of Nuclear Weapons, Final Document, Part I* (NPT/CONF.1995/32 (Part I) and NPT/CONF.1995/32 (Part I)/Corr.2), annex.

[2] United Nations, *Treaty Series*, vol. 729, No. 10485.

[3] *2000 Review Conference of the Parties to the Treaty on the Non-Proliferation of Nuclear Weapons, Final Document*, vols. I–III (NPT/CONF.2000/28 (Parts I and II), NPT/CONF.2000/28 (Part III) and NPT/CONF.2000/28 (Part IV)).

which the Conference noted with concern the continued existence in the Middle East of unsafeguarded nuclear facilities, reaffirmed the importance of the early realization of universal adherence to the Treaty, and called upon all States in the Middle East that had not yet done so, without exception, to accede to the Treaty as soon as possible and to place all their nuclear facilities under full-scope Agency safeguards,

Acknowledging that, in the Final Document of the 2010 Review Conference of the Parties to the Treaty on the Non-Proliferation of Nuclear Weapons,[4] the Conference emphasized the importance of a process leading to full implementation of the 1995 resolution on the Middle East and decided, inter alia, that the Secretary-General of the United Nations and the co-sponsors of the 1995 resolution, in consultation with the States of the region, would convene a conference in 2012, to be attended by all States of the Middle East, on the establishment of a Middle East zone free of nuclear weapons and all other weapons of mass destruction, on the basis of arrangements freely arrived at by the States of the region, and with the full support and engagement of the nuclear-weapon States,

Expressing regret and concern that the conference was not convened in 2012 as mandated and that little progress has been achieved towards the implementation of the resolution on the Middle East adopted by the 1995 Review and Extension Conference of the Parties to the Treaty,

Noting, in this context, the relevant resolutions of the League of Arab States aiming at the establishment of a Middle East zone free of nuclear weapons and all other weapons of mass destruction,

Taking note with appreciation of the report of the Secretary-General,[5]

Recalling that Israel remains the only State in the Middle East that has not yet become a party to the Treaty,

Concerned about the threats posed by the proliferation of nuclear weapons to the security and stability of the Middle East region,

Stressing the importance of taking confidence-building measures, in particular the establishment of a nuclear-weapon-free zone in the Middle East, in order to enhance peace and security in the region and to consolidate the global non-proliferation regime,

Emphasizing the need for all parties directly concerned to seriously consider taking the practical and urgent steps required for the implementation of the proposal to establish a nuclear-weapon-free zone in the region of the Middle East in accordance with the relevant resolutions of the General Assembly and, as a means of promoting this objective, inviting the countries

---

[4] *2010 Review Conference of the Parties to the Treaty on the Non-Proliferation of Nuclear Weapons, Final Document*, vols. I–III (NPT/CONF.2010/50 (Vol. I), NPT/CONF.2010/50 (Vol. II) and NPT/CONF.2010/50 (Vol. III)).

[5] A/72/340 (Part II).

concerned to adhere to the Treaty and, pending the establishment of the zone, to agree to place all their nuclear activities under Agency safeguards,

Noting that 183 States have signed the Comprehensive Nuclear-Test-Ban Treaty,[6] including a number of States in the region,

1.   *Recalls* the conclusions on the Middle East of the 2010 Review Conference of the Parties to the Treaty on the Non-Proliferation of Nuclear Weapons,[7] and calls for the speedy and full implementation of the commitments contained therein;

2.   *Stresses* that the resolution on the Middle East adopted by the 1995 Review and Extension Conference of the Parties to the Treaty[1] is an essential element of the outcome of the 1995 Conference and of the basis on which the Treaty was indefinitely extended without a vote in 1995;

3.   *Reiterates* that the resolution on the Middle East adopted by the 1995 Review and Extension Conference of the Parties to the Treaty remains valid until its goals and objectives are achieved;

4.   *Calls for* immediate steps towards the full implementation of that resolution;

5.   *Reaffirms* the importance of Israel's accession to the Treaty on the Non-Proliferation of Nuclear Weapons[2] and placement of all its nuclear facilities under comprehensive International Atomic Energy Agency safeguards, in realizing the goal of universal adherence to the Treaty in the Middle East;

6.   *Calls upon* that State to accede to the Treaty without further delay, not to develop, produce, test or otherwise acquire nuclear weapons, to renounce possession of nuclear weapons and to place all its unsafeguarded nuclear facilities under full-scope Agency safeguards as an important confidence-building measure among all States of the region and as a step towards enhancing peace and security;

7.   *Requests* the Secretary-General to report to the General Assembly at its seventy-third session on the implementation of the present resolution;

8.   *Decides* to include in the provisional agenda of its seventy-third session the item entitled "The risk of nuclear proliferation in the Middle East".

Action by the General Assembly

Date: 4 December 2017   Meeting: 62nd plenary meeting
Vote: 157-5-20   Report: A/72/412
        173-3-2, p.p. 5
        172-3-1, p.p. 6

---

[6] See resolution 50/245 and A/50/1027.
[7] *2010 Review Conference of the Parties to the Treaty on the Non-Proliferation of Nuclear Weapons, Final Document*, vol. I (NPT/CONF.2010/50 (Vol. I)), part I, *Conclusions and recommendations for follow-on actions*, sect. IV.

Sponsors

Algeria, Bahrain, Comoros, Djibouti, **Egypt** (on behalf of the States Members of the United Nations that are members of the League of Arab States), Iraq, Jordan, Kuwait, Lebanon, Libya, Mauritania, Morocco, Oman, Qatar, Saudi Arabia, Somalia, Sudan, Tunisia, United Arab Emirates, Yemen, State of Palestine

Recorded vote

As a whole

In favour:

Afghanistan, Albania, Algeria, Andorra, Angola, Antigua and Barbuda, Argentina, Armenia, Austria, Azerbaijan, Bahamas, Bahrain, Bangladesh, Barbados, Belarus, Belize, Benin, Bhutan, Bolivia (Plurinational State of), Bosnia and Herzegovina, Botswana, Brazil, Brunei Darussalam, Bulgaria, Burkina Faso, Burundi, Cabo Verde, Cambodia, Chad, Chile, China, Colombia, Comoros, Congo, Costa Rica, Côte d'Ivoire, Croatia, Cuba, Cyprus, Democratic People's Republic of Korea, Democratic Republic of the Congo, Djibouti, Dominican Republic, Ecuador, Egypt, El Salvador, Equatorial Guinea, Eritrea, Estonia, Fiji, Finland, Gabon, Gambia, Ghana, Greece, Guatemala, Guinea, Guinea-Bissau, Guyana, Honduras, Iceland, Indonesia, Iran (Islamic Republic of), Iraq, Ireland, Jamaica, Japan, Jordan, Kazakhstan, Kenya, Kuwait, Kyrgyzstan, Lao People's Democratic Republic, Latvia, Lebanon, Lesotho, Liberia, Libya, Liechtenstein, Madagascar, Malawi, Malaysia, Maldives, Mali, Malta, Mauritania, Mauritius, Mexico, Mongolia, Montenegro, Morocco, Mozambique, Myanmar, Namibia, Nauru, Nepal, New Zealand, Nicaragua, Nigeria, Norway, Oman, Pakistan, Papua New Guinea, Paraguay, Peru, Philippines, Portugal, Qatar, Republic of Korea, Republic of Moldova, Russian Federation, Rwanda, Saint Kitts and Nevis, Saint Lucia, Saint Vincent and the Grenadines, Samoa, San Marino, Saudi Arabia, Senegal, Serbia, Sierra Leone, Singapore, Slovakia, Slovenia, Solomon Islands, Somalia, South Africa, Spain, Sri Lanka, Sudan, Suriname, Swaziland, Sweden, Switzerland, Syrian Arab Republic, Tajikistan, Thailand, the former Yugoslav Republic of Macedonia, Timor-Leste, Togo, Trinidad and Tobago, Tunisia, Turkey, Turkmenistan, Tuvalu, Uganda, Ukraine, United Arab Emirates, United Republic of Tanzania, Uruguay, Uzbekistan, Vanuatu, Venezuela (Bolivarian Republic of), Viet Nam, Yemen, Zambia, Zimbabwe

Against:

Canada, Israel, Micronesia (Federated States of), Palau, United States

Abstaining:

Australia, Belgium, Cameroon, Czech Republic, Denmark, Ethiopia, France, Georgia, Germany, Hungary, India, Italy, Lithuania, Luxembourg, Monaco, Netherlands, Panama, Poland, Romania, United Kingdom

Fifth preambular paragraph*

In favour:

> Afghanistan, Albania, Algeria, Andorra, Angola, Antigua and Barbuda, Argentina, Armenia, Australia, Austria, Azerbaijan, Bahamas, Bahrain, Bangladesh, Barbados, Belarus, Belgium, Belize, Benin, Bolivia (Plurinational State of), Bosnia and Herzegovina, Botswana, Brazil, Brunei Darussalam, Bulgaria, Burkina Faso, Cabo Verde, Cambodia, Canada, Central African Republic, Chad, Chile, China, Colombia, Comoros, Congo, Costa Rica, Côte d'Ivoire, Croatia, Cuba, Cyprus, Czech Republic, Democratic Republic of the Congo, Denmark, Djibouti, Dominican Republic, Ecuador, Egypt, El Salvador, Equatorial Guinea, Eritrea, Estonia, Ethiopia, Fiji, Finland, France, Gabon, Gambia, Germany, Ghana, Greece, Guatemala, Guinea, Guinea-Bissau, Guyana, Haiti, Honduras, Hungary, Iceland, Indonesia, Iran (Islamic Republic of), Iraq, Ireland, Italy, Jamaica, Japan, Jordan, Kazakhstan, Kenya, Kuwait, Kyrgyzstan, Lao People's Democratic Republic, Latvia, Lebanon, Lesotho, Liberia, Libya, Liechtenstein, Lithuania, Luxembourg, Madagascar, Malawi, Malaysia, Maldives, Mali, Malta, Mauritania, Mauritius, Mexico, Monaco, Mongolia, Montenegro, Morocco, Mozambique, Myanmar, Namibia, Nepal, Netherlands, New Zealand, Nicaragua, Nigeria, Norway, Oman, Panama, Papua New Guinea, Paraguay, Peru, Philippines, Poland, Portugal, Qatar, Republic of Korea, Republic of Moldova, Romania, Russian Federation, Rwanda, Saint Kitts and Nevis, Saint Lucia, Saint Vincent and the Grenadines, Samoa, San Marino, Saudi Arabia, Senegal, Serbia, Sierra Leone, Singapore, Slovakia, Slovenia, Solomon Islands, Somalia, South Africa, Spain, Sri Lanka, Sudan, Suriname, Swaziland, Sweden, Switzerland, Syrian Arab Republic, Tajikistan, Thailand, the former Yugoslav Republic of Macedonia, Timor-Leste, Togo, Trinidad and Tobago, Tunisia, Turkey, Turkmenistan, Tuvalu, Uganda, Ukraine, United Arab Emirates, United Kingdom, United Republic of Tanzania, United States, Uruguay, Uzbekistan, Vanuatu, Venezuela (Bolivarian Republic of), Viet Nam, Yemen, Zambia, Zimbabwe

Against:

> India, Israel, Pakistan

Abstaining:

> Bhutan, Nauru

---

* Subsequently, the delegation of Nauru informed the Secretariat that it had not intended to participate in the voting. The voting tally above does not reflect this information.

Sixth preambular paragraph

In favour:

Afghanistan, Albania, Algeria, Andorra, Angola, Antigua and Barbuda, Argentina, Armenia, Australia, Austria, Azerbaijan, Bahamas, Bahrain, Bangladesh, Barbados, Belarus, Belgium, Belize, Benin, Bolivia (Plurinational State of), Bosnia and Herzegovina, Botswana, Brazil, Brunei Darussalam, Bulgaria, Burkina Faso, Burundi, Cabo Verde, Cambodia, Canada, Chad, Chile, China, Colombia, Comoros, Congo, Costa Rica, Côte d'Ivoire, Croatia, Cuba, Cyprus, Czech Republic, Democratic Republic of the Congo, Denmark, Djibouti, Dominican Republic, Ecuador, Egypt, El Salvador, Equatorial Guinea, Eritrea, Estonia, Ethiopia, Fiji, Finland, France, Gabon, Gambia, Germany, Ghana, Greece, Guatemala, Guinea, Guinea-Bissau, Guyana, Haiti, Honduras, Hungary, Iceland, Indonesia, Iran (Islamic Republic of), Iraq, Ireland, Italy, Jamaica, Japan, Jordan, Kazakhstan, Kenya, Kuwait, Kyrgyzstan, Lao People's Democratic Republic, Latvia, Lebanon, Lesotho, Liberia, Libya, Liechtenstein, Lithuania, Luxembourg, Madagascar, Malawi, Malaysia, Maldives, Mali, Malta, Mauritania, Mexico, Monaco, Mongolia, Montenegro, Morocco, Mozambique, Myanmar, Namibia, Nepal, Netherlands, New Zealand, Nicaragua, Nigeria, Norway, Oman, Panama, Papua New Guinea, Paraguay, Peru, Philippines, Poland, Portugal, Qatar, Republic of Korea, Republic of Moldova, Romania, Russian Federation, Rwanda, Saint Kitts and Nevis, Saint Lucia, Saint Vincent and the Grenadines, Samoa, San Marino, Saudi Arabia, Senegal, Serbia, Sierra Leone, Singapore, Slovakia, Slovenia, Solomon Islands, Somalia, South Africa, Spain, Sri Lanka, Sudan, Suriname, Swaziland, Sweden, Switzerland, Syrian Arab Republic, Tajikistan, Thailand, the former Yugoslav Republic of Macedonia, Timor-Leste, Togo, Trinidad and Tobago, Tunisia, Turkey, Turkmenistan, Tuvalu, Uganda, Ukraine, United Arab Emirates, United Kingdom, United Republic of Tanzania, United States, Uruguay, Uzbekistan, Vanuatu, Venezuela (Bolivarian Republic of), Viet Nam, Yemen, Zambia, Zimbabwe

Against:

India, Israel, Pakistan

Abstaining:

Bhutan

Action by the First Committee

Date: 27 October 2017 Meeting: 24th meeting
Vote: 150-4-19 Draft resolution: A/C.1/72/L.2
  164-3-2, p.p. 5
  164-3-2, p.p. 6

Agenda item 103

72/68 Convention on Prohibitions or Restrictions on the Use of Certain Conventional Weapons Which May Be Deemed to Be Excessively Injurious or to Have Indiscriminate Effects

Text

The General Assembly,

Recalling its resolution 71/84 of 5 December 2016,

Recalling with satisfaction the adoption and entry into force of the Convention on Prohibitions or Restrictions on the Use of Certain Conventional Weapons Which May Be Deemed to Be Excessively Injurious or to Have Indiscriminate Effects[1] and its amended article 1,[2] the Protocol on Non-Detectable Fragments (Protocol I),[1] the Protocol on Prohibitions or Restrictions on the Use of Mines, Booby Traps and Other Devices (Protocol II)[1] and its amended version,[3] the Protocol on Prohibitions or Restrictions on the Use of Incendiary Weapons (Protocol III),[1] the Protocol on Blinding Laser Weapons (Protocol IV)[4] and the Protocol on Explosive Remnants of War (Protocol V),[5]

Welcoming the results of the Fifth Review Conference of the High Contracting Parties to the Convention, held in Geneva from 12 to 16 December 2016,

Welcoming also the results of the Eighteenth Annual Conference of the High Contracting Parties to Amended Protocol II, held in Geneva on 30 August 2016,

Welcoming further the results of the Tenth Conference of the High Contracting Parties to Protocol V, held in Geneva on 29 August 2016,

Regretting that in 2017 the Meeting of the Group of Experts of the High Contracting Parties to Amended Protocol II, the Meeting of Experts of the High Contracting Parties to Protocol V and the first session of the Group of Governmental Experts related to emerging technologies in the area of lethal autonomous weapons systems of the High Contracting Parties to the Convention could not take place owing to lack of adequate funding to hold all meetings, and noting the importance of addressing issues arising from the outstanding dues of High Contracting Parties and participating States

---

[1] United Nations, *Treaty Series*, vol. 1342, No. 22495.
[2] Ibid., vol. 2260, No. 22495.
[3] Ibid., vol. 2048, No. 22495.
[4] Ibid., vol. 2024, No. 22495.
[5] Ibid., vol. 2399, No. 22495.

and from the financial and accounting practices recently implemented by the United Nations,

Recalling the role played by the International Committee of the Red Cross in the elaboration of the Convention and the Protocols thereto, and welcoming the particular efforts of various international, non-governmental and other organizations in raising awareness of the humanitarian consequences of various categories of conventional weapons which may be deemed to be excessively injurious or to have indiscriminate effects,

1.   *Calls upon* all States that have not yet done so to take all measures to become parties, as soon as possible, to the Convention on Prohibitions or Restrictions on the Use of Certain Conventional Weapons Which May Be Deemed to Be Excessively Injurious or to Have Indiscriminate Effects[1] and the Protocols thereto, as amended, with a view to achieving the widest possible adherence to these instruments at an early date and so as to ultimately achieve their universality;

2.   *Calls upon* all High Contracting Parties to the Convention that have not yet done so to express their consent to be bound by the Protocols to the Convention and the amendment extending the scope of the Convention and the Protocols thereto to include armed conflicts of a non-international character;

3.   *Emphasizes* the importance of the universalization of the Protocol on Explosive Remnants of War (Protocol V);[5]

4.   *Welcomes* the additional ratifications and acceptances of or accessions to the Convention, as well as the consents to be bound by the Protocols thereto;

5.   *Acknowledges* the continued efforts of the Secretary-General, as depositary of the Convention and the Protocols thereto, and of the respective office holders of the conferences of the High Contracting Parties to the Convention, Protocol V and Amended Protocol II, on behalf of the High Contracting Parties, to achieve the goal of universality;

6.   *Recalls* the following decisions by the Fifth Review Conference of the High Contracting Parties to the Convention:

(a)   To establish an open-ended Group of Governmental Experts related to emerging technologies in the area of lethal autonomous weapons systems in the context of the objectives and purposes of the Convention, adhering to the agreed recommendations contained in document CCW/CONF.V/2, and to submit a report to the 2017 Meeting of the High Contracting Parties to the Convention consistent with those recommendations;

(b)   To add to the agenda of the next Meeting of the High Contracting Parties in 2017 the item "Protocol III";

(c)   To add to the agenda of the next Meeting of the High Contracting Parties in 2017 the item "Mines other than anti-personnel mines";

(d)   To add to the agenda of the next Meeting of the High Contracting Parties in 2017 the item for informal discussion "Consideration of how developments in the field of science and technology relevant to the Convention may be addressed under the Convention";

(e)   To invite the Chairperson-elect to conduct consultations with a view to including on the agenda of the 2017 annual Meeting of the High Contracting Parties the item "Strengthening the respect for international humanitarian law and addressing, in the context and objectives of the Convention and its annexed Protocols, the challenges presented by the use of conventional weapons in armed conflicts and their impact on civilians, particularly in areas where there are concentrations of civilians";

(f)   To include on the agenda of the annual Meetings of the High Contracting Parties the item "Financial issues related to the Convention and its annexed Protocols" and to consider at the next such meeting efficiency and cost-saving measures and a report to be prepared by the Chairperson-elect;

(g)   To retain the practice of keeping summary records only for the final sessions of the future Review Conferences, the meetings of the High Contracting Parties to the Convention, and the Conferences of the High Contracting Parties to Amended Protocol II and Protocol V;

(h)   To continue the Sponsorship Programme;

7.   *Welcomes* the commitment by High Contracting Parties to continue to contribute to the further development of international humanitarian law and in this context to keep under review both the development of new weapons and uses of weapons, which may have indiscriminate effects or cause unnecessary suffering;

8.   *Calls upon* all High Contracting Parties to ensure full and prompt compliance with their financial obligations under the Convention and its annexed Protocols;

9.   *Also calls upon* all High Contracting Parties to explore options to improve the financial situation and ways to ensure financial stability for the operation of the Convention and its annexed Protocols;

10.   *Welcomes* the commitment of High Contracting Parties to Protocol V to the effective and efficient implementation of the Protocol and the implementation of the decisions of the First and Second Conferences of the High Contracting Parties to the Protocol establishing a comprehensive framework for the exchange of information and cooperation;

11.   *Notes* that, in conformity with article 8 of the Convention, conferences may be convened to examine amendments to the Convention or to any of the Protocols thereto, to examine additional protocols concerning other categories of conventional weapons not covered by existing Protocols or to

review the scope and application of the Convention and the Protocols thereto and to examine any proposed amendments or additional protocols;

12. *Acknowledges* the work of the Implementation Support Unit within the Geneva Branch of the Office for Disarmament Affairs of the Secretariat, which was established following a decision by the 2009 Meeting of the High Contracting Parties to the Convention;

13. *Requests* the Secretary-General to render the assistance necessary and to provide such services as may be required for the annual conferences and expert meetings of the High Contracting Parties to the Convention and of the High Contracting Parties to Amended Protocol II and Protocol V, as well as for any continuation of the work after the meetings;

14. *Also requests* the Secretary-General, in his capacity as depositary of the Convention and the Protocols thereto, to continue to inform the General Assembly periodically, by electronic means, of ratifications and acceptances of and accessions to the Convention, its amended article 1[2] and the Protocols;

15. *Decides* to include in the provisional agenda of its seventy-third session the item entitled "Convention on Prohibitions or Restrictions on the Use of Certain Conventional Weapons Which May Be Deemed to Be Excessively Injurious or to Have Indiscriminate Effects".

Action by the General Assembly

Date: 4 December 2017   Meeting: 62nd plenary meeting
Vote: Adopted without a vote   Report: A/72/413

Sponsors

Pakistan

Action by the First Committee

Date: 31 October 2017   Meeting: 26th meeting
Vote: Adopted without a vote   Draft resolution: A/C.1/72/L.16/Rev.1

Agenda item 104

72/69 Strengthening of security and cooperation in the Mediterranean region

Text

The General Assembly,

Recalling its previous resolutions on the subject, including resolution 71/85 of 5 December 2016,

Reaffirming the primary role of the Mediterranean countries in strengthening and promoting peace, security and cooperation in the Mediterranean region,

Welcoming the efforts deployed by the Euro-Mediterranean countries to strengthen their cooperation in combating terrorism, in particular through the adoption of the Euro-Mediterranean Code of Conduct on Countering Terrorism by the Euro-Mediterranean Summit, held in Barcelona, Spain, on 27 and 28 November 2005,

Bearing in mind all the previous declarations and commitments, as well as all the initiatives taken by the riparian countries at the recent summits, ministerial meetings and various forums concerning the question of the Mediterranean region,

Recalling, in this regard, the adoption on 13 July 2008 of the Joint Declaration of the Paris Summit for the Mediterranean, which launched a reinforced partnership, named the "Barcelona Process: Union for the Mediterranean", and the common political will to revive efforts to transform the Mediterranean into an area of peace, democracy, cooperation and prosperity,

Welcoming the entry into force of the African Nuclear-Weapon-Free Zone Treaty (Treaty of Pelindaba)[1] as a contribution to the strengthening of peace and security both regionally and internationally,

Recognizing the indivisible character of security in the Mediterranean and that the enhancement of cooperation among Mediterranean countries with a view to promoting the economic and social development of all peoples of the region will contribute significantly to stability, peace and security in the region,

Recognizing also the efforts made so far and the determination of the Mediterranean countries to intensify the process of dialogue and consultations with a view to resolving the problems existing in the Mediterranean region and to eliminating the causes of tension and the consequent threat to peace

---

[1] A/50/426, annex.

and security, as well as their growing awareness of the need for further joint efforts to strengthen economic, social, cultural and environmental cooperation in the region,

Recognizing further that prospects for closer Euro-Mediterranean cooperation in all spheres can be enhanced by positive developments worldwide, in particular in Europe, in the Maghreb and in the Middle East,

Reaffirming the responsibility of all States to contribute to the stability and prosperity of the Mediterranean region and their commitment to respecting the purposes and principles of the Charter of the United Nations as well as the provisions of the Declaration on Principles of International Law concerning Friendly Relations and Cooperation among States in accordance with the Charter of the United Nations,[2]

Noting the peace negotiations in the Middle East, which should be of a comprehensive nature and represent an appropriate framework for the peaceful settlement of contentious issues in the region,

Expressing concern at the persistent tension and continuing military activities in parts of the Mediterranean that hinder efforts to strengthen security and cooperation in the region,

Taking note of the report of the Secretary-General,[3]

1. *Reaffirms* that security in the Mediterranean is closely linked to European security as well as to international peace and security;

2. *Expresses its satisfaction* at the continuing efforts by Mediterranean countries to contribute actively to the elimination of all causes of tension in the region and to the promotion of just and lasting solutions to the persistent problems of the region through peaceful means, thus ensuring the withdrawal of foreign forces of occupation and respecting the sovereignty, independence and territorial integrity of all countries of the Mediterranean and the right of peoples to self-determination, and therefore calls for full adherence to the principles of noninterference, non-intervention, non-use of force or threat of use of force and the inadmissibility of the acquisition of territory by force, in accordance with the Charter and the relevant resolutions of the United Nations;

3. *Commends* the Mediterranean countries for their efforts in meeting common challenges through coordinated overall responses, based on a spirit of multilateral partnership, towards the general objective of turning the Mediterranean basin into an area of dialogue, exchanges and cooperation, guaranteeing peace, stability and prosperity, encourages them to strengthen such efforts through, inter alia, a lasting multilateral and action-oriented

---

[2] Resolution 2625 (XXV), annex.
[3] A/72/320.

cooperative dialogue among States of the region, and recognizes the role of the United Nations in promoting regional and international peace and security;

4.   *Recognizes* that the elimination of the economic and social disparities in levels of development and other obstacles, as well as respect and greater understanding among cultures in the Mediterranean area, will contribute to enhancing peace, security and cooperation among Mediterranean countries through the existing forums;

5.   *Calls upon* all States of the Mediterranean region that have not yet done so to adhere to all the multilaterally negotiated legal instruments in force related to the field of disarmament and non-proliferation, thus creating the conditions necessary for strengthening peace and cooperation in the region;

6.   *Encourages* all States of the region to favour the conditions necessary for strengthening the confidence-building measures among them by promoting genuine openness and transparency on all military matters, by participating, inter alia, in the United Nations Report on Military Expenditures and by providing accurate data and information to the United Nations Register of Conventional Arms;

7.   *Encourages* the Mediterranean countries to strengthen further their cooperation in combating terrorism in all its forms and manifestations, including the possible resort by terrorists to weapons of mass destruction, taking into account the relevant resolutions of the United Nations, and in combating international crime and illicit arms transfers and illicit drug production, consumption and trafficking, which pose a serious threat to peace, security and stability in the region and therefore to the improvement of the current political, economic and social situation and which jeopardize friendly relations among States, hinder the development of international cooperation and result in the destruction of human rights, fundamental freedoms and the democratic basis of pluralistic society;

8.   *Requests* the Secretary-General to submit a report on means to strengthen security and cooperation in the Mediterranean region;

9.   *Decides* to include in the provisional agenda of its seventy-third session the item entitled "Strengthening of security and cooperation in the Mediterranean region".

Action by the General Assembly

Date: 4 December 2017   Meeting: 62nd plenary meeting
Vote: Adopted without a vote   Report: A/72/414

Sponsors

Algeria, Angola, Austria, Bosnia and Herzegovina, Central African Republic, Egypt, Eritrea, Greece, Ireland, Libya, Malta, Mauritania, Myanmar, Netherlands, Portugal, Sudan, Tunisia, Zambia

Co-sponsors

Andorra, Cyprus, Georgia, Guinea, Jordan, Maldives, Montenegro, Romania, San Marino, Senegal, Serbia, Slovenia, the former Yugoslav Republic of Macedonia, Turkey, United Kingdom

Action by the First Committee

Date: 1 November 2017　　　Meeting:　　　27th meeting
Vote: Adopted without a vote　Draft resolution: A/C.1/72/L.8

Agenda item 105

72/70   Comprehensive Nuclear-Test-Ban Treaty

Text

The General Assembly,

Reiterating that the cessation of nuclear-weapon test explosions or any other nuclear explosions constitutes an effective nuclear disarmament and non-proliferation measure, and convinced that this is a meaningful step in the realization of a systematic process for achieving nuclear disarmament,

Recalling that the Comprehensive Nuclear-Test-Ban Treaty, adopted by the General Assembly by its resolution 50/245 of 10 September 1996, was opened for signature on 24 September 1996,

Stressing that a universal and effectively verifiable Treaty constitutes a fundamental instrument in the field of nuclear disarmament and non-proliferation and will be a major contribution to international peace and security,

Stressing also the vital importance and urgency of achieving the entry into force of the Treaty, as noted also in Security Council resolution 2310 (2016) of 23 September 2016, and affirming its resolute determination, 21 years after the Treaty was opened for signature, to achieve its entry into force,

Encouraged by the signing of the Treaty by 183 States, including 41 of the 44 whose ratification is needed for its entry into force, and welcoming the ratification of the Treaty by 166 States, including 36 of the 44 whose ratification is needed for its entry into force, among which there are 3 nuclear-weapon States,

Recalling its resolution 71/86 of 5 December 2016,

Recalling also the adoption by consensus of the conclusions and recommendations for follow-on actions of the 2010 Review Conference of the Parties to the Treaty on the Non-Proliferation of Nuclear Weapons,[1] in which the Conference, inter alia, reaffirmed the vital importance of the entry into force of the Comprehensive Nuclear-Test-Ban Treaty as a core element of the international nuclear disarmament and non-proliferation regime and included specific actions to be taken in support of the entry into force of the Treaty,

Welcoming the 20 Years CTBT Ministerial Meeting, held in Vienna on 13 and 14 June 2016, which brought together leaders and policymakers to review and reinvigorate efforts to achieve the entry into force of the Treaty,

---

[1] *2010 Review Conference of the Parties to the Treaty on the Non-Proliferation of Nuclear Weapons, Final Document,* vol. I (NPT/CONF.2010/50 (Vol. I)), part I, *Conclusions and recommendations for follow-on actions.*

Welcoming also the Final Declaration adopted by the tenth Conference on Facilitating the Entry into Force of the Comprehensive Nuclear-Test-Ban Treaty, held in New York on 20 September 2017, convened pursuant to article XIV of the Treaty, and recalling the Joint Ministerial Statement on the Comprehensive Nuclear-Test-Ban Treaty, adopted at the ministerial meeting held in New York on 21 September 2016,[2]

Noting that the group of eminent persons, established to support the article XIV process, met in Vienna on 14 June 2016, where they called for new thinking and further engagement with the leadership of the remaining eight annex 2 States with the aim of facilitating their respective ratification processes,

Noting also the establishment in early 2016 of a youth group open to all students and young graduates who are directing their careers towards contributing to global peace and security and who wish to actively engage in promoting the Treaty and its verification regime,

Welcoming continuing progress in the development of the Treaty's verification regime, which advances the Treaty's primary non-proliferation and disarmament objective, including the completion in June 2017 of the hydroacoustic part of the International Monitoring System,

Recognizing the civil and scientific benefits provided by the CTBT global monitoring system,

1. *Stresses* the vital importance and urgency of signature and ratification, without delay and without conditions, in order to achieve the earliest entry into force of the Comprehensive Nuclear-Test-Ban Treaty;[3]

2. *Welcomes* the contributions by the signatory States to the work of the Preparatory Commission for the Comprehensive Nuclear-Test-Ban Treaty Organization, in particular its efforts to ensure that the verification regime of the Treaty will be capable of meeting the verification requirements of the Treaty upon its entry into force, in accordance with article IV of the Treaty, and encourages their continuation;

3. *Underlines* the need to maintain momentum towards completion of all elements of the verification regime;

4. *Urges* all States not to carry out nuclear-weapon test explosions or any other nuclear explosions, to maintain their moratoriums in this regard and to refrain from acts that would defeat the object and purpose of the Treaty, while stressing that these measures do not have the same permanent and legally binding effect as the entry into force of the Treaty;

---

[2] A/71/736.
[3] See resolution 50/245 and A/50/1027.

5.   *Condemns in the strongest terms* the nuclear tests conducted by the Democratic People's Republic of Korea on 3 September 2017 and 6 January and 9 September 2016, as expressed by the Security Council in its resolutions 2375 (2017) of 11 September 2017, 2321 (2016) of 30 November 2016 and 2270 (2016) of 2 March 2016, recalls Council resolutions 1718 (2006) of 14 October 2006, 1874 (2009) of 12 June 2009 and 2094 (2013) of 7 March 2013, urges full compliance with the obligations under the relevant resolutions, including that the Democratic People's Republic of Korea shall not conduct any further nuclear tests, and reaffirms its support for the goal of complete, verifiable and irreversible denuclearization of the Korean Peninsula in a peaceful manner, including through the Six-Party Talks;

6.   *Urges* all States that have not yet signed the Treaty, in particular those whose ratification is needed for its entry into force, to sign and ratify it as soon as possible;

7.   *Urges* all States that have signed but not yet ratified the Treaty, in particular those whose ratification is needed for its entry into force, to accelerate their ratification processes with a view to ensuring their earliest successful conclusion;

8.   *Encourages* further expressions from among the remaining States whose ratification is needed for the Treaty to enter into force of their intention to pursue and complete the ratification process;

9.   *Urges* all States to remain seized of the issue at the highest political level and, where in a position to do so, to promote adherence to the Treaty through bilateral and joint outreach, seminars and other means;

10.   *Welcomes* the report of the Secretary-General submitted pursuant to resolution 70/73 of 7 December 2015;[4]

11.   *Decides* to include in the provisional agenda of its seventy-third session the item entitled "Comprehensive Nuclear-Test-Ban Treaty".

Action by the General Assembly

Date: 4 December 2017   Meeting: 62nd plenary meeting
Vote: 180-1-4   Report: A/72/415
          169-0-11, p.p. 4
          174-0-6, p.p. 7

Sponsors

Albania, Angola, Argentina, **Australia**, Austria, Belgium, Bosnia and Herzegovina, Bulgaria, Canada, Costa Rica, Croatia, Czech Republic, Dominican Republic, El Salvador, Eritrea, Estonia, Finland, France, Georgia, Germany, Ghana, Greece, Hungary, Iceland, Iraq, Ireland,

---

[4] A/71/134 and A/71/134/Add.1/Rev.1.

Italy, Japan, Kazakhstan, Kenya, Lao People's Democratic Republic, Latvia, Liechtenstein, Lithuania, Luxembourg, Malawi, Malta, **Mexico**, Mongolia, Namibia, Netherlands, **New Zealand**, Nigeria, Norway, Panama, Philippines, Poland, Portugal, Republic of Korea, Republic of Moldova, Romania, Samoa, Serbia, Singapore, Slovakia, Slovenia, Spain, Sweden, Switzerland, Thailand, Trinidad and Tobago, Ukraine, United Kingdom, Uruguay

Co-sponsors

Andorra, Armenia, Burkina Faso, Chad, Colombia, Côte d'Ivoire, Cyprus, Denmark, Guinea, Guinea-Bissau, Guyana, Haiti, Honduras, Jamaica, Kyrgyzstan, Madagascar, Malaysia, Maldives, Micronesia (Federated States of), Monaco, Montenegro, Papua New Guinea, Paraguay, Russian Federation, San Marino, Senegal, Sri Lanka, Swaziland, the former Yugoslav Republic of Macedonia, Turkey, Zambia

Recorded vote

As a whole

In favour:

Afghanistan, Albania, Algeria, Andorra, Angola, Antigua and Barbuda, Argentina, Armenia, Australia, Austria, Azerbaijan, Bahamas, Bahrain, Bangladesh, Barbados, Belarus, Belgium, Belize, Benin, Bhutan, Bolivia (Plurinational State of), Bosnia and Herzegovina, Botswana, Brazil, Brunei Darussalam, Bulgaria, Burkina Faso, Burundi, Cabo Verde, Cambodia, Cameroon, Canada, Chad, Chile, China, Colombia, Comoros, Congo, Costa Rica, Côte d'Ivoire, Croatia, Cuba, Cyprus, Czech Republic, Democratic Republic of the Congo, Denmark, Djibouti, Dominican Republic, Ecuador, Egypt, El Salvador, Equatorial Guinea, Eritrea, Estonia, Ethiopia, Fiji, Finland, France, Gabon, Gambia, Georgia, Germany, Ghana, Greece, Guatemala, Guinea, Guinea-Bissau, Guyana, Haiti, Honduras, Hungary, Iceland, Indonesia, Iran (Islamic Republic of), Iraq, Ireland, Israel, Italy, Jamaica, Japan, Jordan, Kazakhstan, Kenya, Kuwait, Kyrgyzstan, Lao People's Democratic Republic, Latvia, Lebanon, Lesotho, Liberia, Libya, Liechtenstein, Lithuania, Luxembourg, Madagascar, Malawi, Malaysia, Maldives, Mali, Malta, Marshall Islands, Mauritania, Mexico, Micronesia (Federated States of), Monaco, Mongolia, Montenegro, Morocco, Mozambique, Myanmar, Namibia, Nauru, Nepal, Netherlands, New Zealand, Nicaragua, Nigeria, Norway, Oman, Pakistan, Palau, Panama, Papua New Guinea, Paraguay, Peru, Philippines, Poland, Portugal, Qatar, Republic of Korea, Republic of Moldova, Romania, Russian Federation, Rwanda, Saint Kitts and Nevis, Saint Lucia, Saint Vincent and the Grenadines, Samoa, San Marino, Saudi Arabia, Senegal, Serbia,

Sierra Leone, Singapore, Slovakia, Slovenia, Solomon Islands, Somalia, South Africa, Spain, Sri Lanka, Sudan, Suriname, Swaziland, Sweden, Switzerland, Tajikistan, Thailand, the former Yugoslav Republic of Macedonia, Timor-Leste, Togo, Tonga, Trinidad and Tobago, Tunisia, Turkey, Turkmenistan, Tuvalu, Uganda, Ukraine, United Arab Emirates, United Kingdom, United Republic of Tanzania, Uruguay, Uzbekistan, Vanuatu, Venezuela (Bolivarian Republic of), Viet Nam, Yemen, Zambia, Zimbabwe

Against:

Democratic People's Republic of Korea

Abstaining:

India, Mauritius, Syrian Arab Republic, United States

Fourth preambular paragraph

In favour:

Afghanistan, Albania, Algeria, Andorra, Angola, Antigua and Barbuda, Argentina, Armenia, Australia, Austria, Azerbaijan, Bahamas, Bahrain, Bangladesh, Barbados, Belarus, Belgium, Belize, Benin, Bhutan, Bosnia and Herzegovina, Botswana, Brunei Darussalam, Bulgaria, Burkina Faso, Burundi, Cabo Verde, Cambodia, Canada, Chad, Chile, China, Colombia, Comoros, Congo, Costa Rica, Côte d'Ivoire, Croatia, Cyprus, Czech Republic, Democratic Republic of the Congo, Denmark, Djibouti, Dominican Republic, Ecuador, El Salvador, Equatorial Guinea, Eritrea, Estonia, Ethiopia, Fiji, Finland, France, Gabon, Gambia, Georgia, Germany, Ghana, Greece, Guatemala, Guinea, Guinea-Bissau, Guyana, Haiti, Honduras, Hungary, Iceland, Iraq, Ireland, Israel, Italy, Jamaica, Japan, Jordan, Kazakhstan, Kenya, Kuwait, Kyrgyzstan, Lao People's Democratic Republic, Latvia, Lebanon, Lesotho, Liberia, Libya, Liechtenstein, Lithuania, Luxembourg, Madagascar, Malawi, Malaysia, Maldives, Mali, Malta, Marshall Islands, Mauritania, Mexico, Micronesia (Federated States of), Monaco, Mongolia, Montenegro, Morocco, Mozambique, Myanmar, Namibia, Nepal, Netherlands, New Zealand, Nigeria, Norway, Oman, Pakistan, Panama, Papua New Guinea, Paraguay, Peru, Philippines, Poland, Portugal, Qatar, Republic of Korea, Republic of Moldova, Romania, Russian Federation, Rwanda, Saint Kitts and Nevis, Saint Lucia, Saint Vincent and the Grenadines, Samoa, San Marino, Saudi Arabia, Senegal, Serbia, Sierra Leone, Singapore, Slovakia, Slovenia, Solomon Islands, Somalia, South Africa, Spain, Sri Lanka, Sudan, Suriname, Swaziland, Sweden, Switzerland, Tajikistan, Thailand, the former Yugoslav Republic of Macedonia, Timor-Leste, Togo, Trinidad and Tobago, Tunisia, Turkey, Turkmenistan, Tuvalu, Uganda, Ukraine, United Arab Emirates, United Kingdom,

United Republic of Tanzania, Uruguay, Uzbekistan, Vanuatu, Venezuela (Bolivarian Republic of), Viet Nam, Yemen, Zambia, Zimbabwe

Against:

None

Abstaining:

Bolivia (Plurinational State of), Brazil, Cuba, Democratic People's Republic of Korea, Egypt, India, Indonesia, Iran (Islamic Republic of), Nicaragua, Syrian Arab Republic, United States

Seventh preambular paragraph

In favour:

Afghanistan, Albania, Algeria, Andorra, Angola, Antigua and Barbuda, Argentina, Armenia, Australia, Austria, Azerbaijan, Bahamas, Bahrain, Bangladesh, Barbados, Belarus, Belgium, Belize, Benin, Bhutan, Bolivia (Plurinational State of), Bosnia and Herzegovina, Botswana, Brazil, Brunei Darussalam, Bulgaria, Burkina Faso, Burundi, Cabo Verde, Cambodia, Canada, Chad, Chile, China, Colombia, Comoros, Congo, Costa Rica, Côte d'Ivoire, Croatia, Cuba, Cyprus, Czech Republic, Democratic Republic of the Congo, Denmark, Djibouti, Dominican Republic, Ecuador, Egypt, El Salvador, Equatorial Guinea, Eritrea, Estonia, Ethiopia, Fiji, Finland, France, Gabon, Gambia, Georgia, Germany, Ghana, Greece, Guatemala, Guinea, Guinea-Bissau, Guyana, Haiti, Honduras, Hungary, Iceland, Indonesia, Iran (Islamic Republic of), Iraq, Ireland, Italy, Jamaica, Japan, Jordan, Kazakhstan, Kenya, Kuwait, Kyrgyzstan, Lao People's Democratic Republic, Latvia, Lebanon, Lesotho, Liberia, Libya, Liechtenstein, Lithuania, Luxembourg, Madagascar, Malawi, Malaysia, Maldives, Mali, Malta, Marshall Islands, Mauritania, Mexico, Micronesia (Federated States of), Monaco, Mongolia, Montenegro, Morocco, Mozambique, Myanmar, Namibia, Nepal, Netherlands, New Zealand, Nicaragua, Nigeria, Norway, Oman, Panama, Papua New Guinea, Paraguay, Peru, Philippines, Poland, Portugal, Qatar, Republic of Korea, Republic of Moldova, Romania, Russian Federation, Rwanda, Saint Kitts and Nevis, Saint Lucia, Saint Vincent and the Grenadines, Samoa, San Marino, Saudi Arabia, Senegal, Serbia, Sierra Leone, Singapore, Slovakia, Slovenia, Solomon Islands, Somalia, South Africa, Spain, Sri Lanka, Sudan, Suriname, Swaziland, Sweden, Switzerland, Tajikistan, Thailand, the former Yugoslav Republic of Macedonia, Timor-Leste, Togo, Trinidad and Tobago, Tunisia, Turkey, Turkmenistan, Tuvalu, Uganda, Ukraine, United Arab Emirates, United Kingdom, United Republic of Tanzania, Uruguay, Uzbekistan, Vanuatu, Venezuela (Bolivarian Republic of), Viet Nam, Yemen, Zambia, Zimbabwe

Against:
  None

Abstaining:
  Democratic People's Republic of Korea, India, Israel, Pakistan, Syrian
  Arab Republic, United States

Action by the First Committee

Date: 27 October 2017   Meeting: 24th meeting
Vote: 174-1-4   Draft resolution: A/C.1/72/L.42
       164-0-11, p.p. 4
       167-0-7, p.p. 7

Agenda item 106

72/71 Convention on the Prohibition of the Development, Production and Stockpiling of Bacteriological (Biological) and Toxin Weapons and on Their Destruction

Text

The General Assembly,

Recalling its previous resolutions relating to the complete and effective prohibition of bacteriological (biological) and toxin weapons and on their destruction,

Noting with satisfaction that, with the ratification and accession of four additional States,[1] there are now 179 States parties to the Convention on the Prohibition of the Development, Production and Stockpiling of Bacteriological (Biological) and Toxin Weapons and on Their Destruction,[2] including all the permanent members of the Security Council, and stressing at the same time that there is a continuing need to achieve its universalization,

Reaffirming its call upon all signatory States that have not yet ratified the Convention to do so without delay, and calling upon those States that have not signed the Convention to become parties thereto at the earliest possible date, thus contributing to the achievement of universal adherence to the Convention which will facilitate its success,

Bearing in mind its call upon all States parties to the Convention to participate in the implementation of the recommendations of the review conferences of the parties to the Convention, including the exchange of information and data agreed to in the Final Declaration of the Third Review Conference of the Parties to the Convention on the Prohibition of the Development, Production and Stockpiling of Bacteriological (Biological) and Toxin Weapons and on Their Destruction, later amended by the Final Declaration of the Seventh Review Conference, and to provide such information and data in conformity with the standardized procedure to the Implementation Support Unit within the Office for Disarmament Affairs of the Secretariat on an annual basis and no later than 15 April,

Welcoming the reaffirmation made in the Final Declarations of the Fourth, Sixth, Seventh and Eighth Review Conferences that under all circumstances the use of bacteriological (biological) and toxin weapons and

---

[1] Liberia, 4 November 2016 (ratification), Nepal, 4 November 2016 (ratification), Guinea, 9 November 2016 (accession) and Samoa, 21 September 2017 (accession).

[2] United Nations, *Treaty Series*, vol. 1015, No. 14860.

their development, production and stockpiling are effectively prohibited under article I of the Convention,

Recognizing the importance of ongoing efforts by States parties to enhance international cooperation, assistance and the fullest possible exchange of equipment, materials and scientific and technological information for the use of bacteriological (biological) agents and toxins for peaceful purposes, recognizing also that there still remain challenges to be overcome in order to enhance international cooperation, and recognizing further the value of building capacity through international cooperation, in line with the Final Document of the Eighth Review Conference,

Reaffirming the importance of national measures, in accordance with constitutional processes, in strengthening the implementation of the Convention by States parties, in line with the Final Document of the Eighth Review Conference,

Reaffirming also the importance of the review of developments in the field of science and technology related to the Convention,

Recalling previous intersessional processes carried out under the Convention,

Noting, in the decisions and recommendations of the Final Document, that the Eighth Review Conference decided that States parties would hold annual meetings and that the first such meeting would start on 4 December 2017, have a duration of up to five days and seek to make progress on issues of substance and process for the period before the next Review Conference, with a view to reaching consensus on an intersessional process,

Recalling the decision of the Eighth Review Conference that the Ninth Review Conference shall be held in Geneva not later than 2021,

1.   *Notes* the consensus outcome of and the decisions on all provisions of the Convention on the Prohibition of the Development, Production and Stockpiling of Bacteriological (Biological) and Toxin Weapons and on Their Destruction[2] reached at the Eighth Review Conference of the Parties to the Convention, and calls upon States parties to the Convention to participate and actively engage in their continued implementation;

2.   *Appreciates* the information and data on confidence-building measures provided by States parties to date, and calls upon all States parties to participate in the exchange of information and data on confidence-building measures called for in the relevant decisions of the review conferences;

3.   *Notes* the decision of the Eighth Review Conference to continue and improve the database established by the Seventh Review Conference to facilitate requests for and offers of exchange of assistance and cooperation, and urges States parties to submit to the Implementation Support Unit, on a voluntary basis, requests for and offers of cooperation and assistance,

including in terms of equipment, materials and scientific and technological information regarding the use of biological and toxin agents for peaceful purposes;

4. *Encourages* States parties to provide, at least biannually, appropriate information on their implementation of article X of the Convention and to collaborate to offer assistance or training, upon request, in support of the legislative and other implementation measures of States parties needed to ensure their compliance with the Convention;

5. *Notes* the decision of the Eighth Review Conference to renew the sponsorship programme established by the Seventh Review Conference in order to support and increase the participation of developing States parties in the annual meetings, welcomes the continued willingness among States parties to provide voluntary contributions, and calls upon States parties in a position to do so to offer voluntary contributions for the programme;

6. *Also notes* the decision of the Eighth Review Conference to renew the mandate of the Implementation Support Unit agreed to at the Seventh Review Conference, mutatis mutandis, for the period from 2017 to 2021, and notes with appreciation the work of the Unit;

7. *Further notes* that the Eighth Review Conference did not reach agreement on a new intersessional programme and that, in its Final Document, it decided that States parties would hold annual meetings and that the first such meeting would be held in Geneva starting on 4 December 2017, have a duration of up to five days and seek to make progress on issues of substance and process for the period before the next Review Conference, with a view to reaching consensus on an intersessional process, and welcomes the efforts of States parties to that end;

8. *Notes with appreciation* the events organized by some States parties, regional organizations and the Office for Disarmament Affairs of the Secretariat for exchanges of views on the implementation of the Convention, and encourages States parties to continue to participate in such informal exchanges and discussions;

9. *Requests* the Secretary-General to continue to render the necessary assistance to the depositary Governments of the Convention and to continue to provide such services as may be required for the conduct and the implementation of the decisions and recommendations of the review conferences;

10. *Notes* the importance of addressing issues arising from the outstanding dues of States parties and participating States and from financial and accounting practices recently implemented by the United Nations under which funds must be available before meetings can be held, encourages States parties to consider ways of addressing these issues at their next opportunity,

and requests the Secretary-General to cooperate with States parties in exploring options to address or reduce the impact of such issues;

11. *Decides* to include in the provisional agenda of its seventy-third session the item entitled "Convention on the Prohibition of the Development, Production and Stockpiling of Bacteriological (Biological) and Toxin Weapons and on Their Destruction".

Action by the General Assembly

Date: 4 December 2017   Meeting: 62nd plenary meeting
Vote: Adopted without a vote   Report: A/72/416

Sponsors

Hungary

Action by the First Committee

Date: 30 October 2017   Meeting: 25th meeting
Vote: Adopted without a vote   Draft resolution: A/C.1/72/L.49

Agenda item 97 (a)

72/250 Further practical measures for the prevention of an arms race in outer space

Text

The General Assembly,

Recalling its resolutions 71/31 and 71/32 of 5 December 2016 and 71/90 of 6 December 2016, as well as its other resolutions on this subject,

Encouraging all States to contribute actively to the prevention of an arms race in outer space, especially the placement of weapons in outer space, as well as the use of force against space objects, with a view to promoting and strengthening international cooperation in the exploration and use of outer space for peaceful purposes, with the objective of shaping a community of shared future for mankind,

Recognizing that the prevention of an arms race, especially of the placement of weapons in outer space, would avert a grave danger for international peace and security,

Reaffirming that practical measures should be examined and taken in the search for agreements to prevent an arms race in outer space,

Recognizing the primary role and responsibility of the Conference on Disarmament in the negotiation of a multilateral agreement or agreements on the prevention of an arms race in outer space,

1. *Expresses its deep regret* over the years of stalemate in the work of the Conference on Disarmament, and looks forward to the Conference again fulfilling its mandate as the world's single multilateral disarmament negotiating forum;

2. *Urges* the Conference on Disarmament to agree on and implement at its earliest opportunity a balanced and comprehensive programme of work that includes the immediate commencement of negotiations on an international legally binding instrument on the prevention of an arms race in outer space, including, inter alia, on the prevention of the placement of weapons in outer space;

3. *Requests* the Secretary-General to establish a United Nations Group of Governmental Experts, with a membership of up to 25 Member States, chosen on the basis of fair and equitable geographical representation, to consider and make recommendations on substantial elements of an international legally binding instrument on the prevention of an arms race in outer space, including, inter alia, on the prevention of the placement of weapons in outer space;

4.   *Decides* that the newly established Group of Governmental Experts will operate by consensus, without prejudice to national positions in future negotiations, and hold two 2-week sessions in Geneva, one in 2018 and the other in 2019;

5.   *Requests* the Chair of the Group of Governmental Experts to organize, in New York, a two-day open-ended intersessional informal consultative meeting, in 2019, so that all Member States can engage in interactive discussions and share their views on the basis of a report on the work of the Group to be provided by the Chair in his own capacity;

6.   *Requests* the Secretary-General to transmit the report of the Group of Governmental Experts to the General Assembly at its seventy-fourth session and to the Conference on Disarmament prior to its 2020 session;

7.   *Decides* that, if the Conference on Disarmament agrees upon and implements a balanced and comprehensive programme of work that includes the negotiation of an international legally binding instrument on the prevention of an arms race in outer space, including, inter alia, on the prevention of the placement of weapons in outer space, the newly established Group of Governmental Experts will conclude its work and submit the results thereof to the Secretary-General for onward transmission to the Conference on Disarmament;

8.   *Also* decides to include in the provisional agenda of its seventy-third session an item entitled "Further practical measures for the prevention of an arms race in outer space".

Action by the General Assembly

Date: 24 December 2017   Meeting: 76th plenary meeting
Vote: 108-5-47   Report: A/72/407

Sponsors

Algeria, Angola, Belarus, **China**, Cuba, Ecuador, Egypt, Guinea, Iran (Islamic Republic of), Kazakhstan, Kenya, Malawi, Myanmar, Nicaragua, **Russian Federation**, Sierra Leone, South Africa, Sudan, Syrian Arab Republic, Venezuela (Bolivarian Republic of), Zambia, Zimbabwe

Co-sponsors

Armenia, Bangladesh, Bolivia (Plurinational State of), Brazil, Ghana, Kyrgyzstan, Lao People's Democratic Republic, Namibia, Nigeria, Sri Lanka, Suriname, Tajikistan, Uzbekistan

*Recorded vote**

In favour:

Afghanistan, Algeria, Antigua and Barbuda, Argentina, Armenia, Azerbaijan, Bahamas, Bahrain, Bangladesh, Barbados, Belarus, Benin, Bhutan, Bolivia (Plurinational State of), Botswana, Brazil, Brunei Darussalam, Burkina Faso, Burundi, Cabo Verde, Cambodia, Cameroon, Chile, China, Colombia, Congo, Costa Rica, Côte d'Ivoire, Cuba, Djibouti, Ecuador, Egypt, El Salvador, Eritrea, Ethiopia, Gabon, Ghana, Guatemala, Guinea, Guyana, Honduras, India, Indonesia, Iran (Islamic Republic of), Iraq, Jamaica, Jordan, Kazakhstan, Kenya, Kuwait, Kyrgyzstan, Lao People's Democratic Republic, Lebanon, Lesotho, Liberia, Libya, Madagascar, Malaysia, Maldives, Mali, Mauritania, Mauritius, Mexico, Mongolia, Morocco, Mozambique, Myanmar, Namibia, Nauru, Nepal, Nicaragua, Nigeria, Oman, Pakistan, Panama, Papua New Guinea, Paraguay, Peru, Philippines, Qatar, Russian Federation, Rwanda, Saint Kitts and Nevis, Saint Lucia, Saudi Arabia, Serbia, Sierra Leone, Singapore, Solomon Islands, South Africa, Sri Lanka, Sudan, Switzerland, Syrian Arab Republic, Tajikistan, Thailand, Togo, Tunisia, Tuvalu, Uganda, United Arab Emirates, United Republic of Tanzania, Uruguay, Uzbekistan, Venezuela (Bolivarian Republic of), Viet Nam, Yemen, Zimbabwe

Against:

France, Israel, Ukraine, United Kingdom, United States

Abstaining:

Albania, Andorra, Angola, Australia, Austria, Belgium, Bosnia and Herzegovina, Bulgaria, Canada, Croatia, Cyprus, Czech Republic, Denmark, Equatorial Guinea, Estonia, Finland, Georgia, Germany, Greece, Hungary, Iceland, Ireland, Italy, Japan, Latvia, Liechtenstein, Lithuania, Luxembourg, Malta, Monaco, Montenegro, Netherlands, New Zealand, Norway, Palau, Poland, Portugal, Republic of Korea, Republic of Moldova, Romania, San Marino, Slovakia, Slovenia, Spain, Sweden, the former Yugoslav Republic of Macedonia, Turkey

Action by the First Committee

Date: 30 October 2017	Meeting:	25th meeting
Vote: 121-5-45	Draft resolution:	A/C.1/72/L.54

---

* Subsequently, the delegation of Timor-Leste informed the Secretariat that it had intended to vote in favour. The voting tally above does not reflect this information.

Agenda item 99 (cc)

72/251 Follow-up to the 2013 high-level meeting of the General Assembly on nuclear disarmament

Text

The General Assembly,

Recalling its resolutions 67/39 of 3 December 2012, 68/32 of 5 December 2013, 69/58 of 2 December 2014, 70/34 of 7 December 2015 and 71/71 of 5 December 2016,

Welcoming the convening of the high-level meeting of the General Assembly on nuclear disarmament, on 26 September 2013, and recognizing its contribution to furthering the objective of the total elimination of nuclear weapons,

Emphasizing the importance of seeking a safer world for all and achieving peace and security in a world without nuclear weapons,

Reaffirming that effective measures of nuclear disarmament have the highest priority, as affirmed at the first special session of the General Assembly devoted to disarmament,

Convinced that nuclear disarmament and the total elimination of nuclear weapons are the only absolute guarantee against the use or threat of use of nuclear weapons,

Acknowledging the significant contribution made by a number of countries towards realizing the objective of nuclear disarmament by the establishment of nuclear-weapon-free zones, as well as by voluntary renunciation of nuclear weapon programmes or withdrawal of all nuclear weapons from their territories, and strongly supporting the speedy establishment of a nuclear-weapon-free zone in the Middle East,

Recalling the resolve of the Heads of State and Government, as contained in the United Nations Millennium Declaration,[1] to strive for the elimination of weapons of mass destruction, particularly nuclear weapons, and to keep all options open for achieving this aim, including the possibility of convening an international conference to identify ways of eliminating nuclear dangers,

Reaffirming the central role of the United Nations in the field of disarmament, and also reaffirming the continued importance and relevance of multilateral disarmament machinery as mandated by the General Assembly at its first special session devoted to disarmament,

---

[1] Resolution 55/2.

Acknowledging the important role of civil society, including non-governmental organizations, academia, parliamentarians and the mass media, in advancing the objective of nuclear disarmament,

Sharing the deep concern at the catastrophic humanitarian consequences of any use of nuclear weapons, and in this context reaffirming the need for all States at all times to comply with applicable international law, including international humanitarian law,

Taking note of the report of the Secretary-General submitted pursuant to resolution 71/71,[2] and welcoming the fact that a large number of Member States contributed their views to this report,

Noting the adoption, with a vote, of the Treaty on the Prohibition of Nuclear Weapons[3] on 7 July 2017 at the United Nations conference to negotiate a legally binding instrument to prohibit nuclear weapons, leading towards their total elimination,

Mindful of the solemn obligations of States parties, undertaken in article VI of the Treaty on the Non-Proliferation of Nuclear Weapons,[4] particularly to pursue negotiations in good faith on effective measures relating to the cessation of the nuclear arms race at an early date and to nuclear disarmament,

Expressing its deep concern that the negotiations in the Conference on Disarmament for the conclusion of a comprehensive convention on nuclear weapons have not yet commenced,

Determined to work collectively towards the realization of nuclear disarmament,

1.   *Underlines* the strong support, expressed at the high-level meeting of the General Assembly on nuclear disarmament, held on 26 September 2013, for taking urgent and effective measures to achieve the total elimination of nuclear weapons;

2.   *Calls for* urgent compliance with the legal obligations and the fulfilment of the commitments undertaken on nuclear disarmament;

3.   *Endorses* the wide support expressed at the high-level meeting for a comprehensive convention on nuclear weapons;

4.   *Calls for* the urgent commencement of negotiations in the Conference on Disarmament on effective nuclear disarmament measures to achieve the total elimination of nuclear weapons, including, in particular, on a comprehensive convention on nuclear weapons;

---

[2] A/72/339.
[3] A/CONF.229/2017/8.
[4] United Nations, *Treaty Series*, vol. 729, No. 10485.

5.   *Decides* to convene, in New York from 14 to 16 May 2018, a United Nations high-level international conference on nuclear disarmament to review the progress made in this regard;

6.   *Also decides* that the United Nations high-level international conference shall include a one-day organizational meeting, to be held in New York on 28 March 2018, which shall be conducted under the rules of procedure of the General Assembly, to decide on all relevant procedural matters;

7.   *Requests* the Secretary-General to send letters to all States Members of the United Nations and members of specialized agencies inviting them to participate in the conference, and encourages all States Members of the United Nations and members of specialized agencies to participate in the conference at the highest level;

8.   *Decides* that the Secretary-General or his designate shall act as Secretary-General of the conference;

9.   *Also decides* that the conference shall be held with the participation of the President of the General Assembly and the Secretary-General;

10.   *Requests* the Secretary-General to invite relevant regional and international organizations, including the International Atomic Energy Agency, the Preparatory Commission for the Comprehensive Nuclear-Test-Ban Treaty Organization, the International Committee of the Red Cross, the International Federation of Red Cross and Red Crescent Societies and institutions related to the treaties establishing nuclear-weapon-free zones, to participate in the conference;

11.   *Encourages* the wider participation of civil society, including non-governmental organizations, academia and parliamentarians, in the conference, and requests the Secretary-General to draw up a list of non-governmental organizations in consultative status with the Economic and Social Council that will participate in the conference;

12.   *Requests* the Secretary-General to provide the conference with the assistance necessary for the performance of its work, including full conference services, essential background information and relevant documents;

13.   *Takes note* of the views provided by Member States with regard to achieving the objective of the total elimination of nuclear weapons, in particular on the elements of a comprehensive convention on nuclear weapons, as reflected in the report submitted by the Secretary-General pursuant to resolution 71/71,[2] and requests the Secretary-General to forward this report to the Conference on Disarmament and the Disarmament Commission for their early consideration;

14. *Welcomes* the commemoration and promotion of 26 September as the International Day for the Total Elimination of Nuclear Weapons devoted to furthering this objective;

15. *Expresses its appreciation* to Member States, the United Nations system and civil society, including non-governmental organizations, academia, parliamentarians, the mass media and individuals that developed activities in promotion of the International Day for the Total Elimination of Nuclear Weapons;

16. *Reiterates its request* to the President of the General Assembly to organize, on 26 September every year, a one-day high-level plenary meeting of the Assembly to commemorate and promote the International Day for the Total Elimination of Nuclear Weapons;

17. *Decides* that the aforementioned high-level plenary meeting shall be held with the participation of Member and observer States, represented at the highest possible level, as well as with the participation of the President of the General Assembly and the Secretary-General;

18. *Requests* the Secretary-General to undertake all arrangements necessary to commemorate and promote the International Day for the Total Elimination of Nuclear Weapons, including through the United Nations Offices at Geneva and Vienna, as well as the United Nations regional centres for peace and disarmament;

19. *Calls upon* Member States, the United Nations system and civil society, including non-governmental organizations, academia, parliamentarians, the mass media and individuals, to commemorate and promote the International Day for the Total Elimination of Nuclear Weapons through all means of educational and public awareness-raising activities about the threat posed to humanity by nuclear weapons and the necessity for their total elimination in order to mobilize international efforts towards achieving the common goal of a nuclear-weapon-free world;

20. *Requests* the Secretary-General to seek the views of Member States with regard to achieving the objective of the total elimination of nuclear weapons, in particular on effective nuclear disarmament measures, including elements of a comprehensive convention on nuclear weapons, and to submit a report thereon to the General Assembly at its seventy-third session, and also to transmit the report to the Conference on Disarmament;

21. *Also requests* the Secretary-General to report on the implementation of the present resolution to the General Assembly at its seventy-third session;

22. *Decides* to include in the provisional agenda of its seventy-third session, under the item entitled "General and complete disarmament", the sub-item entitled "Follow-up to the 2013 high-level meeting of the General Assembly on nuclear disarmament".

Action by the General Assembly

Date: 24 December 2017   Meeting: 76th plenary meeting
Vote: 114-30-14   Report: A/72/409
     97-29-18, p.p. 12

Sponsors

Indonesia (on behalf of the States Members of the United Nations that are members of the Movement of Non-Aligned Countries)

Recorded vote

*As a whole**

In favour:

Afghanistan, Algeria, Antigua and Barbuda, Argentina, Armenia, Austria, Azerbaijan, Bahamas, Bahrain, Bangladesh, Barbados, Belarus, Benin, Bhutan, Bolivia (Plurinational State of), Botswana, Brazil, Brunei Darussalam, Burkina Faso, Cabo Verde, Cambodia, Chile, China, Colombia, Congo, Costa Rica, Côte d'Ivoire, Cuba, Cyprus, Djibouti, Dominican Republic, Ecuador, Egypt, El Salvador, Equatorial Guinea, Eritrea, Ethiopia, Gabon, Ghana, Guatemala, Guinea, Guyana, Honduras, India, Indonesia, Iran (Islamic Republic of), Iraq, Ireland, Jamaica, Jordan, Kazakhstan, Kenya, Kuwait, Kyrgyzstan, Lao People's Democratic Republic, Lebanon, Lesotho, Liberia, Libya, Liechtenstein, Madagascar, Malaysia, Maldives, Mali, Marshall Islands, Mauritania, Mauritius, Mexico, Mongolia, Morocco, Mozambique, Myanmar, Namibia, Nepal, New Zealand, Nicaragua, Nigeria, Norway, Oman, Pakistan, Palau, Panama, Papua New Guinea, Paraguay, Peru, Philippines, Qatar, Republic of Moldova, Saint Kitts and Nevis, Saint Lucia, San Marino, Saudi Arabia, Sierra Leone, Singapore, Solomon Islands, South Africa, Sri Lanka, Sudan, Sweden, Switzerland, Syrian Arab Republic, Tajikistan, Thailand, Timor-Leste, Togo, Tunisia, Tuvalu, Uganda, United Republic of Tanzania, Uruguay, Uzbekistan, Venezuela (Bolivarian Republic of), Viet Nam, Yemen

Against:

Albania, Australia, Belgium, Canada, Croatia, Czech Republic, Denmark, Estonia, France, Germany, Hungary, Israel, Italy, Latvia, Lithuania, Luxembourg, Malta, Monaco, Montenegro, Netherlands, Poland, Republic of Korea, Romania, Russian Federation, Slovakia, Slovenia, Spain, Turkey, United Kingdom, United States

---

* Subsequently, the delegation of the United Arab Emirates informed the Secretariat that it had intended to vote in favour; the delegation of Norway had intended to vote abstain. The voting tally above does not reflect this information.

Abstaining:

Andorra, Angola, Bosnia and Herzegovina, Bulgaria, Finland, Georgia, Greece, Iceland, Japan, Portugal, Serbia, the former Yugoslav Republic of Macedonia, Ukraine, United Arab Emirates

Twelfth preambular paragraph**

In favour:

Afghanistan, Algeria, Antigua and Barbuda, Argentina, Austria, Bahamas, Bahrain, Bangladesh, Barbados, Belarus, Bhutan, Bolivia (Plurinational State of), Botswana, Brazil, Brunei Darussalam, Burkina Faso, Cabo Verde, Chile, Colombia, Congo, Costa Rica, Côte d'Ivoire, Cyprus, Djibouti, Ecuador, Egypt, El Salvador, Equatorial Guinea, Eritrea, Ethiopia, Finland, Gabon, Ghana, Guatemala, Guinea, Guyana, Honduras, India, Indonesia, Iran (Islamic Republic of), Iraq, Ireland, Jamaica, Jordan, Kazakhstan, Kuwait, Kyrgyzstan, Lao People's Democratic Republic, Lebanon, Lesotho, Liberia, Liechtenstein, Madagascar, Malaysia, Maldives, Malta, Mauritania, Mauritius, Mexico, Mongolia, Morocco, Mozambique, Myanmar, Namibia, Nepal, Netherlands, New Zealand, Nicaragua, Norway, Oman, Pakistan, Panama, Papua New Guinea, Paraguay, Peru, Philippines, Qatar, Republic of Moldova, Saint Kitts and Nevis, Saint Lucia, San Marino, Saudi Arabia, Sierra Leone, Singapore, Solomon Islands, South Africa, Sri Lanka, Sudan, Sweden, Switzerland, Tajikistan, Thailand, Timor-Leste, United Republic of Tanzania, Venezuela (Bolivarian Republic of), Viet Nam, Yemen

Against:

Albania, Andorra, Bosnia and Herzegovina, Burundi, China, Croatia, Czech Republic, Denmark, Estonia, France, Germany, Hungary, Israel, Italy, Latvia, Lithuania, Luxembourg, Monaco, Montenegro, Poland, Republic of Korea, Romania, Russian Federation, Slovakia, Slovenia, Spain, Syrian Arab Republic, United Kingdom, United States

Abstaining:

Angola, Armenia, Australia, Belgium, Benin, Bulgaria, Canada, Georgia, Greece, Iceland, Japan, Nigeria, Portugal, Serbia, the former Yugoslav Republic of Macedonia, Turkey, Ukraine, United Arab Emirates

Action by the First Committee

Date: 1 November 2017 Meeting: 27th meeting
Vote: 129-30-12 Draft resolution: A/C.1/72/L.45/Rev.1
123-26-17, p.p. 12

** Subsequently, the delegations of Cuba, the Syrian Arab Republic and the United Arab Emirates informed the Secretariat that they had intended to vote in favour; the delegation of Norway that it had intended to abstain. The voting tally above does not reflect this information.

DECISIONS

Agenda item 94

72/512 Developments in the field of information and telecommunications in the context of international security

Text

The General Assembly decides to include in the provisional agenda of its seventy-third session the item entitled "Developments in the field of information and telecommunications in the context of international security".

Action by the General Assembly

Date: 4 December 2017   Meeting: 62nd plenary meeting
Vote: 185-0-1   Report: A/72/404

Sponsors

Algeria, Angola, Argentina, Belarus, Benin, Bolivia (Plurinational State of), Brazil, China, Cuba, Democratic People's Republic of Korea, Democratic Republic of the Congo, Egypt, Eritrea, Ghana, Guinea, India, Indonesia, Kazakhstan, Kenya, Lao People's Democratic Republic, Mongolia, Myanmar, Nicaragua, **Russian Federation**, Sierra Leone, Sudan, Suriname, Syrian Arab Republic, Tajikistan, Thailand, Venezuela (Bolivarian Republic of), Viet Nam, Zimbabwe

Co-sponsors

Armenia, Azerbaijan, Bangladesh, Burkina Faso, Chad, Chile, Congo, Côte d'Ivoire, Ecuador, El Salvador, Guinea-Bissau, Iran (Islamic Republic of), Kyrgyzstan, Madagascar, Malawi, Mali, Morocco, Nepal, Nigeria, Oman, Pakistan, Qatar, Republic of Korea, Samoa, Senegal, Serbia, Seychelles, Sri Lanka, Swaziland, Tunisia, Uzbekistan, Vanuatu

Recorded vote

In favour:

Afghanistan, Albania, Algeria, Andorra, Angola, Antigua and Barbuda, Argentina, Armenia, Australia, Austria, Azerbaijan, Bahamas, Bahrain, Bangladesh, Barbados, Belarus, Belgium, Belize, Benin, Bhutan, Bolivia (Plurinational State of), Bosnia and Herzegovina, Botswana, Brazil, Brunei Darussalam, Bulgaria, Burkina Faso, Burundi, Cabo Verde, Cambodia, Cameroon, Canada, Central African Republic, Chad, Chile, China, Colombia, Comoros, Congo, Costa Rica, Côte d'Ivoire,

Croatia, Cuba, Cyprus, Czech Republic, Democratic People's Republic of Korea, Democratic Republic of the Congo, Denmark, Djibouti, Dominican Republic, Ecuador, Egypt, El Salvador, Equatorial Guinea, Eritrea, Estonia, Ethiopia, Fiji, Finland, France, Gabon, Gambia, Georgia, Germany, Ghana, Greece, Guatemala, Guinea, Guinea-Bissau, Guyana, Haiti, Honduras, Hungary, Iceland, India, Indonesia, Iran (Islamic Republic of), Iraq, Ireland, Israel, Italy, Jamaica, Japan, Jordan, Kazakhstan, Kenya, Kiribati, Kuwait, Kyrgyzstan, Lao People's Democratic Republic, Latvia, Lebanon, Lesotho, Liberia, Libya, Liechtenstein, Lithuania, Luxembourg, Madagascar, Malawi, Malaysia, Maldives, Mali, Malta, Marshall Islands, Mauritania, Mauritius, Mexico, Micronesia (Federated States of), Monaco, Mongolia, Montenegro, Morocco, Mozambique, Myanmar, Namibia, Nepal, Netherlands, New Zealand, Nicaragua, Nigeria, Norway, Oman, Pakistan, Palau, Panama, Papua New Guinea, Paraguay, Peru, Philippines, Poland, Portugal, Qatar, Republic of Korea, Republic of Moldova, Romania, Russian Federation, Rwanda, Saint Kitts and Nevis, Saint Lucia, Saint Vincent and the Grenadines, Samoa, San Marino, Saudi Arabia, Senegal, Serbia, Sierra Leone, Singapore, Slovakia, Slovenia, Solomon Islands, Somalia, South Africa, Spain, Sri Lanka, Sudan, Suriname, Swaziland, Sweden, Switzerland, Syrian Arab Republic, Tajikistan, Thailand, the former Yugoslav Republic of Macedonia, Timor-Leste, Togo, Tonga, Trinidad and Tobago, Tunisia, Turkey, Turkmenistan, Tuvalu, Uganda, United Arab Emirates, United Kingdom, United Republic of Tanzania, United States, Uruguay, Uzbekistan, Vanuatu, Venezuela (Bolivarian Republic of), Viet Nam, Yemen, Zambia, Zimbabwe

Against:
   None

Abstaining:
   Ukraine

Action by the First Committee

Date: 31 October 2017		Meeting:	26th meeting
Vote: 173-0-1		Draft decision:	A/C.1/72/L.44

Agenda item 99 (a)

72/513 Treaty banning the production of fissile material for nuclear weapons or other nuclear explosive devices

Text

The General Assembly, recalling its resolution 71/259 of 23 December 2016 and previous resolutions on this matter, decides:

(a)   To welcome the commencement of the work of the high-level fissile material cut-off treaty expert preparatory group tasked with making recommendations on substantial elements of a future non-discriminatory, multilateral and internationally and effectively verifiable treaty banning the production of fissile material for nuclear weapons or other nuclear explosive devices, on the basis of document CD/1299 and the mandate contained therein, and examining, with a view to making possible recommendations, the report of the Group of Governmental Experts mandated pursuant to resolution 67/53 of 3 December 2012, as contained in document A/70/81, as well as the views submitted by Member States as contained in documents A/68/154, A/68/154/Add.1, A/71/140/Rev.1 and A/71/140/Rev.1/Add.1;

(b)   To welcome the first informal open-ended consultative meeting in New York, which was open-ended so that all Member States could engage in interactive discussions and share their views on a treaty banning the production of fissile material for nuclear weapons or other nuclear explosive devices;

(c)   To welcome the informal discussions in the Conference on Disarmament on a treaty banning the production of fissile material for nuclear weapons or other nuclear explosive devices;

(d)   To include in the provisional agenda of its seventy-third session, under the item entitled "General and complete disarmament", the sub-item entitled "Treaty banning the production of fissile material for nuclear weapons or other nuclear explosive devices".

Action by the General Assembly

Date: 4 December 2017   Meeting: 62nd plenary meeting
Vote: 182-1-4   Report: A/72/409

Sponsors

Canada, Germany, Netherlands

Recorded vote

In favour:
Afghanistan, Albania, Algeria, Andorra, Angola, Antigua and Barbuda, Argentina, Armenia, Australia, Austria, Azerbaijan, Bahamas, Bahrain, Bangladesh, Barbados, Belarus, Belgium, Belize, Benin, Bhutan, Bolivia (Plurinational State of), Bosnia and Herzegovina, Botswana, Brazil, Brunei Darussalam, Bulgaria, Burkina Faso, Burundi, Cabo Verde, Cambodia, Cameroon, Canada, Central African Republic, Chad, Chile, China, Colombia, Comoros, Congo, Costa Rica, Côte d'Ivoire, Croatia, Cuba, Cyprus, Czech Republic, Democratic Republic of the Congo, Denmark, Djibouti, Dominican Republic, Ecuador, Egypt, El Salvador, Equatorial Guinea, Eritrea, Estonia, Ethiopia, Fiji, Finland, France, Gabon, Gambia, Georgia, Germany, Ghana, Greece, Guatemala, Guinea, Guinea-Bissau, Guyana, Haiti, Honduras, Hungary, Iceland, India, Indonesia, Iraq, Ireland, Italy, Jamaica, Japan, Jordan, Kazakhstan, Kenya, Kiribati, Kuwait, Kyrgyzstan, Lao People's Democratic Republic, Latvia, Lebanon, Lesotho, Liberia, Libya, Liechtenstein, Lithuania, Luxembourg, Madagascar, Malawi, Malaysia, Maldives, Mali, Malta, Marshall Islands, Mauritania, Mauritius, Mexico, Micronesia (Federated States of), Monaco, Mongolia, Montenegro, Morocco, Mozambique, Myanmar, Namibia, Nauru, Nepal, Netherlands, New Zealand, Nicaragua, Nigeria, Norway, Oman, Palau, Panama, Papua New Guinea, Paraguay, Peru, Philippines, Poland, Portugal, Qatar, Republic of Korea, Republic of Moldova, Romania, Russian Federation, Rwanda, Saint Kitts and Nevis, Saint Lucia, Saint Vincent and the Grenadines, Samoa, San Marino, Saudi Arabia, Senegal, Serbia, Sierra Leone, Singapore, Slovakia, Slovenia, Solomon Islands, Somalia, South Africa, Spain, Sri Lanka, Sudan, Suriname, Swaziland, Sweden, Switzerland, Tajikistan, Thailand, the former Yugoslav Republic of Macedonia, Timor-Leste, Togo, Tonga, Trinidad and Tobago, Tunisia, Turkey, Turkmenistan, Tuvalu, Uganda, Ukraine, United Arab Emirates, United Kingdom, United Republic of Tanzania, United States, Uruguay, Uzbekistan, Vanuatu, Venezuela (Bolivarian Republic of), Viet Nam, Yemen, Zambia, Zimbabwe

Against:
Pakistan

Abstaining:
Democratic People's Republic of Korea, Iran (Islamic Republic of), Israel, Syrian Arab Republic

Action by the First Committee

Date: 27 October 2017   Meeting: 24th meeting
Vote: 174-1-4   Draft decision: A/C.1/72/L.50

Agenda item 99 (ii)

72/514 Nuclear disarmament verification

Text

The General Assembly, recalling its resolution 71/67 of 5 December 2016, decides to include in the provisional agenda of its seventy-third session, under the item entitled "General and complete disarmament", the sub-item entitled "Nuclear disarmament verification".

Action by the General Assembly

Date: 4 December 2017   Meeting: 62nd plenary meeting
Vote: Adopted without a vote   Report: A/72/409

Sponsors

Chile, Finland, Mexico, Morocco, Netherlands, **Norway**, Switzerland, United Kingdom

Action by the First Committee

Date: 27 October 2017   Meeting: 24th meeting
Vote: Adopted without a vote   Draft decision: A/C.1/72/L.55

Agenda item 99 (y)

72/515 Treaty on the South-East Asia Nuclear-Weapon-Free Zone (Bangkok Treaty)

Text

The General Assembly, recalling its resolutions 62/31 of 5 December 2007, 64/39 of 2 December 2009, 66/43 of 2 December 2011, 68/49 of 5 December 2013 and 70/60 of 7 December 2015, entitled "Treaty on the South-East Asia Nuclear-Weapon-Free Zone (Bangkok Treaty)", decides to include in the provisional agenda of its seventy-fourth session, under the item entitled "General and complete disarmament", the sub-item entitled "Treaty on the South-East Asia Nuclear-Weapon-Free Zone (Bangkok Treaty)".

Action by the General Assembly

Date: 4 December 2017	Meeting: 62nd plenary meeting
Vote: Adopted without a vote	Report: A/72/409

Sponsors

Philippines (on behalf of the States Members of the United Nations that are members of the Association of Southeast Asian Nations and the States parties to the Treaty on the South-East Asia Nuclear-Weapon-Free Zone (Bangkok Treaty))

Action by the First Committee

Date: 1 November 2017	Meeting: 27th meeting
Vote: Adopted without a vote	Draft decision: A/C.1/72/L.58

ANNEX

List of reports and notes of the Secretary-General

Agenda item 90	**Reduction of military budgets**
(a)	*Reduction of military budgets*
(b)	*Objective information on military matters, including transparency of military expenditures*
A/72/293	Note by the Secretary-General transmitting the report of the Group of Governmental Experts to Review the Operation and Further Development of the United Nations Report on Military Expenditures
A/72/328	Report of the Secretary-General on objective information on military matters, including transparency of military expenditures
Agenda item 91	**Implementation of the Declaration of the Indian Ocean as a Zone of Peace**
A/72/29	Report of the Ad Hoc Committee on the Indian Ocean
Agenda item 92	**African Nuclear-Weapon-Free Zone Treaty**
Agenda item 93	**Prohibition of the development and manufacture of new types of weapons of mass destruction and new systems of such weapons: report of the Conference on Disarmament**
A/72/27	Report of the Conference on Disarmament
Agenda item 94	**Developments in the field of information and telecommunications in the context of international security**
A/72/327	Note by the Secretary-General transmitting the report of the Group of Governmental Experts on Developments in the Field of Information and Telecommunications in the Context of International Security

(f)	*Regional disarmament*
(g)	*Conventional arms control at the regional and subregional levels*
A/72/318	Report of the Secretary-General on conventional arms control at the regional and subregional levels
(h)	*Convening of the fourth special session of the General Assembly devoted to disarmament*
(i)	*Nuclear-weapon-free southern hemisphere and adjacent areas*
(j)	*Observance of environmental norms in the drafting and implementation of agreements on disarmament and arms control*
A/72/309	Report of the Secretary-General on the observance of environmental norms in the drafting and implementation of agreements on disarmament and arms control
(k)	*Follow-up to the advisory opinion of the International Court of Justice on the legality of the threat or use of nuclear weapons*
A/72/321 (sub-items (b), (k) and (o) of agenda item 99)	Report of the Secretary-General on nuclear disarmament; follow-up to the advisory opinion of the International Court of Justice on the legality of the threat or use of nuclear weapons; reducing nuclear danger
(l)	*Implementation of the Convention on the Prohibition of the Development, Production, Stockpiling and Use of Chemical Weapons and on Their Destruction*
A/72/179	Note by the Secretary-General transmitting the report of the Organisation for the Prohibition of Chemical Weapons on the implementation of the Convention on the Prohibition of the Development, Production, Stockpiling and Use of Chemical Weapons and on Their Destruction
(m)	*Implementation of the Convention on the Prohibition of the Use, Stockpiling, Production and Transfer of Anti-Personnel Mines and on Their Destruction*

(n)	*Assistance to States for curbing the illicit traffic in small arms and light weapons and collecting them*
A/72/122 (sub-items (n) and (p) of agenda item 99)	Report of the Secretary-General on the illicit trade in small arms and light weapons in all its aspects and assistance to States for curbing the illicit traffic in small arms and light weapons and collecting them
(o)	*Reducing nuclear danger*
A/72/321 (sub-items (b), (k) and (o) of agenda item 99)	Report of the Secretary-General on nuclear disarmament; follow-up to the advisory opinion of the International Court of Justice on the legality of the threat or use of nuclear weapons; reducing nuclear danger
(p)	*The illicit trade in small arms and light weapons in all its aspects*
A/72/122 (sub-items (n) and (p) of agenda item 99)	Report of the Secretary-General on the illicit trade in small arms and light weapons in all its aspects and assistance to States for curbing the illicit traffic in small arms and light weapons and collecting them
(q)	*Towards a nuclear-weapon-free world: accelerating the implementation of nuclear disarmament commitments*
(r)	*Promotion of multilateralism in the area of disarmament and non proliferation*
A/72/302	Report of the Secretary-General on the promotion of multilateralism in the area of disarmament and non-proliferation
(s)	*Measures to prevent terrorists from acquiring weapons of mass destruction*
A/72/344	Report of the Secretary-General on measures to prevent terrorists from acquiring weapons of mass destruction
(t)	*Confidence-building measures in the regional and subregional context*
A/72/305	Report of the Secretary-General on confidence-building measures in the regional and subregional context

(u)	*Problems arising from the accumulation of conventional ammunition stockpiles in surplus*
(v)	*Transparency and confidence-building measures in outer space activities*
A/72/65 and Add.1	Report of the Secretary-General on transparency and confidence-building measures in outer space activities
(w)	*Follow-up to nuclear disarmament obligations agreed to at the 1995, 2000 and 2010 Review Conferences of the Parties to the Treaty on the Non-Proliferation of Nuclear Weapons*
(x)	*The Arms Trade Treaty*
(y)	*Treaty on the South-East Asia Nuclear-Weapon-Free Zone (Bangkok Treaty)*
(z)	*United action with renewed determination towards the total elimination of nuclear weapons*
(aa)	*Compliance with non-proliferation, arms limitation and disarmament agreements and commitments*
(bb)	*Taking forward multilateral nuclear disarmament negotiations*
A/72/206	Report of the United Nations conference to negotiate a legally binding instrument to prohibit nuclear weapons, leading towards their total elimination
(cc)	*Follow-up to the 2013 high-level meeting of the General Assembly on nuclear disarmament*
A/72/339	Report of the Secretary-General on the follow-up to the 2013 high-level meeting of the General Assembly on nuclear disarmament
(dd)	*Countering the threat posed by improvised explosive devices*
(ee)	*Humanitarian consequences of nuclear weapons*
(ff)	*Humanitarian pledge for the prohibition and elimination of nuclear weapons*
(gg)	*Ethical imperatives for a nuclear-weapon-free world*

(hh)	*Implementation of the Convention on Cluster Munitions*
(ii)	*Nuclear disarmament verification*
A/72/304	Report of the Secretary-General on nuclear disarmament verification
Agenda item 100	**Review and implementation of the Concluding Document of the Twelfth Special Session of the General Assembly**
(a)	*Convention on the Prohibition of the Use of Nuclear Weapons*
A/72/27	Report of the Conference on Disarmament
(b)	*United Nations Regional Centre for Peace and Disarmament in Africa*
A/72/97	Report of the Secretary-General on the United Nations Regional Centre for Peace and Disarmament in Africa
(c)	*United Nations Regional Centre for Peace, Disarmament and Development in Latin America and the Caribbean*
A/72/99	Report of the Secretary-General on the United Nations Regional Centre for Peace, Disarmament and Development in Latin America and the Caribbean
(d)	*United Nations Regional Centre for Peace and Disarmament in Asia and the Pacific*
A/72/98 and Corr.1	Report of the Secretary-General on the United Nations Regional Centre for Peace and Disarmament in Asia and the Pacific
(e)	*Regional confidence-building measures: activities of the United Nations Standing Advisory Committee on Security Questions in Central Africa*
A/72/363	Report of the Secretary-General on regional confidence-building measures: activities of the United Nations Standing Advisory Committee on Security Questions in Central Africa
(f)	*United Nations regional centres for peace and disarmament*

Agenda item 101	**Review of the implementation of the recommendations and decisions adopted by the General Assembly at its tenth special session**
A/72/154	Note by the Secretary-General transmitting the report of the Director of the United Nations Institute for Disarmament Research
A/72/185	Report of the Secretary-General on the work of the Advisory Board on Disarmament Matters
(a)	*Report of the Conference on Disarmament*
A/72/27	Report of the Conference on Disarmament
(b)	*Report of the Disarmament Commission*
A/72/42	Report of the Disarmament Commission for 2017
Agenda item 102	**The risk of nuclear proliferation in the Middle East**
A/72/340 (Part II)	Report of the Secretary-General on the risk of nuclear proliferation in the Middle East
Agenda item 103	**Convention on Prohibitions or Restrictions on the Use of Certain Conventional Weapons Which May Be Deemed to Be Excessively Injurious or to Have Indiscriminate Effects**
Agenda item 104	**Strengthening of security and cooperation in the Mediterranean region**
A/72/320	Report of the Secretary-General on the strengthening of security and cooperation in the Mediterranean region
Agenda item 105	**Comprehensive Nuclear-Test-Ban Treaty**
A/72/180	Note by the Secretary-General transmitting the report of the Executive Secretary of the Preparatory Commission for the Comprehensive Nuclear-Test-Ban Treaty Organization for 2016
Agenda item 106	**Convention on the Prohibition of the Development, Production and Stockpiling of Bacteriological (Biological) and Toxin Weapons and on Their Destruction**